Library Marketing Basics

Library Marketing Basics

Mark Aaron Polger

ROWMAN & LITTLEFIELD
Lanham • Boulder • New York • London

Published by Rowman & Littlefield
An imprint of The Rowman & Littlefield Publishing Group, Inc.
4501 Forbes Boulevard, Suite 200, Lanham, Maryland 20706
www.rowman.com

6 Tinworth Street, London, SE11 5AL, United Kingdom

British Library Cataloguing in Publication Information Available

Library of Congress Cataloging-in-Publication Data

Names: Polger, Mark Aaron, author.
Title: Library marketing basics / Mark Aaron Polger.
Description: Lanham : Rowman & Littlefield, [2019] | Includes
  bibliographical
  references and index.
Identifiers: LCCN 2018049996 (print) | LCCN 2018060095 (ebook) | ISBN
  9781538125816 (electronic) | ISBN 9781442239623 (cloth : alk. paper) |
  ISBN 9781442239630 (pbk. : alk. paper)
Subjects: LCSH: Libraries—Marketing.
Classification: LCC Z716.3 (ebook) | LCC Z716.3 .P65 2019 (print) | DDC
  021.7—dc23
LC record available at https://lccn.loc.gov/2018049996

♾™ The paper used in this publication meets the minimum requirements
of American National Standard for Information Sciences—Permanence of
Paper for Printed Library Materials, ANSI/NISO Z39.48-1992.

Printed in the United States of America

This book is dedicated to my mum Leona Polger, who has always been supportive, an amazing confidant, and my best friend. Your guidance and great advice is always appreciated, even if I don't always take it.

Contents

List of Figures

Foreword

Mark Aaron Polger is one of the most enthusiastic library marketers I know, so I was excited to learn he was writing a book on the topic. When he invited me to contribute the Foreword, I was honored. I wasn't sure what I'd discover in the manuscript, and for months, I eagerly awaited my sneak peek.

I was not disappointed.

Enthusiasm certainly helps with marketing, but it's far from being the most important thing. There's a lot of background knowledge and strategy behind great marketing initiatives. And while it's true that librarians can do some effective marketing and promotional work without being experts in that field, I can tell the difference between projects done by people who've put in some study time and projects done by people who've decided to wing it.

This book, *Library Marketing Basics*, is one of the tools you can study to help you achieve marketing greatness. It's different from many of the library marketing books that have come out in the past five years or so. Those books have been filled with case studies, which share ideas and tactics for implementing projects. But they seldom explain where the ideas came from or why particular tactics were chosen.

This tome, however, explains how to start at the proper beginning, with market research. Polger has long been involved in many local and national marketing organizations, and he drew on his vast experience to pen this new title. Studying *Library Marketing Basics* will enable readers to understand the what, why, and how of the craft. I think that's incredibly important. It's vital to realize what marketing really is (and is not), and to grasp the tenets behind it. People who've done that are more likely to implement projects that are successful.

Right from the get-go, Polger comes out and says that librarians "have the best of intentions, but their [marketing] efforts are very often misguided, sporadic, random, uninformed, and not user-centered" (p. 15). While this might be hard to hear, it's true. Polger has seen that during his wide-ranging activities in this field (chairing LLAMA's PR Xchange Committee and co-chairing the Annual PR Xchange Awards Competition; co-chairing meetings for ACRL's Library Marketing and Outreach Interest Group, and working on the Planning Committee for the Library Marketing and Communications Conference), and he aims to help change those misguided actions with this book.

I like that the author begins with definitions. That might seem pedantic, but please, don't skip these. In my 15 years as a library marketing consultant, I've spoken with hundreds of librarians who don't understand the difference between marketing, promotion, advocacy, outreach, and other related words. In fact, Polger includes some differentiations between words that even I sometimes overlook (i.e., "market research" and "marketing research"). Realizing what the terms really mean will help you get the most out of the rest of this book, and every other thing you read over time on the topic.

Polger carries this logical, helpful approach throughout his book. He explains concepts thoroughly and includes a plethora of citations to guide you to more details about every topic he touches on. And he's included all the concepts you need to know about, from advertising to generation Z. *Library Marketing Basics* gives you a broad look at the field, which includes campaigns, plans, brands, analytics, social media, search engine optimization, etc. But those are just the A-level topics you'd expect from a marketing book in 2019, right? In its quest to be complete, this one also mentions measuring return on investment, understanding eye-tracking studies, using perceptual maps, listing elements that should be part of a marketing plan, identifying touchpoints, and more. If it relates to marketing, it's probably in this tome. And Polger considers, and offers examples from, all types of libraries.

Two points that Polger makes throughout this work are obvious to marketing pros, but still, unfortunately, important lessons for marketing learners:

1. Always start any initiative with market research. That provides the evidence-based information you'll need to complete all of the steps in the marketing cycle.
2. Program and event ideas should spring *from* the market research, rather than coming from what program planners feel like doing. If they are simply asking for "marketing support" just before their events, then the process is upside-down.

So as you read *Library Marketing Basics*, let Polger's process recommendations sink in and truly affect the way you work. And if you also catch his infectious enthusiasm, you'll be in an even better position to do great marketing.

Kathy Dempsey
Editor, *Marketing Library Services*
Author, *The Accidental Library Marketer*
Marketing Consultant and Founder, Libraries Are Essential
Founding Chair, Library Marketing and Communications Conference

Acknowledgments

Thanks to Heath Sledge for being such a supportive editor and for helping me throughout the process of this book project. Thanks to Charles Harmon and everyone at Rowman & Littlefield for believing in this project (and for your patience). Thanks to Sandy Wood for inviting me to write this book and for working with me at the beginning of this project.

Thanks to my parents Leona and David Polger, who have been so supportive throughout my life.

Thanks to Janice Rosen, archives director of the Canadian Jewish Archives in Montreal, Canada. I worked for Janice from 1993–1999 before attending library school and she has always been a wonderful mentor and friend.

Thanks to Kathy Dempsey, my library marketing mentor and friend. Your advice has been invaluable and I am so glad you're only an email away!

Thanks to my small groups of supportive family and dear friends in Montreal, Toronto, and New York City; Keith Saks, Karen Okamoto, Antonio D'Souza, Wendy Furtenbacher, Don Madonna, Vivian Bejerman, Kinga Breining, Peter Kiss, Scott Sheidlower, Elizabeth (Lisa) Palov, Mason Cooper, Julie Miller, Maxine D'Alfonso, Tony D'Alfonso, Beth Hurley, Ryan Hurley, Aaron Boros, Daniel Malen, Marlin Roy, Dimitry Epelbaum, Andrew Grudek, Faline Bobier, Susanne Marcus Solomkin, David Solomkin, Jennie Solomkin, Shari Kopla, Raffi Kopla, Lynn Marcus, Susan Yegendorf, Simon Abecassis, David Abecassis, Jana Stuart, Christy Sich, Dan Sich, Joel Moses, Heidi Furtenbacher, Pamela Pollack, Christine Oakes, and Naomi Gold.

I'd like to thank the many library marketing professionals who gave permission for me to use their library's marketing plans, images from their marketing campaigns, and their social media guidelines; Andrew Hickner, Anne Peters, Linda Hazzan, Gary Marks Jr., Katherine Jardine, Daniel Vinson, Karen Lemke, Robin Bedenbaugh, Toni Tucker, Carolyn Ellis, Kandace Foreman, Laurel Scheinfeld, Kristin Hall, and Heather Buchansky.

Lastly, I would like to thank the College of Staten Island Library Personnel and Budgetary (P&B) Committee who granted me research leave during the summers of 2017 and 2018 so I was able to complete this project.

Introduction

WHY IS LIBRARY MARKETING IMPORTANT?

Let's face it: libraries no longer have a monopoly on providing information. According to a Pew Research study, 77 percent of Americans go online daily, and 26 percent of them are constantly online (Perrin and Jiang, 2018). Libraries now compete against Google, Wikipedia, Amazon, Facebook, and YouTube, and the Internet is winning. According to another Pew Research study, people in the United States most often conduct information searches without visiting the library. Indeed, they are losing their faith in libraries; only 40 percent of participants said that libraries were trustworthy sources of information (Horrigan, 2017). Libraries need to differentiate what they do from what the Internet does: while technology has made it easier to find information, librarians help their users find the *right* information. Libraries have a unique role to play, even in a world where information needs can be immediately gratified, and libraries must market that unique value (Sadeh, 2007).

Library marketing is the mix of promotions, events, user research, and activities that help meet the needs and desires of your target audiences. And although this may be surprising, marketing need not be expensive. The most accessible, affordable type of marketing is web marketing (discussed in chapter 8, "Using the Web to Market the Library"). Unlike traditional marketing channels, web and social media marketing allow you to interact directly with your audience, and they have a very low cost to entry. Most libraries engage in DIY marketing—what this book is designed to teach you to do. In the long run, well-planned, well-executed marketing activities actually save the library money. Libraries cannot afford to waste money providing services that patrons will not use, and good market research about user needs (discussed in chapter 3) helps libraries determine what services and resources to provide in order to use their budget productively.

MARKETING IN LIBRARIES

When we think "marketing," many of us think of large corporations aggressively trying to sell products or services. People assume that marketers are pushy, aggressive salespeople who aim to get their weekly sales quota (and their commissions!) no matter what. Marketing isn't usually associated with libraries, which are one of the few free public spaces left in the world (Vårheim, Steinmo, and Ide, 2008), and which "sell" nothing but access to knowledge and learning. Library employees often believe that libraries' benefits are obvious and apparent—that library users will visit without any active promotion (Kumbar, 2004). But libraries are not baseball fields: we cannot assume that if we build it, they will come (Rodwell and Fairbairn, 2008; Wisniewski, 2007). We cannot passively wait for library users to walk in. Budget cuts are increasing, and librarians cannot be complacent; it is crucial to communicate our value. Librarians must take a proactive approach to informing the community about library benefits and influencing the community to support its libraries.

But how can libraries market themselves successfully and inexpensively? Librarians rarely have training in marketing, for marketing education is not required in library school (Singh, 2017). Not only do most library employees not know how to market, many of them don't believe that marketing duties should be part of their jobs (McClelland, 2014; Goetsch, 2008; Okamoto and Polger, 2012; Yi, Lodge, and McCausland, 2013). Until recently, librarians rarely even imagined working with marketing professionals, let alone doing marketing activities themselves!

This book is designed to reduce your fear of and resistance to library marketing. Unlike other books about the subject, this one is designed

as a beginner's guide, with clear, easy-to-follow language and instructions. It offers an overview of marketing basics as applied to libraries
of all types, including community libraries and university libraries.
It provides clear definitions of marketing terms and presents easy
step-by-step instructions for how to conduct market research, create
a marketing plan, divide your users into segments, think strategically
when using the web and social media for promoting your library, and
implementing a marketing campaign. It teaches librarians and administrators how to engage in low-cost, high-impact campaigns that increase
patronage by defining and meeting users' needs. It uses relatable, real-
world examples from the corporate sector, television, pop culture, and
the media to show that marketing your library is easier than you think.

BROADENING THE DEFINITION OF THE LIBRARY

This book is aimed at marketing both the physical and virtual library.
Chapters will discuss how you can promote both your physical facility and your library's virtual/digital components—the library website
and the suite of the library's subscription database. These physical,
mobile, and digital library services extend library access beyond the
four walls of the library building—what we often call "outreach."
(Indeed, as this book will show, outreach is already a form of library
marketing.) Some of these extensions of the physical library facility
have existed for a long time; for example, bookmobile services have
been in place since World War II, providing library services to communities that are unable to visit the physical library. These mobile
libraries, which were featured in an entire issue of *Library Trends*
(January 1961), are great models of outreach and are also a powerful
marketing tool to raise awareness of library services in the community (Boyce and Boyce, 1991; Smith, 1961). Mobile library services
also serve hospitals, where book carts or laptop carts provide library
outreach to employees and patients who might not have time to visit
the physical library (Polger, 2010); some public libraries also provide
mobile outreach in prisons, with some prison libraries liaising with
colleges to provide educational opportunities for prisoners (Lehmann,
2011; Curry, Wolf, Boutilier, and Chan, 2003; De la Peña McCook,

2004). These mobile libraries are not only outreach tools; they can also be thought of as marketing tools. Raising public awareness of library services helps bring new patrons in.

Other extensions of the physical library are very recent. In addition to traditional physical mobile outreach programs, libraries also now have "virtual" branches that are accessible to anyone with an Internet connection. In fact, the virtual library is the fastest-growing element of library services. The virtual library includes robust library websites and costly web-based electronic subscriptions, as well as expensive searchable commercial databases that have replaced traditional indexes and abstracts. Users can access these virtual libraries on their desktops, laptops, or mobile devices. Library websites thus act as gateways to external websites and provide internal content directly to users. But these, too, like mobile library services, are useful communications and marketing tools that promote both actual content and the library itself—its services, resources, and events).

The library website is often the first place a library user will access, before they ever step inside the physical library building (Welch, 2005). The library website thus needs to be user friendly, user centered, be ADA compliant, and intuitive. Content must be easily discoverable, not buried under several levels of clicks. Chapter 8 discusses how to perform usability testing on your library website.

CHANGING STEREOTYPES THROUGH LIBRARY MARKETING

To successfully market your library, you must understand the stereotypes about libraries and librarians that you are trying to counteract. Libraries are seen by funders as dinosaurs—extinct, irrelevant, and therefore a low priority for funding. Yet even as funding continues to decline, costs continue to increase (those expensive database subscriptions!). Librarians, who have been portrayed as unmarried spinsters, bookish, sexually repressed, unattractive, and uptight (Mosley, 2003; Kneale, 2014a), are often seen not as information professionals but as hobbyists who primarily shelve and stamp books or shush loud talkers; librarianship, which is often seen as women's work, has struggled for years to be recognized as a profession (Gray, 2013; Goode, 1961;

Asheim, 1978; Hanks and Schmidt, 1975). Over the last twenty years, though, as an influx of younger librarians have joined the profession, the stereotype has swung in the opposite direction. Recent books, blogs, and online videos have portrayed modern librarians as sexy, super heroic, tech-savvy activists who are cultured, sophisticated, and innovative (Kneale, 2014b; Kroll, 2004). But no matter which stereotype happens to be ascendant at the moment, librarianship remains a misunderstood, sometimes mysterious, profession—one that is difficult to successfully market. Marketing can help to address these negative (and outdated) stereotypes of librarians and libraries.

In addition to the problem of stereotypes, there is the problem of diversification and specialization: how do you market a profession that is so heterogeneous? Libraries have many departments that perform many different functions, and over the last twenty-five years, librarians' work has diversified and specialized. Some library employees hold "public service" positions, which means they serve library users at the circulation, reserves, or reference desks. Some library employees provide instruction, teaching one-shot library instruction classes or offering slightly longer-term instruction in the use of specialized software. In public libraries, some librarians coordinate special programs for children, teenagers, and the elderly. Other librarians are hidden away in technical services, where they are responsible for cataloguing, acquisitions, serials, and the library website. In academic libraries, many librarians are required to hold a second master's degree, and most librarians have expertise in particular subjects; academic librarians are becoming increasingly specialized (Goetsch, 2008; Croneis and Henderson, 2002; Grimes and Grimes, 2008; Meier, 2010; Shank, 2006). It is difficult to explain, let alone promote, the entire profession when each librarian's responsibilities are unique and specific.

MARKETING: A BAD WORD?

Some librarians think that the term "marketing" does not belong in libraries. "Marketing" sounds like "selling," and many librarians are already uncomfortable with the commodification of libraries (Singh, 2009; Estall and Stephens, 2011; Shontz, Parker, and Parker, 2004).

Many library employees believe that marketing is manipulative, a waste of time, and outside the parameters of their professional work (Kumbar, 2004). But these conceptions of marketing are wrong. In the corporate world, marketing may be about selling, but in the nonprofit realm of libraries, it is about building relationships and ensuring that the needs of specific audiences are met.

Marketing is not synonymous with promotion. Creating a flyer, sign, bookmark, or brochure is not marketing. These materials are part of the marketing equation, but only a small part. As the marketing iceberg principle, originally adapted from Ernest Hemingway's theory of omission (Trodd, 2007; Monash University, 2018) illustrates, the visible components of marketing—the promotions—are a very small portion of the library's marketing efforts. The visible portion of the iceberg might represent the library website, its social media postings, the library displays, and other promotional materials such as newsletters. The invisible part of the iceberg represents what cannot be seen: the library's strategic plan, their marketing plan, and their market research data (more about this in chapter 3)—all the things that underpin the marketing activities and initiatives the library undertakes.

Marketing is especially important now for libraries, who must compete with bookstores, Google, Amazon, Facebook, YouTube, and the rest of the Internet to provide information. The library no longer has a monopoly on information access. We need to step up and serve our users proactively rather than passively waiting for users to walk in our doors. Waiting around for patrons hasn't been working. In the last decade, circulation and reference desk transactions have declined (Martell, 2008; Applegate, 2008; Martell, 2007; Dubnjakovic, 2012). To attract new users and better serve existing patrons, we need to have an attractive facility with knowledgeable, friendly, and accessible employees; we need intuitive, user-friendly websites; and we must create collections, services, and resources that meet our users' needs. Marketing involves studying our users' needs and ensuring that we fulfill those needs in our communications, products, and services.

The overarching goal of this book is to help libraries and librarians develop relationships with users by tailoring services, collections, electronic resources, and communication channels (signage, printed promotional materials, websites, and social media) to meet users' needs.

We know that library services and resources should be user centered, but we often do not know what that looks like—what our users truly want. This book aims to teach you how to better understand your users' needs by using the assessment methods and tools of marketing.

GROWTH IN DEMAND FOR LIBRARY MARKETING SKILLS

Library marketing has become an increasingly hot topic over the last two decades. Koontz, Gupta, and Webber (2006) reviewed the field, examining the number of books and articles published about library marketing during two periods: 1957 and 1978 (76 articles) and 3,382 papers from 1979 to 2006. A cursory WorldCat search for publications about library marketing since 2006 indicates that 45 books have been published since Koontz, Gupta, and Webber (2006) carried out their study, and the EBSCO Library and Information Science database shows citations to 4,593 articles published between 2006 and 2018. This increase in published books and articles in the last 12 years, and 2015's inaugural Library Marketing and Communications Conference in Addison, Texas, suggest that interest in library marketing is growing.

This increase in interest in library marketing is also apparent in changes in library job advertisements, which now often ask for marketing skills. Between 2000 and 2010, there has also been an increase in the number of jobs posted seeking librarians with the skills to help market their libraries (Okamoto and Polger, 2012), and the number of specialized library positions whose main responsibilities include marketing and public relations. Many other job advertisements have coded mentions of marketing duties: the words "outreach," "communications," and "engagement" often denote jobs whose major responsibilities include marketing, and positions such as community engagement librarians, communications librarians, and public relations librarians all require marketing skills (Gerolimos, Malliari, and Iakovidis, 2015; Triumph and Beile, 2015). Libraries are thus slowly embracing marketing as a legitimate set of skills for librarians (Spalding and Wang, 2006).

In many public and large academic libraries, library marketing is done by professionals with marketing or graphic design backgrounds, and some libraries with even larger budgets have a full time graphic designer on staff. The professional library marketers, who often do not hold MLIS degrees, typically do not engage in traditional librarian activities such as reference, instruction, or collection development. There is sometimes a disconnect between library marketers without MLIS degrees and those with formal academic training in marketing. Some marketers without MLIS degrees do not think like librarians, and they often need to work with a professional librarian to successfully realize their vision when planning marketing activities.

According to Siess (2003), library marketing is a crucial step in increasing library visibility in order to combat declining budgets, the easy access to information offered by the Internet, and the public perception that libraries are extinct. She argues that librarians must market themselves as highly qualified research experts, and that while downsizing and outsourcing have become the "new normal," librarians must lobby for more employees and more funding by marketing their libraries. Library marketing is a tool for library survival.

WHAT TO EXPECT FROM THIS BOOK

This book provides a beginner's guide for readers interested in actively raising the profile of their library to their users. Many libraries and librarians have had success with informal efforts to market their libraries, implementing initiatives piecemeal, informally conducting marketing activities without a marketing plan, or conducting community research. However, these marketing efforts can be improved upon and made more efficient.

This book offers an overview of basic marketing principles and application. It contains library-specific marketing examples, as well as many examples from the corporate sector, which can be adapted to use in libraries. Libraries do not have the multimillion-dollar marketing budgets of large corporations, but librarians are creative, and they can use these corporate campaigns to inspire activities and strategies that will work for them.

Chapter 1 provides definitions of the basic marketing terms that are used throughout the book. It also clarifies the differences between marketing and promotion, publicity and public relations, outreach and communications, and advocacy and lobbying.

Chapter 2 delves into market segmentation—the process of dividing your users into different subgroups to more accurately identify each subgroup's needs. The chapter shows how to create profiles for your different users and how to identify your target audience.

Chapter 3 discusses how to gather data about your local library users. It gives an overview of the basic principles of market research, explaining how to conduct a SWOT analysis or an environmental scan. It also explains how to use existing census or survey data to better understand your community.

Chapter 4 identifies the steps to creating a library marketing plan. Marketing plans can be created for specific events, services, or resources, or as part of a broader library marketing campaign. This chapter includes sample marketing plans from academic, public, and special libraries.

Chapter 5 identifies the components of a library marketing campaign and the planning process involved in implementing such a campaign: preliminary research, outlining goals and objectives, developing a call to action (CTA), using different communication channels to spread the message, and using different assessment tools to evaluate the campaign's effect. This chapter includes discussions of many campaigns (marketing, advertising, public awareness, and advocacy campaigns) from libraries, nonprofits, and the corporate sector, including some John Cotton Dana Award–winning campaigns.

Chapter 6 examines how to develop a unique library brand. It discusses how to conduct a brand audit, maintain brand loyalty, manage your brand, co-brand, and maintain brand awareness.

Chapter 7 explains how to market the physical space of the library, including the furniture, the entrance, signage, displays, and exhibits.

Chapter 8 surveys online tools for library marketing: the library website, email marketing software, website advertisements, Google advertisements, and website analytics programs for learning more about how your users interact with the library website.

Chapter 9 provides an introduction to social media marketing, with a discussion of Facebook, Twitter, Instagram, YouTube and Pinterest. Social media advertisements and analytics tools are also addressed in this chapter.

Chapter 10 discusses library advocacy, an important component of your library's marketing efforts. Advocacy is the essence, spirit, and heart of marketing, and library marketing can only be successful when the library's core values include advocacy. Library employees must become advocates for libraries, and this chapter offers some techniques of advocacy, including elevator speeches, word-of-mouth marketing, compelling presentations, outreach, and community partnerships.

All ten chapters should inspire the reader to think about libraries from a marketing frame of mind. Each chapter provides practical examples from the corporate and nonprofit sector that are relatable to all types of libraries. This book is written in plain language and will help library employees understand the steps to successfully implement marketing activities in their libraries.

REFERENCES

Applegate, Rachel. 2008. "Whose decline? Which academic libraries are 'deserted' in terms of reference transactions?" *Reference & User Services Quarterly*, 176–189.

Asheim, Lester. 1978. "Librarians as professionals." *Library Trends* 27, 3: 225–257.

Boyce, Bert, and Judith Boyce. 1991. "The Bookmobile: A service mechanism for the nineties?" *Wilson Library Bulletin* 66, no. 2: 31–34.

Croneis, Karen S., and Pat Henderson. 2002. "Electronic and digital librarian positions: A content analysis of announcements from 1990 through 2000." *The Journal of Academic Librarianship* 28, no. 4: 232–237.

Curry, Ann, Kris Wolf, Sandra Boutilier, and Helen Chan. 2003. "Canadian federal prison libraries: A national survey." *Journal of Librarianship and Information Science* 35, no. 3: 141–152.

de la Peña McCook, Kathleen. 2004. "Public libraries and people in jail." *Reference & User Services Quarterly* 44, no. 1: 26–30.

Dubnjakovic, Ana. 2012. "Electronic resource expenditure and the decline in reference transaction statistics in academic libraries." *The Journal of Academic Librarianship* 38, no. 2: 94–100.

Estall, Carole, and Derek Stephens. 2011. "A study of the variables influencing academic library employees' attitudes toward marketing." *New Review of Academic Librarianship* 17, no. 2: 185–208.

Gerolimos, Michalis, Afrodite Malliari, and Pavlos Iakovidis. 2015. "Skills in the market: An analysis of skills and qualifications for American librarians." *Library Review* 64, no. 1/2: 21–35.

Goetsch, Lori A. 2008. "Reinventing our work: New and emerging roles for academic librarians." *Journal of Library Administration* 48, no. 2: 157–172.

Goode, William J. 1961. "The librarian: From occupation to profession?" *The Library Quarterly* 31, no. 4: 306–320.

Gray, Sara Wingate. 2013. "Locating librarianship's identity in its historical roots of professional philosophies: Towards a radical new identity for librarians of today (and tomorrow)." *IFLA Journal* 39, no. 1: 37–44.

Grimes, Marybeth F., and Paul W. Grimes. 2008. "The academic librarian labor market and the role of the Master of Library Science degree: 1975 through 2005." *The Journal of Academic Librarianship* 34, no. 4: 332–339.

Hanks, Gardner, and C. James Schmidt. 1975. "An alternative model of a profession for librarians." *College & Research Libraries* 36, no. 3: 175–187.

Horrigan, John B. 2017. "How people approach facts and information." September 11. http://www.pewinternet.org/2017/09/11/how-people-approach-facts-and-information/ (Accessed July 1, 2018).

Kneale, Ruth. 2014a. *You don't look like a librarian: Shattering stereotypes and creating positive new images in the internet age.* Medford: Information Today, Inc.

Kneale, Ruth. 2014b. "Librarians and pop culture: What's the skinny, anyway?" *OLA Quarterly* 14, no. 1: 21.

Koontz, Christie M., Dinesh K. Gupta, and Sheila Webber. 2006. "Key publications in library marketing: A review." *IFLA Journal* 32, no. 3: 224–231.

Kroll, Elyse. 2004. "Breaking the mold: Information professionals as action figures and reality show characters. What's next . . . a nude librarian calendar? Yes!" *Information Outlook* 8, no. 2: 17–21.

Kumbar, Rajashekhar D. 2004. "The importance of marketing and total quality management in libraries." *Electronic Journal of Academic and Special Librarianship* 5, no. 2–3. http://southernlibrarianship.icaap.org/content/v05n02/kumbar_r01.htm

Lehmann, Vibeke. 2011. "Challenges and accomplishments in US prison libraries." *Library Trends* 59, no. 3: 490–508.

Martell, Charles. 2007. "The elusive user: Changing use patterns in academic libraries 1995 to 2004." *College & Research Libraries* 68, no. 5: 435–445.

Martell, Charles. 2008. "The absent user: Physical use of academic library collections and services continues to decline 1995–2006." *The Journal of Academic Librarianship* 34, no. 5: 400–407.

McClelland, Timothy. 2014. "What exactly do you do here? Marketing-related jobs in public and academic libraries." *Journal of Library Administration* 54, no. 5: 347–367.

Meier, John J. 2010. "Are today's science and technology librarians being overtasked? An analysis of job responsibilities in recent advertisements on the ALA JobLIST web site." *Science & Technology Libraries* 29, no. 1–2: 165–175.

Monash University. 2018. "Iceberg Principle." February. https://www.monash.edu/business/marketing/marketing-dictionary/i/iceberg-principle (Accessed July 24, 2018).

Mosley, Pixey Anne. 2003. "Shedding the stereotypes: Librarians in the 21st century." *The Reference Librarian* 37, no. 78: 167–176.

Okamoto, Karen, and Mark Aaron Polger. 2012. "Off to market we go: A content analysis of marketing and promotion skills in academic librarian job ads." *Library Leadership and Management* 26, 2: 1–20.

Perrin, Andrew, and Jingjing Jiang. 2018. "About a quarter of U.S. adults say they are 'almost constantly' online." March 14. http://www.pewresearch.org/fact-tank/2018/03/14/about-a-quarter-of-americans-report-going-online-almost-constantly/ (Accessed July 1, 2018).

Polger, Mark Aaron. 2010. "Information takeout and delivery: A case study exploring different library service delivery models." *Journal of Hospital Librarianship* 10, no. 1: 3–22.

Rodwell, John, and Linden Fairbairn. 2008. "Dangerous liaisons? Defining the faculty liaison librarian service model, its effectiveness and sustainability." *Library Management* 29, no. 1/2: 116–124.

Sadeh, Tamar. 2070. "Time for a change: New approaches for a new generation of library users." *New Library World* 108, no. 7/8: 307–316.

Shank, John D. 2006. "The blended librarian: A job announcement analysis of the newly emerging position of instructional design librarian." *College & Research Libraries* 67, no. 6: 514–524.

Shontz, Marilyn L., Jon C. Parker, and Richard Parker. 2004. "What do librarians think about marketing? A survey of public librarians' attitudes toward the marketing of library services." *The Library Quarterly* 74, no. 1: 63–84.

Siess, Judith A. 2003. *The visible librarian: Asserting your value with marketing and advocacy*. American Library Association.

Singh, Rajesh. 2009. "Does your library have an attitude problem towards 'marketing'? Revealing inter-relationship between marketing attitudes and behaviour." *The Journal of Academic Librarianship* 35, no. 1: 25–32.

Singh, Rajesh. 2017. "Marketing competency for information professionals: The role of marketing education in library and information science education programs" *Marketing Libraries Journal* 1, no. 1: 60–83.

Smith, Stewart W. 1961. "Potentialities and capabilities of bookmobiles for library service," *Library Trends* 9, no. 3: 296–302.

Spalding, Helen H., and Jian Wang. 2006. "The challenges and opportunities of marketing academic libraries in the USA: Experiences of US academic libraries with global application." *Library Management* 27, no. 6/7: 494–504.

Trodd, Zoe. 2007. "Hemingway's camera eye: The problem of language and an interwar politics of form." *The Hemingway Review* 26, no. 2: 7–21.

Triumph, Therese F., and Penny M. Beile. 2015. "The trending academic library job market: An analysis of library position announcements from 2011 with comparisons to 1996 and 1988." *College & Research Libraries* 76, no. 6: 716–739.

Vårheim, Andreas, Sven Steinmo, and Eisaku Ide. 2008. "Do libraries matter? Public libraries and the creation of social capital." *Journal of Documentation* 64, no. 6: 877–892.

Welch, Jeanie M. 2005. "The electronic welcome mat: The academic library web site as a marketing and public relations tool." *The Journal of Academic Librarianship* 31, no. 3: 225–228.

Wisniewski, Jeff. 2007. "Build it (and customize and market it) and they will come." *Internet Reference Services Quarterly* 12, no. 3–4: 341–355.

Yi, Zhixian, Damian Lodge, and Sigrid McCausland. 2013. "Australian academic librarians' perceptions of marketing services and resources." *Library Management* 34, no. 8/9: 585–602.

CHAPTER 1

What Marketing Really Is

IN THIS CHAPTER

- Identifying the different branches of marketing
- Learning marketing-related terms used throughout the book
- Applying the 4Ps of marketing
- Illustrating the 5 elements of the promotional mix
- Understanding the cycle of true marketing
- Discovering why library employees confuse marketing terminology

UNDERSTANDING THE TERM "MARKETING"

Librarians want to spread their message, so they use a variety of communication tools to promote and highlight their library's services and resources. They have the best of intentions, but their efforts are very often misguided, sporadic, random, uninformed, and not user-centered. Librarians think they *know* what is best for their users, but they are ill informed because they haven't taken the time to conduct research. Librarians build collections, subscribe to databases, develop programs and events, hold workshops, and develop elaborate information literacy programs, but they don't consult their users enough. Major funding may bring renovations, new furniture, a new entrance, updated classrooms, and a new cafe, but very little of those decisions take into consideration the thoughts and feelings of library users. Unfortunately, librarians often conduct user surveys after the fact and not during the planning stages of any large-scale renovation or improvement project.

This chapter briefly defines the components of the marketing umbrella. So many library employees confuse and misunderstand the terms below. It is important to illustrate how each term is related to marketing. Further, the chapter identifies how the terms differ from each other. As an example, many pair the terms "marketing and promotion," but in fact, promotion is a component of marketing. Many will also pair "marketing and outreach," but outreach represents a small part of marketing. All of the marketing terms defined here will be used throughout the book; it is important to correctly understand what marketing is and not confuse the terms. Terms will be defined, including some examples of how the concept is used in the business world, followed by brief examples of how they relate to librarians and librarians. Chapters later in the book will expand on these marketing concepts.

MARKETING DEFINED

This book will use an adaptation of the modern definitions of marketing by McCarthy (1960) and Kotler (1967). Marketing represents the long-term planned activities and communication strategies an organization engages in so they can connect their products and services with their intended users. Marketing involves strategic planning, assessment, and evaluation of its users; it matches users' needs and wants with the organization's products and services. Both McCarthy and Kotler's definition of marketing includes the concept of the marketing mix. The marketing mix is comprised of the 4Ps: price, place, promotion, and product. The 4Ps will be discussed more in depth later in this chapter.

Commercial marketing deals mostly with products, but since libraries fall into the category of nonprofit institutions, the central focus of this book will be on services marketing. The branches of marketing defined here are: (1) content marketing, (2) relationship marketing, (3) services marketing, (4) social marketing, and (5) branding.

Content Marketing

Content marketing is a technique of creating and distributing valuable, relevant, and consistent content to attract and acquire a clearly defined audience (Steimle, 2014). Content marketing can be exemplified as the compelling content that is used to target potential customers. Examples include a blog post, a newsletter article, a webinar, podcast, a website slide (in a rotating slide show), a Facebook post, a tweet, or an original photograph taken at a library event (Solomon, 2016). Where marketing content represents all aspects of the marketing components, content marketing relates to the creation of textual and visual content that culminates the entire marketing process.

Internal Marketing

Internal marketing is synonymous with buy-in. It is the way an organization communicates its products and services to its employees. As Mitchell (2002) argues, the "internal" market are the employees of the institution, who are just as important as the customers. Unfortunately, many companies ignore this target audience. It strives to help employees connect to the products and services they are selling. Some strategies to target your internal audience may include staff meetings, targeted communications, and sharing your institution's strategic plan with your staff. Dowd, Evangeliste, and Silberman (2010) also argue that keeping everyone in the communication loop with transparency helps. Internal marketing builds employee loyalty and commitment. It relates to keeping employees informed through the same communication channels as customers, but internal marketing is also about convincing employees to trust the company and its products and services.

Relationship Marketing

Relationship marketing is also known as customer relationship management (CRM) (Olenski, 2013). It focuses on customer loyalty and long-term engagement, rather than the short-term goals of profit, customer acquisition, and individual sales (Gruen, Summers, and Acito, 2000). Relationship marketing examines in-person relationships, relationship building, and customer retention. Relationship marketing is about creating emotional connections with customers. For example, Starbucks attempts to create friendly and interactive relationships between the barista and customers. In particular, they build these connections in neighborhood stores when they make it a point to re-member customer names (Haskova, 2015). Very often, both relation-ship marketing and services marketing are used together to develop memorable customer experiences.

Services Marketing

Services marketing relates to the promotion of services rather than products. In services marketing, organizations deliver value to their customers; customers are at the center of services marketing rather than products. Since services are intangible, services marketing delves into the value of customer relationships, as opposed to a particular product. For services marketing, the 4Ps have been expanded to the 7Ps: price, product, placement, promotion, and three more Ps—physical evidence, people, and process (Gummesson, 1994).

Services marketing is a series of activities implemented through different interactions. Traditionally, companies were evaluated on the products they produced, but as the manufacturing industry became more automated and moved abroad, companies were evaluated more on their services than their products. Trader Joe's cashiers are trained to engage their customers in conversations about their purchases at checkout. They are trained to sound interested in customers' purchases, although at times it may feel forced and inauthentic (Byrne, 2004). An-other important quality of Trader Joe's is its mission to offer customers high-quality specialty food at a lower price in a casual environment. Employees are dressed in Hawaiian shirts, and the experience is meant to be fun and playful (Anitsal, Anitsal, and Girard, 2012). Groceries and big box stores like Wal-Mart compete for customer service and customer loyalty. Low pricing is not the only factor that keeps custom-ers returning (Allaway et al., 2011). Porter Airlines, a Canadian airline headquartered in Toronto, Canada, prides itself for being unique and for being customer centric. They treat every customer as a VIP, offer free alcohol on board, have customer lounges with free coffee, snacks, and free iMac Internet connected computer workstations. They have their own mascot (a raccoon) and their own publication, *re:Porter*. They brand themselves as "flying refined" aiming to create memorable customer experiences (Gooderham, 2010).

Libraries fit into this branch of marketing because library employees want to connect library services with their users by establishing meaningful relationships and interactions. Whether librarians promote interlibrary loan service, laptop lending, iPad and calculator lending, or virtual chat reference that is offered 24/7, services marketing highlights library services as "products."

Social Marketing

Social marketing involves the use of marketing principles and techniques to advance a social cause, idea, or behavior (Kotler and Zaltman, 1971). Social marketing should not be confused with social media marketing, which will be explained in its own chapter. It attempts to introduce a new set of behaviors, reject undesirable behavior, or modify behavior. It has been used greatly in obesity prevention (Bellows et al., 2008; Herrick, 2007), recycling (McKenzie-Mohr, 2000), smoking prevention (Gordon et al., 2006), and alcohol abuse (Glider et al., 2001).

Branding

Branding establishes a visual identity for your organization; it involves linking an image, mascot, logo, name, color scheme, slogan, play on words, or phrase with the library. The library brand represents a visual aid in storytelling. Branding establishes an emotional connection between a customer and the organization.

Branding starts with a catchy tagline. A classic example is Maxwell House's coffee tagline "Good to the last drop," popularized by Cora the storekeeper (played by Margaret Hamilton, better known as the Wicked Witch of the West from the 1939 film *The Wizard of Oz*) (Kalter, 1979). In addition, having a logo or image is important as it enables people to remember the product.

Although brands are most associated with products, some brands are so strong that their products are secondary. Kleenex brand tissues are often called "Kleenex." Apple's Christmas commercials with the slogan "open your heart" do not even show the products they sell (MacBooks, iPads, iPods, etc.) (Mazza, 2016). Coca Cola (Page and Thorsteinsson, 2009) and Google have such strong brand power that people think of them as unique products. Google has become a verb and an adjective (Rosencrance, 2008), and Coca Cola (or simple Coke) has become synonymous with cola. Starbucks' brand is so strong, it no longer needs the text "Starbucks Coffee" below its iconic mermaid logo (Fuller, 2011).

Branding can be so powerful that people can recognize a product or organization simply by the visuals associated with it. Brands such as IKEA, Coca Cola, Starbucks, Apple, and even Oprah have garnered global attention. In the library world, many library users will read a book listed on Oprah's book club because of Oprah's brand power (Maleeny, 2015). Further, her brand power is so strong that if she endorses any author from her book club, they will most likely enjoy much financial success and power themselves. This phenomenon is known as the "Oprah effect" (Loroz and Braig, 2015).

A library brand involves developing an image or a set of images that encompass positive feelings about the library. Creating your own library brand can be implemented by color-coded signs, font types in the promotional materials, consistent clothing worn by library employees, the standards of customer service delivered by staff, a specific set of furniture colors that correspond to the colors of the website, a logo, a newsletter, and other promotional material.

Some libraries have taglines that sit below their logo such as, "your open door to learning." A tagline is typically a brief phrase that relates to the overall mission of your library. Branding, brand management, and brand loyalty will be further addressed in chapter 6.

CYCLE OF TRUE MARKETING

The marketing process involves an ongoing process of activities that include constant communication with your users, assessment and evaluation, and developing a set of concrete, tangible goals for your library. The following steps, described/defined here, comprise the marketing process (Dempsey, 2009).

1. **Market Research:** Understanding your library users.
2. **Market Segmentation:** You have different types of users. It is important to treat them differently.

3. **Set Goals:** Set qualitative and quantitative goals for each group you want to target.
4. **Understand Your Segment:** Get to know your target market more by asking them questions.
5. **Identify and Create Products and Services:** According to market research, identify their wants and needs and create products and services for your different segments.
6. **Evaluate:** Evaluate the effects of giving your users what they want.
7. **Promote:** Promote the products and services to your target groups.
8. **Deliver:** Deliver products and services with your evaluation tools in place.
9. **Get Feedback:** Get feedback from individuals to ascertain whether you've met their needs.
10. **Tweak and Review:** Review your evaluations and update your programs, services, and goals to ensure quality service.
11. **Improve:** Update and improve your products and services and start the cycle again.

The cycle of true marketing will be discussed in greater detail in the chapter on library marketing plans (chapter 4).

THE 4Ps OF MARKETING—THE MARKETING MIX

Marketing involves understanding the different users of the organization, assessing their preferences and needs, and developing specific initiatives that target specific groups (or segments) of your population. As mentioned earlier, marketing consists of the 4Ps: product, pricing, place, promotion (McCarthy, 1960).

Known as the marketing mix, true marketing involves these elements working together in a cyclical manner. For libraries, some aspects of the marketing mix must be adapted accordingly (Olu Adeyoyin, 2005; Das and Karn, 2008).

In 1981, Booms and Bitner expanded the 4Ps to the 7Ps, adding physical evidence, people, and process to the mix above (Gummesson,

1994). More recently, in 1973 Professor Koichi Shimizu adapted the 4Ps to the 4Cs model: commodity, cost, communication, channel. He further expanded the 4Cs into the 7Cs (corporation, commodity, cost, communication, channel, consumer, circumstance) (Madhav, Sandeep, and Caleb, 2014). In 1990, Lauterborn offered an alternative 4C model (consumer, cost, communication, convenience) (Paul and Bihani, 2014). For the sake of simplicity, most of this book will focus on the 4Ps—the marketing mix.

Product

The "product" relates to what the organization or company is selling to the customer. McDonald's sells hamburgers and other meat-based products. In the early 1990s, McDonald's came out with pizza in Canada and the United States, and it was not very successful (Csanady, 2015). Starbucks focuses more on the customer experience rather than products. Customers can buy a cup of coffee for as little as one dollar at McDonald's, but Starbucks aims to provide an experience where every drink is crafted and customized to the customer's liking (Mascarenhas et al., 2006).

The library "product" can be identified as the plethora of library services and resources that are offered to the community. The library product can be somewhat related to the "user experience" of the physical facility and the virtual places of the library, and include the experiences users feel when they use the facility and interact with a library staff person. Products include the library's collection of books, electronic resources, furniture, computers, laptops, iPads, and other technology. The product can extend to the library website, the electronic resources provided, the cleanliness of the restrooms, the design of the entrance, or the overall "look and feel" of the reference desk. The product is the overall aesthetic of the library, both in physical and virtual formats.

Price

The "price" represents the value of the product that is being sold. The price determines the place, promotion, branding, and the profit margins. In Canada, the "no name" brand (owned by Loblaws Grocery) is a lower-end, more generic food brand that is considered a lower level version of the Loblaws grocery chain. The "no name" brand and its "no frills" stores are not as decorative and not high-end like the Loblaws chain. Less money is spent on marketing and advertising (Shaw, 2014). Starbucks' coffee prices are more expensive than Dunkin' Donuts because of its marketing strategy and its goal to provide a higher-end customer experience. More money is spent on the design of the café and the ambiance. Dunkin' Donuts' goal is more practical with its tagline—"America runs on Dunkin"—which is targeted to the "average Joe" (Champagne and Iezzi, 2014)

The library's "price" represents the value the library allocates each service or resource. Library users are often disconnected from pricing since all library services appear to be free. In fact, each library service costs significant staff time, and resources can cost in the millions each year. Library users are unaware that due to the declining use of the print collection, many libraries are spending more of their annual budget on electronic resources (databases, e-journals, e-newspapers, e-magazines, and e-books). The library's price for programs, resources, and services relates to what percentage of their annual budget is allocated to a specific program or resource.

Place

The "place" represents the physical and virtual spaces where the company sells its products. Many stores have "brick and mortar" locations like Macy's or Wal-Mart, while some stores are online only (like Wayfair or Amazon, until recently). When a new Whole Foods or Trader Joe's grocery store opens in a neighborhood, it opens there because market research has revealed that there is a need to have this grocery presence. Starbucks does not open in random corners of the city. Market research is conducted to determine if there is a customer base that would purchase Starbucks products.

The library's "place" represents the physical facility and the virtual places the library positions itself within the larger organizational context. For a college library, the place is important because the library needs to position itself as the center of knowledge, and in an ideal world, the physical library would be located at the center of campus.

The college library must ensure that it has a place at the table by advocating for increased funding, exposure, increased staffing, and increased services.

A college library may convince the college's administration and IT department to have their URL placed prominently on the college website. This is a small form of advocacy. The library must emphasize its place within the college hierarchy. Further, the college library will often fight for autonomy when developing their website. They don't want to be controlled by the college IT department and want to manage their own website content and design. Having a solid place (both physical and virtual) is very important as it gives the library more credibility.

The fact that many libraries want their own buildings and don't want to be hidden on a few floors or in a shopping mall illustrates the importance of "the library as place" (Waxman et al., 2007). The library as "place" matters. Some libraries spend hundreds of thousands of dollars on items that many users might not notice: fancier, updated chairs, ergonomic furniture, updated technology, updated electrical systems, and new carpeting. Virtually, libraries need to invest in infrastructure that can support improved wireless and wired connectivity. The concept of "place" is sometimes overlooked by library users. Improved lighting, updated restrooms, new library signage, painting, repairing the roof, and upgrading the web server for a library website renovation are just some more examples of the importance of library as "place" in the marketing mix.

Promotion

Promotion represents how organizations communicate their value to their customers. Traditionally, there are marketing departments with publicists, communication specialists, advertising departments, social media managers, and graphic designers who create promotional material. Promotion is the act of raising awareness to the community that you wish to target. Similar to the way an employee gets a promotion from one position to another, or a raise in salary, the term "promotion" in the context of marketing relates to getting your message across and making your message central in people's minds. Promotion is only a small part of marketing, but many people confuse the two terms as one and the same.

Promotion actually represents the tip of the marketing iceberg (Kac-zynski, 2008; Kotler and Goldgehn, 1981). The marketing iceberg represents a visual depiction of the entire marketing process, where everything visible is the creative activities that a marketer might do to get their message across. This might include television advertisements, press releases, promotional swag, YouTube videos, radio interviews, posters, flyers, banners, and social media buzz. The hidden part of the marketing iceberg metaphor represents the long-term planning, assess-ment, and ongoing evaluation of the entire campaign.

Promotion is the "fun" part of marketing since it relates to the cre-ative endeavors that so many librarians dismiss as "fluff." Promotion is the part of marketing that comes last. It is where all library employees should be involved. It would be more productive if the library staff collectively worked together to promote its value. The library's promo-tional efforts should not be supported by just one person, but by a team of people or even the entire library staff. At the root of promotion is the importance of communicating the value of the library.

When librarians are asked to create a flyer, a brochure, or a poster to promote an event, database, author talk, or film series, what they are actually doing is the promotion part of marketing. Most librarians pro-mote the value of the physical facility, the print collection, a collection of electronic resources, their website, or an audio video collection, and the staff that support these library services and resources. Unlike a large-scale marketing campaign, promoting is often piecemeal, informal, and typically not assessed or evaluated. Promotion is not usually targeted to a specific audience, and often times the promotional vehicle used may be the wrong one. Librarians should think carefully when selecting their promotional outlet to use. For example, promoting computer training classes for senior citizens (who might not be tech savvy), should not be posted on social media, as it may be counterproductive. It should be pro-moted on a platform that will attract the appro-priate audience, such as a printed newsletter.

Promotional Mix

Advertising
Direct Marketing
Personal Selling
Public Relations
Sales Promotions

Promotion can be further subdivided into what is called the Promotional Mix (see text-box). Each of these promotional methods is used extensively by businesses and can be adapted successfully for use in libraries.

Advertising

Advertising usually includes any paid dissemination of information to both traditional news media and to social media. Advertising is non-personal and generic. Unlike other components of promotion, the advertiser does not have a direct connection to the customer. Advertisements represent the visible parts of the "marketing iceberg," as mentioned in the introduction. Advertisements are what bombard our daily lives—on television; as full-page newspaper columns; on subway station platforms and in subway cars; on city buses, bus stops, park benches, billboards, all over Times Square; and in subtle ways like the Macy's Thanksgiving Day Parade. The Macy's Thanksgiving Day Parade in New York City provides New Yorkers with entertainment, but it also relays a positive message about Macy's (i.e., public relations), while at the same time advertising their company with the Macy's brand. In addition to advertising Macy's, other companies like Ocean Spray, Kentucky Fried Chicken, and Hallmark pay to be included in the parade (Pollack, 2015).

Advertisements are often confused with public service announcements and propaganda. Where all three types are highly visual, they are different. Advertisements are concerned with the selling of goods and services, while public service announcements are intended to raise awareness of an issue for the public good. In other words, they are probably paying money to be seen on television, radio, newspapers, magazines, but they are not asking for money. Propaganda, on the other hand, is the use of audio and visual media to sell a particular ideology or political belief. Very often, propaganda is disseminated in the form of posters, flyers, and through the news media. People for the Ethical Treatment of Animals (PETA) spends a great deal of their marketing budget on the placement of propaganda, which displaces traditional advertisements.

Libraries use another form of advertising when they create free promotional merchandise to give to their patrons. Known as swag, promotional merchandise offers a low-cost way to promote and advertise a library with branded items. Some popular examples of swag include staples, book bags, conference folders, pens, pencils, stationery, mousepads, and USB sticks. Swag is widely available at many online retailers such as VistaPrint or 4Imprint, and it provides a simple solution to promote your library and your brand. Branding and swag will be discussed in greater length in the branding chapter.

Direct Marketing

Direct marketing refers to a direct form of communication from seller to customer. Where advertisements direct their attention to the masses, direct marketing is focused on a specific customer subset. If someone purchases a product at an online store such as Wayfair or Overstock, they usually register for an online account. They might check off "receive announcements on new products and discounts." This is where direct marketing comes in. Direct marketing uses customer information (name, address, email, phone numbers) from online stores and starts to send messages about products, sales, and other incentives. Traditionally, telemarketing was rampant in the 1980s and still exists today, but email marketing has taken over. Where telemarketers were generally perceived as annoying and unnatural since many read from a script, email marketing sometimes has the same effect.

In the print world, direct marketing is sometimes referred to as "junk mail." Examples may include printed store catalogs and the constant letters from credit card companies inviting (almost begging) you to join. If done correctly, direct marketing can be informative and helpful and may influence you to purchase the product or services.

There is a fine line between useful information and harassment. Sometimes direct marketing can be poorly planned and not enough market research was involved (see chapter 3). Telemarketers who "cold call" people who live in Manhattan asking about car insurance did not conduct appropriate market research since many Manhattanites don't drive but take public transit.

When using email marketing software, the message must be highly visual, useful, current, and not too text-heavy. If libraries wish to pursue email marketing as a means to directly connect with users, they must find the balance between frequency, content depth, the number of articles in each email, and the number of photos (Giles, Perkins, and Crossno, 1998). It is important to note that libraries who conduct email marketing should only use emails from consenting library users. Thus, the library must ask users for permission to continue receiving messages from the library (Tezinde, Smith, and Murphy, 2002).

Personal Selling

Personal selling represents the direct, in-person interaction between buyer and seller. This can be characterized by the retail staff who work on commission and may make a more concerted effort in personal selling than those staff who make an hourly wage or annual salary. Personal selling represents all the interactions the customer receives from the seller. In personal selling, the customers are already there, as opposed to advertising which is generated to the masses.

Personal selling also exists online. When a customer purchases a product on eBay or Etsy, the seller not only sends an auto confirmation of their product and price paid but also the websites are set up to ask for feedback, with both the purchaser (customer) and seller providing a review or grade for each other.

In a library, personal selling involves the interactions between the library employees and users at the circulation desk, reference desk, via email, via livechat, and via social media. Personal selling is more about individual communications and less about the physical/digital divide. It offers a unique opportunity for librarians and staff to promote library services and resources in their conversations, the reference interview, or even in their elevator speeches with administration (which will be discussed in chapter 5). Personal selling is a more intimate form of communication because it is in-person, direct, and is more engaging than other forms of communication.

Public Relations

Publicity and public relations are often thought of as being the same. Publicity represents one aspect of public relations. Publicity involves any type of exposure or dissemination to the media. Publicity is not paid and it involves promoting your message to the media. Popular examples of publicity can include newspaper articles, magazine articles, radio announcements, interviews, live events, and web-based promotional materials. With the advent of the Internet, the term "media" has evolved. The media used to be a controlled group of one-way communicators but now with social media and the Internet, the general population is creating their own content and promoting the library via their websites and social media. The purpose of publicity is similar to promotion—to raise awareness around a product, service, or brand.

Public relations focuses on the larger picture. Public relations represents the activities an organization will do to communicate a favorable image to its potential customers. Public relations is very similar to advertisements but where advertising is more visual, public relations is more textual. Public relations departments attempt to create a consistent message to relay to the public about the organization. Each employee should be cognizant of public relations when they speak about their workplace. Public relations involves defending your employer, and communicating positive words about your organization. Public relations relates to a sense of workplace pride.

Public relations uses different methods to influence the behavior of specific audiences. The purpose of public relations is to create and preserve a positive reputation of the organization. The Macy's Thanksgiving Day Parade is both an advertising and public relations campaign at the same time. Since it's branded as "Macy's," there is no doubt that the customer thinks of the large department store. This is where branding is important (library branding will be discussed in chapter 6). Whether subtle or overt, the Macy's Thanksgiving Day Parade advertises Macy's since at some point, the parade even passes by the iconic store. More broadly, it is a public relations campaign because having such a famous, joyous (free) celebration obviously gives good exposure to the Macy's name and this in turn creates a favorable image of the company (Piffer, 2016). In Toronto, Canada, Honest Ed's discount department store (which closed permanently on December 31, 2016, after 68 years) held its annual free turkey giveaway during Canadian Thanksgiving in early October (Lalani, 2016). Both stores were not selling their products that day per se, but they were trying to present their company in a positive way to the community. Where advertising is about selling products using visuals, public relations is about selling the good-natured qualities of your organization through words and actions.

Publicity in a library could be a website slide show, a press release, a social media posting, an individual newsletter article, or media coverage about a summer reading program. Public relations might be accomplished through the development of annual reports, newsletters, announcements from the library director, email blasts, and blog posts.

In a library, if there is a flood, rodent infestation, or property damage from a fire, it is traditionally the publicist (or the library director) who can clearly articulate the message in a positive and hopeful angle. The publicist is the link between the organization they represent, the public, and the media. They typically manage public relations activities by providing the official information before the media picks it up and spins it in an unfavorable way. Publicity only represents a small aspect of public relations. Public relations looks at the entire organization as a whole and attempts to develop a specific image of itself to the media and the public.

Social media has introduced a new era in public relations. Public relations has now become a two-way communication street with celebrities having Facebook, Twitter, and Instagram presences. Social media has blurred the lines between publicity and public relations. Traditionally, the publicist would be the gatekeeper who would write curated messages to the public for the celebrities and organizations they represent. Now with social media, the messages are more unmoderated, informal, unfiltered, and organic. Celebrities and organizations have a closer reach to promote their products or services, or simply engage their audience. Social media eliminates the middleman of the traditional press.

In a library, it is important to utilize a social media policy so that all publicity disseminated via social media is curated for consistency in tone. Social media allows a more direct line to the customer to promote library services, events, programs, and resources. Social media marketing will be discussed in greater length in chapter 9.

Sales Promotions

Sales promotion includes promo codes, loyalty programs, points programs, coupons, in-store demonstrations, free food tastings at supermarkets, displays, contests, and incentive programs. A perfect example would be a rewards card where customers receive points for making purchases. Incentive programs are great ways to draw people in. Whenever an organization has sales, discounts, rebates, or "2 for 1 specials," they are rewarding you for choosing to do business with them.

At a library, asking people to complete a questionnaire or participate in a focus group might be sweetened by providing an Amazon gift card. Another example is when the library offers two weeks of amnesty where library users are forgiven of their overdue books (Doyle, 2011). For libraries, sales promotions might include receiving a free book for being a library member for a certain amount of years, or giving away a free library t-shirt for taking out a certain number of books. Sales promotions are usually in the corporate world and usually relate to rewarding customers for being good. The provision of free promotional merchandise (known as swag) will be discussed in chapter 5.

OTHER TERMS LIBRARY STAFF CONFUSE

In addition to the terms mentioned above, librarians need to become familiar with some additional terms that will help them to market their library and its services and programs. These terms are:

- Advocacy
- Communications
- Outreach

Advocacy

Advocacy relates to activities that promote and defend a particular organization. Advocacy is about arguing in favor of a cause. Lobbying is a form of advocacy where people try to influence legislation. Public libraries lobby the local government for increased funding and academic libraries lobby their administration for policy changes. Where all lobbying represents a form of advocacy, not all advocacy is about lobbying. Lobbying attempts to influence specific legislation at the local, state, or federal level, while advocacy relates to educating people about a specific issue (Braun, 2011).

Libraries aim to find advocates who will promote the library to various stakeholders. Library advocates attempt to educate, influence, and lobby change. They try to target the community, the media, and legislators. Advocates can be library users, library trustees, friends of the library, library employees, socialites, and celebrities. However, library advocates usually tend to be members of the community (who are not library employees). Library advocacy can be thought of as an extension of public relations. Examples of library advocacy include publishing research articles, public speaking, writing reports, lobbying politicians, publishing testimonials on the library website, and curating a short elevator speech. Advocacy changes peoples' attitudes through user awareness and education. Library advocacy identifies specific issues, raises awareness, and asks influential people to speak on the library's behalf.

The American Library Association has developed various advocacy campaigns such as the Libraries Transform Campaign, I Love My Librarian, Library Card Signup Month, and National Library Week (ALA, 2017a). Advocacy is closely connected with activism and politics. Where public relations focuses on positive public perception, advocacy focuses on changing public perception. Public relations is about managing a public image but advocacy is about influencing to affect change.

Communication

Communication is the way people share meaning. Communication is cultural and contextual. It is also fragile because someone may express themselves in one way and the receiver of that information may interpret it differently. Companies use different communication platforms (print, radio, television, web, and social media) in order to reach their potential customers to sell their products and services. Communication is a powerful way to connect with your audience. Traditionally, most companies communicated visually using advertisements on television, in newspapers, and on billboards. Websites and social media now represent a "low/no cost" communication method for companies to relay their message out to the masses. Web and social media marketing will be discussed in greater length in chapters 8 and 9.

In libraries, communication is the vehicle for librarians to conduct marketing activities. Libraries explore different communication channels such as using word of mouth, print, web, radio, television, and social media. Libraries traditionally have used print to communicate their message. Pathfinders, brochures, newsletters, annual reports, memos, flyers, posters, press releases, banners, and signage were prevalent in libraries. In the 1990s, electronic media became not only trendy but the norm in communicating information to the masses. Library websites began to lead as a major communication tool. Some libraries consider their website to be another branch, while other libraries use their websites as their primary means to communicate with their audience. It is now considered an expectation that library websites be updated daily with current, timely information. E-newsletters, blog posts, email blasts, virtual exhibits, YouTube videos, digital signage, and social media all provide a free platform for libraries to communicate their value. It is important that libraries utilize the appropriate communication tools to relay their message and not use the wrong technology. As an example, the public library might use Pinterest to showcase new book covers and use YouTube to promote an upcoming author visit.

Outreach

Outreach is not synonymous with marketing, even though many library employees conflate the term. Outreach, like its name suggests, involves "reaching out." Traditionally, outreach serves a purpose for nonprofit organizations to target underserved populations who may not have access to your services. Outreach involves identifying gaps in service and trying to fill in those gaps by addressing the specific users who are "missing out." Outreach serves an educational role as many nonprofit organizations do not sell any products or services. They are simply offering a public service. Outreach is typically conducted by nonprofit organizations and often targets marginalized groups of people or specific communities. Placing your services at targeted satellite locations is also an example of outreach. Outreach is implemented when organizations step outside their own boundaries and provide services to others at their point of need. In the field of health care, physicians making housecalls or health care professionals visiting shopping malls to give flu shots are examples of outreach.

In the context of libraries, outreach is a way of providing services beyond the walls of the library. Librarians use outreach to develop partnerships with various communities that may be underserved by the library. Outreach may be part of a library's marketing plan as well as part of the library's strategic plan. For a public library, outreach might mean visiting high schools to promote the summer reading program the library is coordinating. Children's librarians at public libraries may visit local daycares to promote the use of public libraries. Public librarians may visit the college library and set up a booth where college students can sign up for a free library card. This last activity is often offered in September of each year as that month is designated as the American Library Association's library card signup month (ALA, 2017b).

At an academic library, outreach may constitute visiting nearby public library branches and collaborating on a joint event. College librarians may visit the high school and provide library instruction sessions to high school students, or they may visit campus departments such as the office of admissions and meet with parents and high school students to discuss library services. The academic library may coordinate a roving reference service in which librarians visit student residence halls and provide reference services to students' point of need. At a hospital library, the medical librarian may visit the clinical units and provide an information delivery service if staff are too busy to visit the library (Polger, 2010).

WHY PEOPLE MISUNDERSTAND THE TERMS

Many library employees misunderstand the true meaning of marketing, so they often use the term interchangeably with promotion or publicity. Promotion and publicity are part of the marketing umbrella but promoting a summer reading program is not true marketing. Placing an ad in the newspaper to promote a famous author visit is a paid advertisement but that only constitutes a small part of marketing. Some feel that marketing is synonymous with selling but that is an oversimplification of the term. Some library employees are uncomfortable using the word "marketing," either because they don't understand the term or they think that marketing is limited to commerce. Some librarians or library staff feel that creating a flyer or bookmark to promote their event is "marketing," but it's only a small part of the marketing process. Marketing represents the big picture. It involves strategic planning that requires market research, community analysis, a community needs assessment (chapter 2), and market segmentation (discussed in chapter 2). After market research and segmentation, different promotional activities will be targeted via a full-scale marketing campaign (as discussed in chapter 5). When planning the campaign, formal evaluation of activities must be conducted before and after the campaign to measure effectiveness (see chapter 2 and chapter 5).

KEY POINTS

This chapter defined marketing-related terms that will be used throughout the book. This chapter also provided an introduction to the 4Ps of marketing, the five components of the promotional mix, and the cycle of true marketing. Lastly, this chapter provided definitions of other terms that library employees conflated with marketing.

- Marketing relates to a variety of strategic activities organizations employ to connect their products and services with their users.
- Many library employees engage in promoting their libraries but few engage in true marketing.
- Many library employees promote services, resources, and programs without conducting market research to understand their users.
- Library employees must understand what true marketing is so they can provide services and resources that are relevant to their users.
- Marketing involves a planned process of market research, market segmentation, promotional activities, and evaluation.

Chapter 3 will examine various types of tools to best understand library users—market research, focus groups, interviewing, community analysis, and anecdotal evidence. These tools are needed to better understand library users before undertaking a large-scale library marketing campaign.

REFERENCES

Allaway, Arthur W., Patricia Huddleston, Judith Whipple, and Alexander E. Ellinger. 2011. "Customer-based brand equity, equity drivers, and customer loyalty in the supermarket industry." *Journal of Product & Brand Management* 20, no. 3: 190–204.

American Library Association. 2017a. "Libraries transform campaign." American Library Association. January 10. http://www.ala.org/advocacy/

American Library Association. 2017b. "September is library card sign-up month." American Library Association. January 10. http://www.ala.org/conferencesevents/celebrationweeks/card

Anitsal, M. Meral, Ismet Anitsal, and Tulay Girard. 2012. "The core of retail mission statements: Top 100 US retailers." *Academy of Strategic Management Journal* 11, no. 1: 131.

Bellows, Laura, Jennifer Anderson, Susan Martin Gould, and Garry Auld. 2008. "Formative research and strategic development of a physical activity component to a social marketing campaign for Obesity Prevention in Preschoolers." *Journal of Community Health* 33, no. 3: 169–178.

Braun, Linda. 2011. "Advocacy and lobbying—What's the difference?" *Young Adult Library Services Association* (blog). October 4. http://yalsa.ala.org/blog/2011/10/04/advocacy-and-lobbying-whats-the-difference/

Byrne, John A. 2004. "Lessons from our customer champions." *Fast Company* 87 (October): 16.

Champagne, Christine, and Teresa Iezzi. 2014. "Dunkin' Donuts and Starbucks: A tale of two coffee marketing giants," August 21. https://www.fastcocreate.com/3034572/coffee-week/dunkin-donuts-and-starbucks-a-tale-of-two-coffee-marketing-giants

Csanady, Ashley. 2015. "Attention children of the '90s: You can still get McDonald's pizza." Canada.com. January 20. http://o.canada.com/life/food/attention-children-of-the-90s-you-can-still-get-mcdonalds-pizza

Das, Basanta Kumar, and Sanjay Kumar Karn. 2008. "Marketing of library and information services in global era: A current approach." *Webology* 5, no. 2: 56. http://www.webology.org/2008/v5n2/a56.html

Dempsey, Kathy. 2009. *The accidental library marketer.* Medford, NJ: Information Today.

Dowd, Nancy, Mary Evangeliste, and Jonathan Silberman. 2010. *Bite-sized marketing: Realistic solutions for the overworked librarian.* American Library Association.

Doyle, John. 2011. "New York Public Library grants amnesty to 143K kids with outstanding fines to get them reading again." *New York Daily News*,

July 25. http://www.nydailynews.com/new-york/new-york-public-library -grants-amnesty-143k-kids-outstanding-fines-reading-article-1.157889.

Fuller, Elizabeth. 2011. "Starbucks logo change: No name. More mermaid. Will it sell more coffee?" *Christian science monitor.* January 6. http://www .csmonitor.com/Business/new-economy/2011/0106/Starbucks-logo-change -No-name.-More-mermaid.-Will-it-sell-more-coffee.

Giles, Sharon, Jeffrey Perkins, and Jon Crossno.1998. "Email marketing for libraries." October. Poster session presented at the meeting of the South Central Chapter of the Medical Library Association, Fort Worth, TX. https://repositories.tdl.org/utswmed-ir/handle/2152.5/1047.

Glider, Peggy, Stephen J. Midyett, Beverly Mills-Novoa, Koreen Johannessen, and Carolyn Collins. 2001. "Challenging the collegiate rite of passage: A campus-wide social marketing media campaign to reduce binge drinking." *Journal of Drug Education* 31, no. 2: 207–220.

Gooderham, Mary. 2010. "Customer experience: Three who got it right." *The Globe and Mail.* October 21. http://www.theglobeandmail.com/report-on -business/small-business/sb-marketing/customer-experience-three-who-got -it-right/article4258801/.

Gordon, Ross, Laura McDermott, Martine Stead, and Kathryn Angus. 2006. "The effectiveness of social marketing interventions for health improvement: What's the evidence?" *Public Health* 120, no. 12: 1133–1139.

Gruen, Thomas W., John O. Summers, and Frank Acito. 2000. "Relationship marketing activities, commitment, and membership behaviors in professional associations." *Journal of Marketing* 64, no. 3: 34–49.

Gummesson, Evert. 1994. "Making relationship marketing operational." *International Journal of Service Industry Management* 5, no. 5: 5–20.

Haskova, Katerina. 2015. "Starbucks marketing analysis." *cris Bulletin* 2015, no. 1: 11–29.

Herrick, Clare. 2007. "Risky bodies: Public health, social marketing and the governance of obesity." *Geoforum* 38, no. 1: 90–102.

Kaczynski, Andrew T. 2008. "A more tenable marketing for leisure services and studies." *Leisure sciences* 30, no. 3: 253–272.

Kalter, Suzy. 1979. "A character star gets her perks playing coffee's Mrs. Olson." *People Magazine,* April 30. http://people.com/archive/a-character -star-gets-her-perks-playing-coffees-mrs-olson-vol-11-no-17/.

Kotler, Philip.1967. *Marketing management: Analysis, planning, implementation and control.* Englewood Cliffs, NJ: Prentice-Hall.

Kotler, Philip, and Gerald Zaltman. 1971. "Social marketing: An approach to planned social change." *The Journal of Marketing* 35, no. 3: 3–12.

Kotler, Philip, and Leslie A. Goldgehn. 1981. "Marketing: A definition for community colleges." *New Directions for Community Colleges* 1981, no. 36: 5–12.

Lalani, Azzura. 2016. "Honest Ed's annual turkey giveaway lives on." *Toronto Star.* December 18. https://www.thestar.com/news/gta/2016/12/18/honest-eds-annual-turkey-giveaway-lives-on.html

Lauterborn, Robert F. 1990. "New marketing litany: Four Ps passé: C-words take over." *Advertising Age* 61, no. 41: 26.

Loroz, Peggy Sue, and Bridgette M. Braig. 2015. "Consumer attachments to human brands: The 'Oprah effect'." *Psychology & Marketing* 32, no. 7: 751–763.

Madhav, Ashok Kumar, Mr. Sandeep, and Mervin Felix Caleb. 2014. "Need for paradigm shift of traditional management education services marketing mix from traditional to modern marketing approaches." *Asian Journal of Management* 5, no. 2: 255–260.

Maleeny, Tim. 2015. "This is why Oprah will remain a powerful brand in 2016." *Fortune Magazine.* December 28. http://fortune.com/2015/12/28/oprah-winfrey-millennials/

Mascarenhas, Oswald A., Ram Kesavan, and Michael Bernacchi. 2006. "Lasting customer loyalty: A total customer experience approach." *Journal of Consumer Marketing* 23, no. 7: 397–405.

Mazza, Ed. 2016. "Apple's touching new 'Frankenstein' Christmas ad will bring tears to your eyes." *Huffington Post*, November 22. http://www.huffingtonpost.com/entry/apple-frankenstein-christmas-commercial_us_5833b7cbe4b030997bc10ff9

McCarthy, Edmund J. 1960. *Basic marketing: A managerial approach.* Chicago: R.D. Irwin Publishers.

McKenzie-Mohr, Doug. 2000. "Fostering sustainable behavior through community-based social marketing." *American Psychologist* 55, no. 5: 531.

Mitchell, Colin. 2002. "Selling the brand inside." *Harvard Business Review* 80, no. 1: 99–101.

Olenski, Steve. 2013. "This is the most important word when it comes to relationship marketing." *Forbes Magazine*, May 9. http://www.forbes.com/sites/marketshare/2013/05/09/this-is-the-most-important-word-when-it-comes-to-relationship-marketing/

Olu Adeyoyin, Samuel. 2005. "Strategic planning for marketing library services." *Library Management* 26, no. 8/9: 494–507.

Page, Tom, and Gisli Thorsteinsson. 2009. "Brand power through effective design." *i-Manager's Journal on Management* 4, no. 1: 11–25.

Paul, Tarak, and Pankaj Bihani. 2014. "Expectation based customer oriented marketing mix—A conceptual framework." *International Journal of Research and Development—A Management Review (IJRDMR)* 3, no. 1: 53–60.

Piffer, Marissa L. 2016. "The hidden messages of PR stunts." *Prowl Public Relations.* December 16. https://prowlpr.com/2016/12/06/the-hidden-messages -of-pr-stunts/

Polger, Mark Aaron. 2010. "Information takeout and delivery: A case study exploring different library service delivery models." *Journal of Hospital Librarianship* 10, no. 1: 3–22.

Pollack, Judann. 2015. "Macy's Thanksgiving Day Parade by the numbers: You won't believe how many clowns!" November 18. http://adage.com/ article/cmo-strategy/macy-s-thanksgiving-day-parade-numbers/301418/

Rosencrance, Linda. 2008. "Report: Google is again no. 1 in brand power." *Computer World.* April 21. http://www.computerworld.com/article/2536639/e -commerce/report-google-is-again-no-1-in-brand-power.html

Shaw, Hollie. 2014. "No frills, food basics, FreshCo's discount gaps shrinking as food fight heats up." March 26. http://business.financialpost.com/news/ retail-marketing/how-canadas-grocery-war-is-eating-into-the-discount -gap-between-stores-like-loblaw-no-frills

Solomon, Laura. 2016. *The librarian's nitty-gritty guide to content marketing.* Chicago: American Library Association.

Steimle, Josh. 2014. "What is content marketing?" *Forbes,* September 19. http://www.forbes.com/sites/joshsteimle/2014/09/19/what-is-content -marketing/#2d6449651d70

Tezinde, Tito, Brett Smith, and Jamie Murphy. 2002. "Getting permission: Exploring factors affecting permission marketing." *Journal of Interactive Marketing* 16, no. 4: 28–36.

Waxman, Lisa, Stephanie Clemons, Jim Banning, and David McKelfresh. 2007. "The library as place: Providing students with opportunities for socialization, relaxation, and restoration." *New Library World* 108, no. 9/10: 424–434.

CHAPTER 2

Segmentation
Identifying Your Target Market

IN THIS CHAPTER

- Overview of market segmentation, targeting, and positioning
- Different ways of segmenting markets
- Differences between target market and target audience
- Positioning statements, product differentiation, and perceptual maps
- Library-specific differentiation techniques

MARKET SEGMENTATION

Market segmentation is the process of subdividing a market into smaller groups, or segments, that have similar demographics, interests, and needs. Segmenting enables the marketer to customize and tailor marketing messages to particular audiences (Thomas, 2016).

Segmenting is especially important for libraries, for, as Matthews (1984) argues, "no library or any agency can reach all members of the community" (p. 20). Although public libraries are for the "public," libraries can best serve users by dividing the "public" into segments. Libraries and other organizations spend time and money on their marketing activities with the intention of serving everyone, but a library's marketing efforts cannot resonate with the entire market. They must be tailored and adapted to meet the varying needs of its users (Matthews, 1984). Libraries must discover the needs and wants of specific user groups by conducting market research (see chapter 3), segmenting their user base into subgroups that share similar needs and wants and marketing specifically to those groups.

To successfully target a market segment, the segment must meet three criteria: the members of the segment must share identical characteristics; the segment must be accessible and available for targeting; and the segment must be large enough to be measurable. For cost effectiveness, segments that are too similar can be merged (De Sáez, 2002).

According to Wedel and Kamakura (2012), there are four ways to segment a market: by geography, by demographic characteristics, by psychographic characteristics, and by behavior. Other methods of segmentation include division by generation or by culture. The following sections discuss these types of segmentation in detail.,

GEOGRAPHIC SEGMENTATION

This broad segment groups users by location: country, state/province, city, or region. Geographic segmentation is often used for mass marketing, where one basic marketing strategy is used to appeal to a broad range of consumers (Kotler, 1982). But further segmentation is usually necessary for library marketing, because geography is often related to demographics and particular areas may be occupied by different cultural groups. Neighborhood public library branches' collections often reflect their geographic placements, just as certain grocery store branches carry specific foods that reflect the cultural and geographic characteristics of the communities they serve.

DEMOGRAPHIC SEGMENTATION

This fundamental way of dividing a larger market splits consumers into groups by variables such as age group, family status, race/ethnicity, gender, sexuality, income level, occupation, nationality, education level, and employment status (De Sáez, 2002).

Below is a sample matrix of some of the demographics that can be used to divide large consumer markets into segments that can be targeted. This example matrix splits consumers into different segments based on family status and children's ages: whether they are single or coupled and whether they have no children, small children, teenagers, or adult children.

Table 2.1.   Sample Matrix of Different Demographic Segments

Number of Children	Single	Coupled
No children	0SP	NCNC
No children	0RP	RCNC
Baby	BSP	BTP
Child	CSP	CTP
Teen	TSP	TTP
Adult children	ASP	ATP
2 or more babies	2BSP	2BTP
2 or more children	2CSP	2CTP
2 or more teens	2TSP	2TTP
2 or more dependent adult children	2ASP	2ATP

Demographic groups that marketers often target include YUPPIEs (young, urban professional), DINKs (double income, no kids), Tweens (between a child and teenager), and WASPs (White Anglo-Saxon Protestant) (Mallegg, 2011).

SAMPLE MATRIX: DEMOGRAPHIC SEGMENTING BY FAMILY TYPE

0SP: Single person, no children

0RP: Retired person, no children

NCNC: Newly married couple with no children

RCNC: Retired couple with no children

BSP: Single parent with baby

2BSP: Single parent with two or more babies

BTP: Two parents with baby

2BTP: Two parents with two or more babies

CSP: Single parent with child

2CSP: Single parent with two or more children

CTP: Two parents with child

2CTP: Two parents with two or more children

TSP: Single parent with teenager

2TSP: Single parent with two or more teenagers

TTP: Two parents with teenager

2TTP: Two parents with two or more teenagers

ASP: Single parent with dependent adult children

ATP: Two parents with dependent adult children

2ASP: Single parent with two or more dependent adult children

2ATP: Two parents with two or more dependent adult children

PSYCHOGRAPHIC SEGMENTATION

A more in-depth type of segmentation than demographics, psychographic segmentation divides consumers by psychological characteristics, such as lifestyle habits, personality traits, beliefs, opinions, emotions, values, and hobbies (Thomas, 2016). For example, a thirty-year-old young, upwardly mobile professional may be willing to spend the extra money on organic food because they feel that it is healthier than conventional food, or because they feel that buying ethically grown, non-mass-produced food is a political decision (Nuttavuthisit and Thøgersen, 2017). Other consumers feel that it suits their values to purchase "cruelty-free" products—products that are not tested on animals (Brinkmann, 2004; Lee, 2008). Still other consumers boycott certain products because of where they are produced. For example, some consumer segments support the BDS (boycott, divestment, and sanctions) movement against Israel for religious or ethical reasons, refusing to purchase goods made by Israelis, by Israeli-owned companies, or by companies that support Israel (Hallward, 2013; Benstead and Reif, 2017; Sari, Mizerski, and Liu, 2017; Halimi, 2017). Market research to segment your user base psychographically should be conducted using qualitative research methods in order to obtain reliable, substantive data.

BEHAVIORAL SEGMENTATION

Behavioral segmentation divides consumers by their attitude toward products or service. While it overlaps with the psychographic segmentation (above), behavioral segmentation also measures usage occasion, user status, loyalty status, attitude, awareness, and adopter status (Kotler, 1982). This segment is characterized by brand loyalty: for example, a consumer may shop at a particular clothing store because of their feelings toward the brand rather than because of the price. Similarly, some library users who are not avid readers may often visit their local library branch because of their positive feelings about the library system or their local library branch.

GENERATIONAL SEGMENTATION

Marketers also create *generational segments*, including Baby Boomers, Generation X, Generation Y (millennials), and Generation Z. This type of segmentation is useful for libraries, who often divide their users (and their physical spaces) by age categories. Some libraries have separate children's departments, and some larger libraries have separate areas for teens or young adults—patrons between the ages of 12 and 17.

Generational segments typically offer the marketer a relatively consistent set of beliefs, attitudes, needs, and wants across a same-age group. Millennials, for example, are characterized as having an affinity for technology, engaging in political activism on social media, changing jobs every few years, and valuing the environment (Gurău, 2012; Stewart, Oliver, Cravens, and Oishi, 2017; Zabel et al., 2017). Millennials are not known for direct political involvement; only half of eligible millennial voters went to the polls in the 2016 election, and 58 percent of this generational segment choose community involvement over political involvement, with most of their political activism conducted through social media engagement (Silverstein, 2017).

Millennials are a large user group in both public and academic libraries, and libraries should understand their needs and wants: millennials (who make up the largest percentage of the U.S. labor force) are attuned to technology, display independent information-seeking behavior, and tend to be self-directed learners. They grew up with the Internet, and their personal and professional lives are often led online; they use technology more than any other group and are more educated than any other group (Fry, 2018a; Jiang, 2018).

Millennials are also strongly committed to public libraries. According to Geiger (2017), 53 percent of U.S. millennials visited a public library annually, compared to 45 percent of Generation Xers and 43 percent of Baby Boomers. While Baby Boomers (born between 1946 and 1964) currently make up the largest segment of the U.S. population, they will likely be outnumbered by millennials by 2019, when the country will have 73 million millennials to 72 million Baby Boomers (Fry, 2018b). However, Baby Boomers hold significant economic, political, and cultural power, and libraries may wish to address their particular needs as this generation reaches retirement. Retired Boomers living on reduced incomes likely have free time to use the library and volunteer on library committees, and some Boomers remain relatively affluent in retirement, donating monies to libraries, sitting on library boards, and participating in "Friends" groups.

CULTURAL SEGMENTATION

In the world of commerce, cultural segmentation helps large corporations make decisions about the products and services that particular communities may need and want. Understanding culture helps marketers tailor their activities to a targeted audience. For example, when a grocery chain moving into a new neighborhood conducts market research (see chapter 3) and learns that a large Greek community lives in the area to be served by the new store, they should survey the local Greek community to discover what products they should carry to meet this group's needs. This is why merchandise at national chain stores like Costco Wholesale differ in various locations: they offer products tailored to the geographic, demographic, and cultural segments that frequent each location (Soni, 2016; Page, 2015).

This logic also works for libraries, since many library branches are located in neighborhoods with distinct cultural groups—automatic market segments that can be taken into account when developing library collections and new library services. When cities develop new local library branches, they conduct market research into the cultural segments of particular neighborhoods, and public library collections and services differ in each neighborhood because they reflect the demographic, psychographic, and cultural segments of their users. If one local library branch has a multilingual collection of East Asian materials, it is because census data identified a significant segment of East Asian users in that library's service area.

TARGETING PARTICULAR MARKET SEGMENTS

After performing market research and segmenting their users, an organization can focus its marketing efforts by targeting specific audiences. A *target market* is a segment of consumers to whom a company tailors its products, services, and marketing activities. Companies should have a single primary target market; it may also try to reach a secondary target market. The target market must be large enough to penetrate, accessible, responsive to marketing activities, and distinct from other markets.

When the target market is too small or too difficult to identify (a common situation for libraries, which aim to be all things to all people), it may be merged with another segment. For example, in academic library settings, the first-year college student segment is often merged with the transfer student segment, even though transfer students are usually in their second or third year of college.

Examples of Corporate Target Market Segments

Clothing. The GAP clothing company has segmented its customer base into three target markets: classic, modern, sophisticated consumers, who are willing to pay above-average prices for simple designs and classic colors (the GAP brand), middle-class urban professionals with refined taste (Shpanya, 2015) who seek more fitted, formal pieces (Banana Republic), and hip, fun consumers who seek disposable casual clothes at low prices (Old Navy).

Groceries. In Canada, the Loblaw company segments its grocery division into two brands that serve two different markets: Loblaws and NoFrills. Loblaws targets a specific demographic segment in the grocery industry, middle-class yuppies who will pay more money for higher-quality products. (Their private label, *Presidents Choice*, does offer reduced prices on a variety of store-brand upscale grocery items, similar to the Whole Foods 365 brand.) The NoFrills chain, owned by the same parent corporation, targets a different segment, offering much lower-priced products under a no-name brand.

Coffee shops. Coffee shops also cater to different target markets. Companies like 7-Eleven, Dunkin' Donuts, and McDonald's "McCafe" have traditionally offered relatively low-cost coffee, but they have increasingly aimed at penetrating the upscale coffee market segment dominated by Starbucks; all three companies now offer flavored coffees, espresso drinks, and a variety of non-dairy options (Dupre, 2016; Monllos, 2016; Wohl, 2018; Wright, Frazer, and Merrilees, 2007).

Starbucks typically targets urban professionals, developing customer loyalty by customizing unique drinks and creating memorable customer experiences (Harrington, Ottenbacher, and Fauser, 2017; Mason, Cole, and Goza, 2017). More recently, Starbucks has begun to try to compete against the local and organic "mom and pop" coffee shops that have taken over a large share of the coffee market in the last twenty years. Starbucks is now trying to market itself as a "green" coffee shop, offering more fair trade and ethically sourced coffee (Chen and Lee, 2015). Green marketing is a new marketing strategy that targets newly emerging consumer segments, rebranding or redeveloping products and services aimed at millennials and Baby Boomers: recycled furniture, electric cars, energy-efficient homes, fair-trade coffee, organic and locally produced food, and other consumer goods made in small quantities (Allen and Spialek, 2017; Dangelico and Vocalelli, 2017).

TARGET AUDIENCES

A *target audience* is a specific subset of a target market (Tambien, 2017). For example, a children's book may have a target *market* of children between the ages of six and eight years old. The book may be marketed to target *audiences* of people who might purchase the book for these children: parents, grandparents, teachers, and college students studying children's literature.

In academic libraries, the target market served is nearly always the broad group of students and faculty. However, a specific academic research database such as JSTOR may have target audiences of faculty, upper-level undergraduate students, and graduate students, and a library service such as Interlibrary Loan may have target audiences of faculty, graduate students, and researchers.

In figures 2.1, 2.2, and 2.3 are examples of how target markets can be segmented from a whole market, and of the target audiences that are segmented from those target markets.

Target Markets- Academic Library

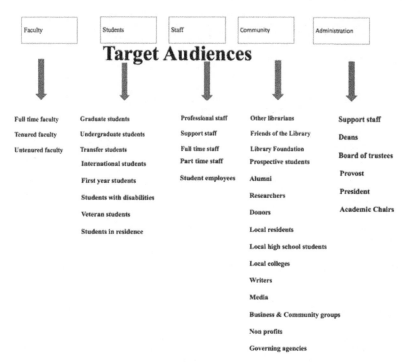

Faculty	Students	Staff	Community	Administration

Target Audiences

Full time faculty	Graduate students	Professional staff	Other librarians	Support staff
Tenured faculty	Undergraduate students	Support staff	Friends of the Library	Deans
Untenured faculty	Transfer students	Full time staff	Library Foundation	Board of trustees
	International students	Part time staff	Prospective students	Provost
	First year students	Student employees	Alumni	President
	Students with disabilities		Researchers	Academic Chairs
	Veteran students		Donors	
	Students in residence		Local residents	
			Local high school students	
			Local colleges	
			Writers	
			Media	
			Business & Community groups	
			Non profits	
			Governing agencies	

Figure 2.1.   Target markets and audiences in an academic library

Target Markets- Public Library

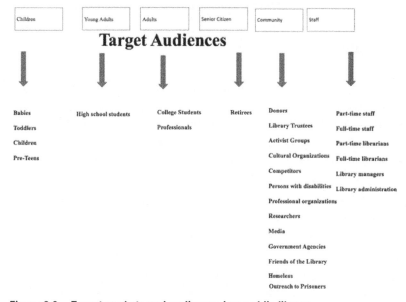

Children	Young Adults	Adults	Senior Citizen	Community	Staff

Target Audiences

Babies	High school students	College Students	Retirees	Donors	Part-time staff
Toddlers		Professionals		Library Trustees	Full-time staff
Children				Activist Groups	Part-time librarians
Pre-Teens				Cultural Organizations	Full-time librarians
				Competitors	Library managers
				Persons with disabilities	Library administration
				Professional organizations	
				Researchers	
				Media	
				Government Agencies	
				Friends of the Library	
				Homeless	
				Outreach to Prisoners	

Figure 2.2.   Target markets and audiences in a public library

Target Markets- Medical Library

Figure 2.3. *Target markets and audiences in a special library (hospital)*

POSITIONING

After you segment your users and target particular markets and audiences, you position your organization in the larger market, aligning your products and services with what your target market wants and needs. Organizations may position themselves as the *only* product or service that meets consumers' needs, as being *better* than their competition, as offering something *unique* that other brands do not, or as being the most *affordable* option. Organizations need to conduct thorough market research, understand their target market, and clearly convey the benefits of their brands to their target audiences (Daye, 2006). In other words, your organization's *position* is the sum of the thoughts, insights, and feelings that a consumer has about a product or service (Daye, 2009); it expresses your brand's essence in the consumer's mind (Ewers and Austen, 2006).

Libraries and librarians position themselves differently for different target markets. For target markets of students, libraries position themselves as supporting student success (Sanabria, 2013; Pun and Kubo, 2017; Soria, Fransen, and Nackerud, 2013; Bowles-Terry, 2012). For target markets of faculty, libraries position themselves as supporting faculty research and teaching (Christiansen, Stombler, and Thaxton, 2004; Kotter, 1999; Ducas and Michaud-Oystryk, 2004; Julien and Pecoskie, 2009) and as supporting them in teaching academic honesty (Snyder Gibson and Chester-Fangman, 2011; Gunnarsson, Kulesza, and Pettersson, 2014). One thing librarians should not do is position libraries defensively, against technologies such as Google—which is what happens when Google is called the "competition" (Potter 2012). Instead, librarians should position themselves as helping users use Google more efficiently.

POSITIONING STATEMENTS

A *positioning statement* shows how a product or service fills a particular consumer need for a particular target audience better than the competition (Hiam 2014). A compelling positioning statement must target a specific audience, relay what is unique about its product or service, illustrate how it fulfills the needs of the target audience, and show how it is better than the competition (Stayman, 2015). Stayman (2015) offers an easy positioning statement template: *For [Target Market], the [product or service] is the [unique feature or benefit] compared to [competition] because [unique feature or benefit].*

For example, ZipCar's positioning statement is, "To urban-dwelling, educated techno-savvy consumers, when you use Zipcar car-sharing service instead of owning a car, you save money while reducing your carbon footprint" (Bouty, 2017). The target market is identified as "urban-dwelling, educated, techno-savvy consumers," the competition is car ownership ("instead of owning a car"), and the points of difference are economic and environmental ("you save money while reducing your carbon footprint").

A library's positioning statement targets a specific group and includes a supporting paragraph that provides them the reasons for choosing their products or services, and not their competition (Keller,

2008). The positioning statement must be familiar to library employees, as it should guide marketing and communications for the institution (Keller, 2008). It may contain the slogans or catch phrases that summarize the type, personality, or goals of the library as defined in the vision and mission (ACRL, 2003, p. 9).

Other simplified library position statements might include some of the following benefits and differentiators:

1. Libraries help college students learn to identify fake news better than social media
2. Librarians help researchers get better results in their Google searches
3. Medical libraries help physicians support patient care with high-quality health information not available on WebMD

PERCEPTUAL MAPS

Perceptual maps are diagrams that enable marketers to visually map out their product's strengths and weaknesses relative to the competition. Perceptual maps usually have only two dimensions (an X and a Y axis), so they are relatively simple to produce and limited in scope. They allow the marketer to reflect on their target market, the products and services they are marketing, and how those products and services differ from others on the market. The following sample perceptual map compares a select list of competing research tools used by a target market (here, first-year college students). The two opposing axes are user-friendliness and cost. Research tools that are positioned close to one another are similar, signifying close competitors; a marketer would need to carefully differentiate these tools from each other (Krawczyk and Xiang, 2016; Pyo, 2015). Marketers may use perceptual maps to make decisions when developing products and services for their users. They help evaluate consumer characteristics, identify the competition, understand some of the strengths and weaknesses, and helps identify different marketing techniques.

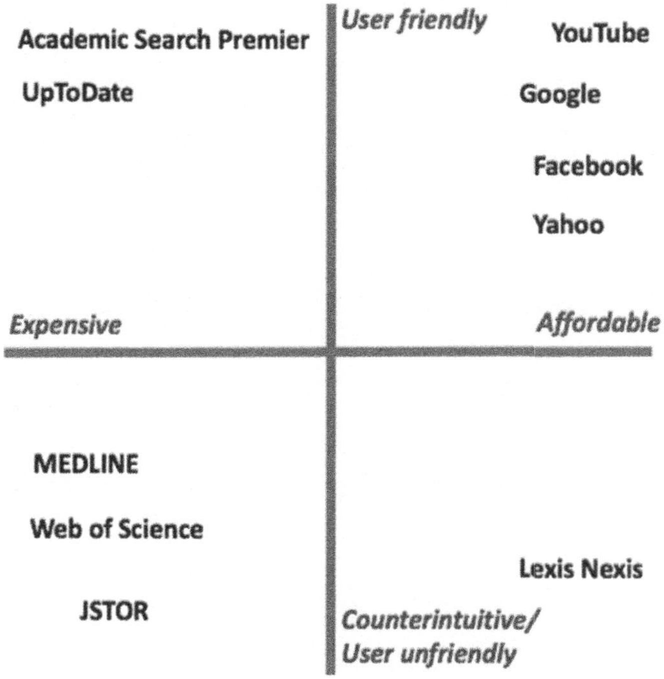

Academic Search Premier	*User friendly*	YouTube
UpToDate		Google
		Facebook
		Yahoo
Expensive		*Affordable*
MEDLINE		
Web of Science		
		Lexis Nexis
JSTOR	*Counterintuitive/*	
	User unfriendly	

Figure 2.4. *Perceptual Map of Competing Databases Used by First Year Students*

PRODUCT / SERVICE DIFFERENTIATION

When marketers *differentiate* a product or service, they identify its unique attributes, match it to a specific target market, and show why it is better than competing products or services for that target market. Companies typically differentiate their offerings by price, product (either choice or quality), or brand/organizational characteristics. When creating a differentiation plan, marketers must brainstorm how the product or service stands out. Table 2.2 is a list of how some products and services have marketed themselves using differentiation.

Table 2.2.   Product Differentiation

Company	Differentiation
Trader Joe's	Smaller stores with fewer, specialized choices; 80% of products are house branded. In-store experience is unique, fun. A trendsetter with affordable prices for high-quality products (Tobak, 2010)
Vitamix	Aimed at health-conscious, affluent individuals who want a powerful product that will last a lifetime. Marketing must engage customer beyond purchase since repeat purchases are rare (Melnik, 2015; Price, 2013)
Amazon	Earth's largest online store, fast delivery, vast product selection, streaming media, content provider (producer of television programming and original television programs and movies) (Mellahi and Johnson, 2000)
Costco Wholesale	Exclusive membership-driven buying club; membership fees subsidize low prices for high-quality products in bulk (Tai and Chuang, 2014). They are a remarkable employer that offer stellar employee benefits and fair wages (Cascio, 2006)
Dyson	First "bagless" vacuum cleaner that is powerful with high suction (Eng, 2017)
eBay	First auction site. Offers a vast collection of new and used consumer products (Chafey, 2018)
Netflix	First streaming media (TV and film) service (Frick, 2017)
Etsy	Artist-driven, unique, custom-made, handmade products (Church and Oakley, 2018)

DIFFERENTIATING THE LIBRARY FROM COMMERCIAL ENTERPRISES

To draw patrons into the library, increase their awareness and use of library services, and engage them in library programming, libraries must differentiate themselves from other organizations that provide information, education, recreation, and community services. There are several ways that libraries differ from competing services like Amazon, Google, and YouTube: first, library services are tax-supported rather than for-profit, meaning that they are effectively free to use; second, libraries offer access to resources that are prohibitively expensive for the average home user, such as academic databases; and finally, libraries offer community programming.

FREE SERVICES

How can libraries differentiate themselves from bookstores? Both libraries and bookstores have helpful, knowledgeable staff, and both organize their collections by subject and author. But libraries, unlike bookstores, offer free access to books and other media. (Of course, libraries are not entirely free; they are nonprofit organizations that are supported by tax revenues, fundraising, and donations. But for the end user, they are effectively free.) Librarians also offer personalized, expert help in searching. They help patrons search effectively for particular materials in collections—something no "you might also like . . ." algorithm can replace. They also teach patrons the principles of good searches so that they can effectively find reliable information on their own.

ACCESS TO SUBSCRIPTION DATABASES

Libraries can differentiate themselves from commercial competitors such as Google, Facebook, YouTube, Amazon, and Twitter by highlighting the access they offer to reliable information via subscription-only databases. Libraries not only provide free access to these very expensive databases, they also employ librarians to teach users how to find the best information on those databases. To differentiate itself from other content providers, an academic library might market particular databases as meeting the particular needs of certain segments of users: for example, they might highlight Web of Science for faculty and Opposing Viewpoints in Context for first-year students.

PROGRAMMING

Public libraries are unique in that they offer free programming to all members of the community. Not many organizations offer ESL classes, resume and cover letter writing classes, computer training, storytime, book talks, author talks, and classes on how to complete income taxes, all for free. Public libraries are true community spaces, and they develop partnerships with other community actors: local schools, community centers, and government agencies. Libraries should differentiate themselves by reminding users that they offer a broad array of free services that promote literacy, civic engagement, and education.

CONCLUSION

This chapter has explained how to *segment* your user market into groups that share needs and desires. It has also explained how to *target* specific segments of users and *position* your products and services as meeting their needs and desires. Finally, it has explained how to *differentiate* your organization from other players in your market, using perceptual maps to understand the competition and identifying the unique characteristics that make your products or services stand out.

REFERENCES

Allen, Myria W., and Matthew L. Spialek. 2017. "Young millennials, environmental orientation, food company sustainability, and green word-of-mouth recommendations." *Journal of Food Products Marketing*: 1–27.

Association of College and Research Libraries. 2003. "Strategic marketing for academic and research libraries: Facilitator guide." http://www.ala.org/acrl/sites/ala.org.acrl/files/content/issues/marketing/FacilitatorGuide.pdf

Benstead, Lindsay J., and Megan Reif. 2017. "Coke, Pepsi or Mecca Cola? Why product characteristics affect the likelihood of collective action problems and boycott success." *Politics, Groups, and Identities* 5, no. 2: 220–241.

Bouty, Laurent. 2017. "What is positioning in marketing strategy?." August 10. https://laurentbouty.com/blog/2017/what-is-positioning-in-marketing-strategy (Accessed July 26, 2018).

Bowles-Terry, Melissa. 2012. "Library instruction and academic success: A mixed-methods assessment of a library instruction program." *Evidence Based Library and Information Practice* 7, no. 1: 82–95.

Brinkmann, Johannes. 2004. "Looking at consumer behavior in a moral perspective." *Journal of Business Ethics* 51, no. 2: 129–141.

Cascio, Wayne F. 2006. "Decency means more than 'always low prices': A comparison of Costco to Wal-Mart's Sam's Club." *Academy of Management Perspectives* 20, no. 3: 26–37.

Chafey, Dave. 2018. "eBay case study." January 6. https://www.smartinsights.com/ecommerce/ecommerce-strategy/ebay-case-study-2/

Chen, Mei-Fang, and Chia-Lin Lee. 2015. "The impacts of green claims on coffee consumers' purchase intention." *British Food Journal* 117, no. 1: 195–209.

Christiansen, Lars, Mindy Stombler, and Lyn Thaxton. 2004. "A report on librarian-faculty relations from a sociological perspective." *The Journal of Academic Librarianship* 30, no. 2: 116–121.

Church, E. Mitchell, and Richelle L. Oakley. 2018. "Etsy and the long-tail: How microenterprises use hyper-differentiation in online handicraft market-places." *Electronic Commerce Research*: 1–16.

Dangelico, Rosa Maria, and Daniele Vocalelli. 2017. "'Green Marketing': An analysis of definitions, strategy steps, and tools through a systematic review of the literature." *Journal of Cleaner Production* 165: 1263–1279.

Daye, Derrick. 2006. "Positioning your brand." August 30. https://www.brandingstrategyinsider.com/2006/08/positioning_you.html (Accessed July 26, 2018).

Daye, Derrick. 2009. "Brand positioning and perceptual maps." September 1. https://www.brandingstrategyinsider.com/2009/09/brand-positioning-and-perceptual-maps.html (Accessed July 26, 2018).

De Sáez, Eileen Elliott. 2002. *Marketing concepts for libraries and information services*. London: Facet Publishing.

Ducas, Ada M., and Nicole Michaud-Oystryk. 2004. "Toward a new venture: Building partnerships with faculty." *College & Research Libraries* 65, no. 4: 334–348.

Dupre, Elyse. 2016. "7-Eleven redefines convenience for the modern age." November 3. https://www.dmnews.com/channel-marketing/multi-omnic hannelrticle/13035395/7eleven-redefines-convenience-for-the-modern-age

Eng, Dinah. 2017. "How James Dyson created a $3 billion vacuum empire." September 9. http://fortune.com/2017/09/09/james-dyson-vacuum/

Ewers, Barbara, and Gaynor Austen. 2006. "A framework for market orientation in libraries." In *Marketing library and information services: International perspectives*, edited by Dinesh K. Gupta and Christie Koontz, [21]–30. Munich: K. G. Saur.

Frick, Walter. 2017. "How can companies compete with Amazon? Netflix has the answer." June 19. *Harvard Business Review*. https://hbr.org/2017/06/how-can-companies-compete-with-amazon-netflix-has-the-answer (Accessed August 7, 2018).

Fry, Richard. 2018a. "Millennials are the largest generation in the U.S. labor force." April 11. http://www.pewresearch.org/fact-tank/2018/04/11/millen nials-largest-generation-us-labor-force/ (Accessed July 23, 2018).

Fry, Richard. 2018b. "Millennials projected to overtake Baby Boomers as America's largest generation." March 1. http://www.pewresearch.org/fact -tank/2018/03/01/millennials-overtake-baby-boomers/ (Accessed August 6, 2018).

Geiger, Abigail. 2017. "Millennials are the most likely generation of Americans to use public libraries." June 21.   http://www.pewresearch.org/fact-tank/2017/06/21/millennials-are-the-most-likely-generation-of-americans-to-use-public-libraries/ (Accessed January 25, 2019).

Gunnarsson, Jenny, Wlodek J. Kulesza, and Anette Pettersson. 2014. "Teaching international students how to avoid plagiarism: Librarians and faculty in collaboration." *The Journal of Academic Librarianship* 40, no. 3–4: 413–417.

Gurău, Călin. 2012. "A life-stage analysis of consumer loyalty profile: Comparing Generation X and Millennial consumers." *Journal of Consumer Marketing* 29, no. 2: 103–113.

Halimi, Tariq Abdullatif. 2017. "Examining the variation in willingness to buy from offending product's origin among fellow nationals: A study from the Arab/Muslim-Israeli conflict." *Journal of Islamic Marketing* 8, no. 2: 243–260.

Hallward, Maia Carter. 2013. "The history and theory of boycott, divestment, and sanctions." In *Transnational Activism and the Israeli-Palestinian Conflict*, pp. 1–32. New York: Palgrave Macmillan.

Harrington, Robert J., Michael C. Ottenbacher, and Simon Fauser. 2017. "QSR brand value: Marketing mix dimensions among McDonald's, KFC, Burger King, Subway and Starbucks." *International Journal of Contemporary Hospitality Management* 29, no. 1: 551–570.

Hiam, Alexander. 2014. *Marketing for dummies*. Hoboken: John Wiley & Sons.

Jiang, Jingjing. 2018. "Millennials stand out for their technology use, but older generations also embrace digital life." May 2. http://www.pewresearch.org/fact-tank/2018/05/02/millennials-stand-out-for-their-technology-use-but-older-generations-also-embrace-digital-life/ (Accessed July 23, 2018).

Julien, Heidi, and Jen J.L. Pecoskie. 2009. "Librarians' experiences of the teaching role: Grounded in campus relationships." *Library & Information Science Research* 31, no. 3: 149–154.

Keller, James. 2008. "Branding and marketing your library." *Public Libraries* 47, no. 5: 45–51.

Kotler, Philip. 1982. *Marketing for nonprofit organizations*. Englewood Cliffs, NJ: Prentice-Hall.

Kotter, Wade R. 1999. "Bridging the great divide: Improving relations between librarians and classroom faculty." *The Journal of Academic Librarianship* 25, no. 4: 294–303.

Krawczyk, Matthew, and Zheng Xiang. 2016. "Perceptual mapping of hotel brands using online reviews: A text analytics approach." *Information Technology & Tourism* 16, no. 1: 23–43.

Lee, Kaman. 2008. "Opportunities for green marketing: Young consumers." *Marketing Intelligence & Planning* 26, no. 6: 573–586.

Loblaw Companies Limited. 2018. "Our web sites." https://www.loblaw.ca/en/contact-us/our-websites.html (Accessed August 8, 2018).

Lynn, Michael. 2007. "Brand segmentation in the hotel and cruise industries: Fact or fiction?" *Cornell Hospitality Report* 7, no. 4: 6–15.

Mallegg, Kristin. 2011. *Acronyms, initialisms & abbreviations dictionary A guide to acronyms, abbreviations, contractions, alphabetic symbols, and similar condensed appellations.* Detroit: Gale.

Mason, Andrew, Tracy Cole, and Nina Goza. 2017. "Starbucks: A case study of effective management in the coffee industry." *Journal of International Management Studies* 17, no. 1: 43–48.

Matthews, Anne J. 1984. "Library market segmentation: An effective approach for meeting client needs." *Journal of Library Administration* 4, no. 4: 19–31.

Mellahi, Kamel, and Michael Johnson. 2000. "Does it pay to be a first mover in e.commerce? The case of Amazon.com." *Management Decision* 38, no. 7: 445–452.

Melnik, Alison. 2015. "Engage customers beyond the purchase: Market like Vitamix." March 17. https://www.pr2020.com/blog/engage-customers-beyond-the-purchase-market-like-vitamix

Monllos, Kristina. 2016. "After a decade, Dunkin' Donuts is evolving its 'America runs on Dunkin' campaign." June 3. https://www.adweek.com/brand-marketing/after-decade-dunkin-donuts-evolving-its-america-runs-dunkin-campaign-171820/

Nuttavuthisit, Krittinee, and John Thøgersen. 2017. "The importance of consumer trust for the emergence of a market for green products: The case of organic food." *Journal of Business Ethics* 140, no. 2 (2017): 323–337.

Page, Vanessa. 2015. "Costco's business model is smarter than you think." July 7. https://www.investopedia.comrticles/investing/070715/costcos-business-model-smarter-you-think.asp (Accessed July 23, 2018).

Potter, Ned. 2012. *The library marketing toolkit.* London: Facet Publishing.

Pun, Raymond, and Hiromi Kubo.2017. "Beyond career collection development: Academic libraries collaborating with career center for student success." *Public Services Quarterly* 13, no. 2: 134–138.

Price, Catherine. 2013. "Can a $400 blender change your life?" October. https://slate.com/human-interest/2013/10/vitamix-a-history-of-the-company-and-analysis-of-the-blenders-appeal.html (Accessed August 7, 2018).

Pyo, Sungsoo. 2015. "Integrating tourist market segmentation, targeting, and positioning using association rules." *Information Technology & Tourism* 15, no. 3: 253–281.

Sanabria, Jesus E. 2013. "The library as an academic partner in student retention and graduation: The library's collaboration with the freshman year seminar initiative at the Bronx Community College." *Collaborative Librarianship* 5, no. 2: 94–100.

Sari, Dessy Kurnia, Dick Mizerski, and Fang Liu. 2017. "Boycotting foreign products: A study of Indonesian Muslim consumers." *Journal of Islamic Marketing* 8, no. 1: 16–34.

Shpanya, Ari. 2015. "Three brands that prove the relationship between pricing and positioning." March 31. https://www.econsultancy.com/blog/66249 -three-brands-that-prove-the-relationship-between-pricing-and-positioning (Accessed July 1, 2018).

Silverstein, Haley. 2017. "The changing face of millennial engagement in politics." September 11. https://www.eastwest.ngo/idea/changing-face-mil lennial-engagement-politics (Accessed July 23, 2018).

Snyder Gibson, Nancy, and Christina Chester-Fangman. 2011. "The librarian's role in combating plagiarism." *Reference Services Review* 39, no. 1: 132–150.

Soni, Phalguni. 2016. "How have Costco's geographic segments performed?" January 16. https://marketrealist.com/2016/01/analyzing-performance-pros pects-costcos-segments (Accessed July 23, 2018).

Soria, Krista M., Jan Fransen, and Shane Nackerud. 2013. "Library use and undergraduate student outcomes: New evidence for students' retention and academic success." *portal: Libraries and the Academy* 13, no. 2: 147–164.

Stayman, Doug. (2015). "How to Write Market Positioning Statements." March 20. http://blog.ecornell.com/how-to-write-market-positioning-statements/

Stewart, Jeanine S., Elizabeth Goad Oliver, Karen S. Cravens, and Shigehiro Oishi. 2017. "Managing millennials: Embracing generational differences." *Business Horizons* 60, no. 1: 45–54.

Tai, Fang-Mei, and Po-Yao Chuang. 2014. "Strategic differentiation management: A transnational study of Costco." *The Journal of International Management Studies* 9, no. 2: 126–141.

Tambien, Erica. 2017. "The difference between a target market & target audience." September 26. https://bizfluent.com/about-6747097-difference -target-market-target-audience.html (Accessed August 6, 2018).

Thomas, Jerry W. 2016. "Market segmentation." https://www.decisionanalyst .com/whitepapers/marketsegmentation/ (Accessed July 1, 2018).

Tobak, Steve. 2010. "10 secrets to Trader Joe's success." August 26. https:// www.cbsnews.com/news/10-secrets-to-trader-joes-success/ (Accessed August 7, 2018).

Wedel, Michel, and Wagner A. Kamakura. 2012. *Market segmentation: Conceptual and methodological foundations. Vol. 8.* New York: Springer Science & Business Media.

Wohl, Jessica. 2018. "Dunkin Donuts CMO: We took our coffee message for granted." February 8. Ad Age. http://adage.com/article/cmo-strategy/dunkin -donuts-cmo-coffee-message-granted/312313/ (Accessed August 6, 2018).

Wright, Owen, Lorelle Frazer, and Bill Merrilees. 2007. "McCafe: The McDonald's co-branding experience." *Journal of Brand Management* 14, no. 6: 442–457.

Zabel, Keith L., Benjamin BJ Biermeier-Hanson, Boris B. Baltes, Becky J. Early, and Agnieszka Shepard. 2017. "Generational differences in work ethic: Fact or fiction?" *Journal of Business and Psychology* 32, no. 3: 301–315.

CHAPTER 3

Data Drives Decisions
Understanding Market Research

IN THIS CHAPTER

- Defining market research
- Distinguishing *market* research from *marketing* research
- Market Research Steps

  1. Assessing your current situation
  2. Conducting a SWOT analysis
  3. Conducting a community needs assessment

- Identifying your target market
- Designing your research approach
- Using primary and second research methods
- Evaluating data and making informed decisions

INTRODUCTION

Many libraries develop vast book collections and extensive menus of services without ever asking what their users want. This frustrates users and wastes funds. To avoid this, libraries must study their audience and its needs before making decisions. The notion of "user centered design" has been extensively studied in the context of library websites (Comeaux, 2008; Bordac and Rainwater, 2008; Sonsteby and Dejonghe, 2013; Manzari and Trinidad-Christensen, 2006).[1] Libraries should apply the same notion of user-centeredness to their collection and service development processes. Unfortunately, there is little research into how to make library services user centered (Bowler et al., 2011; Hauser, 2017; Bias, Marty, and Douglas, 2012).

Therefore, this chapter explains how to ensure that your services and offerings meet user needs: by conducting user research. It illustrates the importance of audience research, community analysis using existing data, and the collection of new data about your specific users so that you can better understand your users. It explains how you can collect primary data (by conducting surveys and interviews) and access secondary data (statistics from other sources) to support your decision making. It explains how to identify gaps in your existing services by conducting a community needs assessment and a SWOT analysis. In short, this chapter teaches you to make informed library management decisions based on targeted, specific data about who your users are and what they want.

Defining Market Research

Market research is the activity of gathering information about a target market. Although "market research" is often confused with the similar phrase "marketing research," the terms are different. *Marketing* research is concerned specifically with research that supports marketing processes; *market* research simply means gathering and analyzing information about a specific target audience, then using that information to support decision making. This chapter primarily focuses on market research, and it includes information about both qualitative data collection (focus groups and interviews) and quantitative data collection (polls and surveys, administered via telephone, paper, or online).

Conducting market research is important because the library needs information about its audience *before* launching products or services. For example, a collection development policy must be developed in alignment with the community it serves. In academia, collections are built based on the teaching and learning needs of students and faculty. Market research seeks to understand what courses are being taught and the different research faculty are engaged in. In public libraries, market research seeks to understand the demographics of the community *before* selecting materials for a library collection. Collection development policies must be based on the needs of the library audiences: academic librarians must collect materials that support the teaching and learning of each academic department, and public libraries must support the research and learning needs of the community. To create effective collection development policies, libraries must conduct market research to learn about their audiences' needs. It would be wasteful to implement new services or collections that no one used.

Differences Between Market Research and Marketing Research

Market research investigates markets (customers), while *marketing* research studies marketing activities themselves. Marketing research is the systematic collection, analysis, and reporting of data relevant to a specific marketing activities (Andreasen, Kotler, and Parker, 2008); it links the consumer to the marketer through information that identifies marketing opportunities, evaluates marketing actions, and monitors marketing performance (Marketing Research, 2009). Where marketing research covers all of the 4Ps (discussed in chapter 1), market research is a subset and only focuses on the target market (Claessens, 2018).

MARKET RESEARCH STEPS

The process of doing market research has several distinct stages: self-assessment, community needs assessment, research design planning, data collection, and an examination of the findings. The rest of the chapter will go over each of these stages in detail.

STEP 1: SELF-ASSESSMENT

In this step, the library performs an audit of its current state in order to identify gaps in services and resources. This phase, which happens before the target audience is selected, involves a lot of professional soul searching. We must evaluate our physical space, our signage, our displays, our furniture, our circulating and non-circulating collection, and our website (see chapter 8 for information about how to perform a website audit).

Assessing Physical Spaces

Chapter 7 provides a checklist for assessing the physical environment (Dempsey, 2009). To assess the library's physical spaces, look at all areas of the library. Examine outdoor areas, including signage, parking lot, sidewalk, entrance, landscaping, directional signage, the book return bin, and the overall cleanliness (Dempsey, 2009, p. 29). Inside the facility, look at the entryway, the elevators, furniture, the bump points (see chapter 7), the service desks, displays, bulletin boards, seating, public and staff areas, computers, and the electrical outlets (Dempsey, 2009, p. 30). The service desks (circulation and reference) should not be cluttered, for clutter presents an unprofessional image. Library employees should regularly shelf-read the collection to ensure that the call number ranges correspond to the signage in that aisle. Annual checkups of internal telephone lists, business cards, and letterhead are also recommended.

Assessing Virtual Environments

The library's virtual spaces, such as its website, should also be assessed annually (see chapter 8 for a detailed explanation of how to conduct a website audit and usability test). The front page should display links to the library's hours, services, resources, current events, the newsletter, FAQ, contact information, and to the search page for books and articles (Dempsey, 2009). The website should use plain language that is consistent across all communications channels. In other words, use the same language on library websites, signage, and promotional material (Polger, 2011; Polger, 2014). Links should be checked and the website optimized for search engines (Chapter 8 will discuss ways to automate the fixing of broken links and search engine optimization [SEO] tools). The Electronic Resources librarian should run regular checks to ensure that the library's proxy server is working and users are able to access the library's collection of subscription databases.

Customer Service

An annual assessment of customer service practices, including in-person, phone, email, and live chat service, can identify ongoing problems and help set priorities for the upcoming year. Evaluate how staff interact with library users. Check the outgoing voice mail message, ensuring that it provides current information. Check live chat transcripts to see how librarians respond to reference questions online. Check that policy enforcement is consistent across staff.

Have regular staff meetings to keep staff up-to-date on policies and procedures. Policy updates should be clearly communicated via email and through an internal blog or staff intranet. Part-time employees should have specific professional development days for customer service training (Jones, 2011), as should all staff in public service positions: circulation, reference, and instruction.

Some libraries may wish to develop scripts that staff can use to handle difficult library patrons; these scripts should keep communications friendly and non-confrontational, and staff should receive ongoing training in how to use them. Although some literature does not support using scripted messages (Good, 2018; Kinsman, 2010; Walsh and Hammes, 2017; Victorino, Verma, and Wardell, 2013; Victorino and Bolinger, 2012; West, 2006), other research suggests that it provides a consistent way to communicate policy (Levin, 2016).

STEP 2: PLAN YOUR COMMUNITY NEEDS ASSESSMENT

A community needs assessment—another name for a specific phase of market research, that of gathering information about user needs—gathers information from the community about their concerns and expectations and how to meet their needs. It identifies existing gaps between what the organization offers and what the community wants—improve the organization's effectiveness at responding to user needs.

As the first step in planning your Community Needs Assessment (CNA), make specific plans: choose specific goals and objectives, identify start and end dates, decide what audiences you will collect data from, design your research approach (including choosing the assessment instruments that will be used and your sample size), and decide whether and how you will use the collected data for marketing activities after the CNA ends.

The second step in planning your CNA is to select your target audiences—the people whose input you want in your CNA. When planning market research, you must establish a specific, manageable target audience, because it would be too time-consuming and costly to survey every possible user from every possible market segment. Chapter 2 explains in detail how to divide the market into different groups, or segments, that share common interests and other characteristics. It also explains how to subdivide this target market into target audiences. For example, the target market might be all first-year college students, while a target audience might be first-year students enrolled in a specific class.

STEP 3: CONDUCT A SWOT ANALYSIS

A SWOT analysis is a structured form of self-reflection about the internal effectiveness of your organization. Increasingly, libraries are undertaking this exercise in order to assess their *strengths, weaknesses, opportunities,* and *threats* (Fernandez, 2009; Kumar, 2012; Morgenstern and Jones, 2012; Mapulanga, 2013; Hijji, 2012; Harris, 2018; Shilpa and Aswath, 2016; Gil, 2017). A SWOT analysis helps organizations make better decisions by identifying the internal (*strengths* and *weaknesses*) and external (*opportunities* and *threats*) factors that may affect success. A SWOT analysis allows an organization to identify its challenges, use resources effectively, understand the competition, and operate more efficiently (Hill, 2018). A SWOT analysis can be performed on any aspect of the library, such as reference services, the library instruction program, course textbook loans, the laptop lending program, the library website, or the library's social media accounts. Table 3.1 is an example of a SWOT analysis of a library's reference service.

STEP 4: RESEARCH DESIGN

Research design should take into account the sample targeted, the sampling method, the survey instrument, the kinds of questions posed, and the method of data analysis that will be used.

Table 3.1. A SWOT Analysis for Reference Services

Strengths	Weaknesses	Opportunities	Threats
Teaching opportunities at the reference desk Librarians provide highest quality information Reference service offered in person, telephone, email, and via live chat Library users are empowered when librarians teach information literacy skills Librarians teach users how to avoid plagiarism and find information efficiently Library users won't waste time finding incorrect information	Budget cuts Lack of resources in providing reference services Decline in reference questions Librarians increasingly frustrated with decline in reference questions	Internal partnerships (for college libraries, campus departments, public libraries) External partnerships (for public libraries, community groups, public schools, daycare, community centers)	Reduced library hours Google Wikipedia Facebook Twitter Ask.com YouTube Fake news

In qualitative research, some questions should be open-ended, some should have Likert scale responses, and some should be closed-ended. Include at least some open-ended questions using the five Ws (who, what, where, when, and why), because these offer the richest results. Surveys should be brief, or respondents will not want to complete them. Survey Monkey or Qualtrics are great online survey management tools. They quickly tabulate data and provide great visuals such as graphs, tables, and charts to represent the data visually.

Data should be collected using several methods; some members of the community may prefer speaking on the phone, while others may prefer paper or online surveys. All methods have benefits and drawbacks. Sending out a link to an online survey is easy, but some users may not have computer or Internet access; paper surveys are fast for users and the data is captured right away, but they are not good for the environment and data must be manually entered in Excel or a database for analysis.

Surveys should also be distributed using several methods so as to reach as many users from your target audience as possible: using the library website, social media, email marketing software, *and* circulating paper copies of your data collection instrument will likely reach more users and garner more responses than any one of these channels on its own.

Incentives may increase your response rate. If you have the budget to do so, you may wish to offer incentives for completion. These incentives can be small and inexpensive. Some sample incentives might include entering names into a drawing for a gift card or giving away small gifts (library swag such as branded staplers, mousepads, pens, notepads, or USB flash drives; chocolate, candy, or bottled water; coupons for the library café or college bookstore; or library tote bags) to users who complete surveys.

Primary versus Secondary Research Data

Primary research refers to the data directly collected by library employees during a community needs assessment. This data reflects the current state of affairs in your particular community, and it is always changing. Therefore, community needs assessments should be performed frequently to capture the changes in community needs. *Secondary* research refers to preexisting data relevant to your users: government statistics, community surveys, trade publications, market research reports, professional associations, think tanks, case studies, and published reference materials. Below is a description of the types of primary and secondary research data that libraries can use to make operational and marketing decisions.

Primary Data Collection

Primary data can be collected using qualitative methods (interviews, focus groups, and open-ended surveys) or quantitative methods (questionnaires and objective surveys).

Interviews and Focus Groups

Interviews are typically one-on-one interviews, held between two people; focus groups are tailored group discussions, typically with between six and eight participants. These two qualitative assessment tools are more expensive and time-consuming than surveys, but they offer richer, more robust data. Qualitative research methods reveal respondents' feelings and opinions. The probing questions engage with issues on a deeper level (Mersdorf, 2016; Walters, 2004).

Focus groups can elicit the same kinds of deep engagement and rich data, but at a slightly lower opportunity cost, since there are more participants per interviewer and session. According to Walters (2004), the four elements of managing a focus group are identifying a target audience; having time and physical space to carry out the focus group; having a trained facilitator; and engaging participants in semi-structured discussions.

Interview and focus group questions are different from survey questions. Interview questions reveal people's interpretations; unlike surveys and questionnaires, these types of questions do not seek absolute facts. According to Spradley (2016), questions should focus on respondents' experiences and emotions, eliciting users' reflections and feelings. Questions should start with one of the five Ws (who, what, where, when, why) or with "how."

There are four types of interview questions: *descriptive, experience, structural,* and *contrast. Descriptive* questions are open-ended and ask interviewees for a detailed account. *Experience* questions ask interviewees to provide more details of their feelings about a specific experience. *Structural* questions seek to elicit how interviewees organize their knowledge, and *contrast* questions measure how interviewees understand the differences between two topics.

Interviewers cannot record their subjects verbatim. Instead, obtain permission from participants to record the proceedings, then transcribe the answers using special software (Dragon is one example) or pay for professional transcription. Below are some examples of interview questions from the four categories above:

Descriptive

What are your general feelings about using this library? How do you feel about the services this library provides? How can this library further improve their services for you?

Experience

How was your experience with the reference librarian today? What information were you seeking? How did the librarian help you (or not)?

Structural

What are your steps in finding a book at the library? Can you outline them for me?

Contrast

What are some of the differences between what you expect to find in a public library versus an academic library?

Questionnaires and Surveys

A survey is an assessment tool that is used to collect quantitative information for analysis (including statistical analysis) and interpretation. Surveys are very inexpensive to administer, and they collect data from a large sample of respondents. Surveys can be administered either through analog channels (in person, over the telephone, or as a printed questionnaire, which may be distributed on-site or by postal mail) or digital channels (via email, social media, or online). A printed questionnaire is one of the most popular types of survey instruments. Most use the terms "survey" and "questionnaire" interchangeably.

Social Media Monitoring

Marketers often use social media monitoring software to observe activity on social platforms to better understand how their product (or company) is perceived. The data these tools collect give insights into an organization's social media profile and reputation. Organizations can also look at the metrics for their own social media; tools include Facebook insights, Twitter analytics, Google+ insights, and Instagram analytics. Quantifiable social media metrics, which include comments, likes, reach, Tweets, mentions, follows, followers, and engagement, are discussed in detail in chapter 9.

Sample Questions

Sample Multiple-Choice Survey Questions

1. How often do you visit the library? (select one)

   Once a week
   3–5 times a week
   Twice a month
   Once a month
   Every three months
   Twice a year
   Once a year

2. What time of day do you use the library? (select one)

   Morning
   Evening
   Afternoon
   Later evening

Sample Open-Ended Questions

   What three things did you learn from today's library instruction class?
   How can we improve library services? List three recommendations.
   What additional services would you like the library to provide?
   How often do you use the library?
   How did you learn about the library's hours?
   Where is a good place in the library to speak on cell phones?
   What are the three databases you most often use for research?

Sample Closed-Ended Questions

   Are you writing a research paper?
   Do you use the library website to find information?
   Did you find what you were looking for today?
   Do you bring food into the library?
   Did you visit the library to print out a document?

Did you receive help from a reference librarian today?
Were library staff friendly today?
Was the library clean?
Do you think the library is too noisy?
Would you benefit from color printing in the library?

Sample True/False Questions

I use the library primarily to conduct research
I use the library primarily to study
I use the library primarily to interact with my friends
Library staff were friendly and helpful
The library's hours are sufficient
The directional signage was straightforward
The library website is intuitive and user friendly
The library has books related to my research topic
The library book collection is outdated
I drove to the library
I used public transit to get to the library
The library is walking distance to my home
I only live on campus during the academic year

Sample Demographic Questions

Age group: _____
Grade level: _____
Gender: _____
Email address: _____
Level of education attained:_____
Race/ethnicity: _____
Income level: _____
Rent or own: _____

Sample Likert Questions (strongly agree, agree, disagree, strongly disagree)

1. This library's book collection is current and timely
2. The library catalog is easy to use

3. Reference librarians provided me with the right information
4. Circulation staff were friendly and helpful
5. The software is current and up to date
6. The library website was easy to navigate
7. I can easily check my printing balance online

Sample Questions: Multiple Responses

1. What is the purpose of the visit today? (you may select more than one response)

Study
Research
Find a book
Find an article
Meet friends
Homework
Write a paper
Read
Go online

Secondary Research Data

To supplement primary data collected from surveys, focus groups, and interviews with their specific user bases, libraries may also use data collected by governmental organizations and other groups. For example, government statistics offer valuable aggregate information about local communities—information that can be vital when lobbying for more funding. For example, if statistical data reveals that many families in your community have young children, local governments can request more funding to build public schools and parks, and the library may allocate a larger part of its budget to children's story hour or to developing picture book collections. Government statistics provide valuable information for planning and decision making. Following is a list of organizations that offer reliable, accessible secondary data that libraries may find useful in justifying funding requests or planning.

Government data

The U. S. Census (http://www.census.gov) is a decennial (every ten years) survey that offers a snapshot of demographic data for the entire nation's population. The census website offers free access to population tables that give publicly accessible information about gender, age, race/ethnicity, immigration status, employment, income level, marital status, and home ownership, broken down by city, state, county, zip code, and town. (Census data collected after 2010 is available only in short form.) Census data can be used to determine the location of new housing and public facilities (including public transportation, roadways, police and fire stations, and public schools) and to analyze demographic information across communities, cities, and states.

The American Community Survey (ACS) (https://www.census.gov/programs-surveys/acs/) is an annual survey, begun in 2005, that collects information from the long form of the decennial census. Topics include demographic questions about ancestry, citizenship, educational attainment, fertility, marital history and status, place of birth, school enrollment, and economic questions about housing, vehicles, home ownership, computer and Internet access, employment status, commuting, food stamps, health insurance coverage, and income and earnings (ACS, 2018). This survey, which is administered by the U.S. Census Bureau, targets approximately 295,000 households per month. It captures a smaller percentage of the population on each survey than the full census, but by rotating the households it surveys, it attempts to build a more detailed picture of the population at the local level than the census can.

The National Center for Education Statistics (NCES) (https://nces.ed.gov/) collects library statistics surveys; it also publishes public school district financial information and statistics on education, including survey data at the national and international level, broken down by age bracket (early childhood education, elementary education, secondary education, and postsecondary education). It includes data from the following surveys and studies from K–12 and postsecondary education:

- National Assessment of Educational Progress
- National Assessments of Adult Literacy
- Early Childhood Longitudinal Studies

- National Household Education
- Beginning Teacher Longitudinal Study
- Career/Technical Education Statistics
- Common Core of Data
- Crime and Safety
- School Climate
- Education Finance
- Education Longitudinal Study
- High School and Beyond
- High School Longitudinal Study
- Middle Grades Longitudinal Study
- National Education Longitudinal Study
- National Household Education
- National Teacher and Principal
- Private School
- Rural Education
- School Attendance
- Crime
- Schools and Staffing
- State Education Reform
- Statewide Longitudinal Data
- Integrated Postsecondary Education Data System
- Career and Technical Education
- National Postsecondary Student Aid
- National Study of Postsecondary Faculty
- Baccalaureate and Beyond
- Urban Education survey

The American Factfinder (https://factfinder.census.gov/) is the U.S. Census Bureau's online search tool that provides access to data sets from different surveys and censuses. They include:

- The American Community Survey
- American Housing Survey
- Annual Survey of Manufactures
- Business Patterns
- Nonemployer Statistics

- The Annual Surveys of Governments
- The Census of Governments
- The Commodity Flow Survey
- The Decennial Census
- The Economic Census (every five years)
- The Survey of Business Owners
- The Equal Employment Opportunity (EEO) Tabulation
- The Population Estimates Program
- The Puerto Rico Community Survey

The National Center for Health Statistics (NCHS) (https://www
.cdc.gov/nchs) provides statistical information aimed at improving the
health of the American people. It is part of the Centers for Disease
Control and Prevention (CDC), under the umbrella of the United States
Department of Health and Human Services (HHS). It includes data
from the following four surveys:

- National Vital Statistics System
- National Health Interview Survey
- National Health and Nutrition Examination Survey
- National Health Care Surveys

The Bureau of Labor Statistics (BLS) (https://www.bls.gov/) is a
statistical agency under the United States Department of Labor. It is
responsible for measuring labor market activity, working conditions,
and price changes in the economy. It collects, analyzes, and publishes
economic information to support public and private decision making. It
provides data about unemployment, employment, inflation and prices,
salary and benefits, consumer spending, workplace injuries, productiv-
ity, and import/export. Select publications from the BLS include the
Occupational Outlook Handbook, the *Economics Daily*, the *Monthly
Labor Review*, *Career Outlook*, and *Geographic Profile*.

Nongovernmental Data That Is Credible and Accessible

Think tanks are nongovernmental agencies that conduct research and
advocacy on issues facing society and provide factual information via

original research reports. Many are topical, focusing on specific social issues. Most are nonprofit and receive funding from the government and private corporations. Think tanks are divided into the following broad categories: independent; policy research (economics, environment, health care, etc.); government-created; corporate; political; and global. Although think tanks are credible sources for data, many of them are partisan.

The Pew Research Center (http://www.pewresearch.org) is a think tank that conducts research and provides factual data to the public about a variety of divisive issues. Known as a fact tank, they are nonprofit, nonpartisan and non-advocacy. Methodologies include public opinion polling, demographic research, content analysis, and other data-driven social science research. Pew Research conducts studies on U.S. politics, journalism and the media, social and demographic trends, religion, Internet and technology, science, Hispanic trends, and global attitudes and trends. Pew research reports have covered topics such as technology use, gun legislation, same-sex marriage, immigration, abortion, online shopping, poverty, health care, death penalty, terrorism, race relations, media ownership, family roles, voter participation, social media, socioeconomic status, taxes, and war and international conflict.

The American National Election Studies (ANES) (https://election studies.org/about-us/) are national surveys distributed to U.S. voters before and after each presidential election. Established in 1977 by a National Science Foundation grant, ANES is coordinated by Stanford University and the University of Michigan in partnership. It collects data from surveys on public opinion, voting, and voter participation and supports the research of social scientists, teachers, students, policy makers, and journalists (ANES, 2018).

Nielsen Media (http://www.nielsen.com) is a large market research company that examines television audience data, as well as collecting consumer data in other areas (food preferences, podcasting habits, sports, finances, innovation, etc.). Nielsen runs a proprietary audience measurement system that determines audience size and composition for television programming in the United States, and their most popular product is the Nielsen ratings. The Nielsen ratings are freely available, but the company does offer more in-depth audience research for a fee. The Nielsen rating methodology uses two techniques to measure audience participation: viewer diaries and set meters that evaluate consumers' television program choices. The Nielsen top ten provides weekly, monthly, and quarterly reports of audience preferences, listing the top ten television programs, music, video games, and social media. The TV ratings are ranked by the percentage of U.S. homes tuned into television (Nielsen, 2018). The music rating is derived from the Billboard charts, and the video game rating is culled from a weekly survey Nielsen poses each week. The social rating is measured by the total social media activity on Facebook and Twitter. Since 2017, Nielsen has expanded their data collection technology to track data on streaming music, movies, and television, including subscription streaming services like Netflix (Steinberg, 2017). Although Nielsen ratings have been criticized for not measuring consumption on mobile devices, the company claims that they are updating their data collection techniques to account for this viewership.

Gallup (http://www.gallup.com) is an American consulting company that conducts research via worldwide public opinion polling and provides large organizations with analytics to help them solve problems (Gallup, 2018a). Its key research areas focus on employee engagement, customer engagement, talent management, and wellbeing (Boudway, 2012). Gallup poll data measures public attitudes about controversial topics, politics, and social and economic issues, and it has been used in U.S. presidential election forecasting. Gallup's daily tracking is comprised of two different surveys: the Gallup U.S. Daily (Gallup, 2018b) and the Gallup-Sharecare Well-Being Index (Gallup, 2018c). The Gallup U.S. Daily gauges Americans' opinions on economics, politics, and current events. They interview U.S. adults 18 years of age and older in all 50 states and the District of Columbia using both landline and cell phone numbers, interviewing 500 people per day, 350 days out of the year (175,000 per year). Gallup's Well-Being Index uses telephone and in-person polling and interviews to collect data from over 160 countries worldwide, surveying approximately 1,000 persons per country (Gallup, 2018a).

The General Social Survey (GSS) (http://gss.norc.org) is a project of the National Opinion Research Center (NORC) at the University of Chicago. This publicly available national resource was founded in

1972 to provide factual information on what Americans think about; it monitors societal change as American society grows more complex. It is one of the most frequently analyzed sources of information in the social sciences. It contains a standard core of demographic, behavioral, and attitudinal questions, plus questions about topics of special interest, including civil liberties, crime and violence, intergroup tolerance, morality, national spending priorities, psychological well-being, social mobility, and stress and traumatic events (National Opinion Research Center, 2018).

STEP 5: ANALYSIS OF DATA

Data analysis is the second-to-last stage of market research. In this stage, all the primary and secondary data is collected for evaluation and interpretation (Devault, 2017) to draw conclusions and make decisions based on those conclusions.

Quantitative studies provide descriptive, factual data, but they do not provide interpretation of that data; the numeric data collected through quantitative research is interpreted through statistical analysis. There are two types of statistical analysis. Descriptive statistics includes the mean, median, and standard deviation of the data; inferential statistics includes t tests, ANOVAs, and multiple regression correlations (Madrigal and McClain, 2012).

There are several software tools that make statistical analysis relatively accessible. Examples of software for quantitative analysis include the following programs and packages:

- **SPSS:** Statistical Package for Social Sciences, https://www.ibm .com/analytics/spss-statistics-software
- **SAS:** Statistical Analysis System, http://www.sas.com
- **STATA:** Statistics and data, https://www.stata.com/

Qualitative data is analyzed via content analysis. In this process, codes and categories are assigned to user responses, which are sorted and grouped to interpret the responses. The most basic and simple method of organizing qualitative data is with Microsoft Excel. More robust qualitative analysis software includes the following, some of which are affordable for personal use.

- **NVivo**, http://www.qsrinternational.com/nvivo/nvivo-products
- **Dedoose**, https://www.dedoose.com/
- **MAXQDA**, https://www.maxqda.com/
- **Atlas.ti**, https://atlasti.com/
- **QDA**, Miner https://provalisresearch.com/products/qualitative -data-analysis-software/

STEP 6: DATA-DRIVEN DECISION MAKING

The collected and analyzed data can be used to make decisions and to support funding requests. Using evidence in decision-making is crucial when allocating resources for materials, activities, and marketing. In many libraries, funds are spent on resources that are underutilized (in some instances, never used at all). This cannot happen when market research is conducted, for it lets you know whether the particular user group the resource was acquired for wanted it to begin with. Libraries are good at assessing whether resources should be retained, but they often do this only after the fact. For example, most academic libraries consult the annual usage statistics offered by database companies such as EBSCO, ProQuest, JSTOR, and publishers like Elsevier. These annual usage statistics give information about page views, searches, and article downloads for the past year of subscription. Let's say that an academic library that supports 30,000 students and faculty subscribes to a database with an annual cost of $30,000, and that that database has had only 10 page views, 5 article downloads, and 10 searches in the past year. Most sensible libraries conclude that the cost per search and download is too expensive and that the database should be canceled. But this decision is made after spending $30,000. Market research might have revealed that users were unaware of this database, or that the community's learning and teaching needs did not require this database. Consulting usage statistics each year is very important, but libraries need to research what their users want and need *beforehand*, not after the money is spent.

DATA DRIVES DECISIONS   83

CONCLUSION

This chapter laid out the case that libraries should carry out market re-search to support library decision making about how best to serve their target audience. This chapter identified the steps involved in planning market research, including a self-assessment with a SWOT analysis, an inventory of the physical and virtual library space, and a brief problem statement with tangible goals and objectives for the market research. It offered an overview of how to conduct market research (identify a target audience, select primary and secondary research data sources, identify a sampling method) and a brief discussion of how to collect and analyze market data to support decision making and bolster funding requests. Since market research is time consuming and costly, the next chapter illustrates how to identify different groups in your market. Once the data is obtained from the target market, the marketer can evaluate and make informed decisions on how to implement a market-ing campaign and other marketing activities.

NOTE

1. User-centered design for library websites and physical library facilities is discussed in detail in chapters 7 and 8.

REFERENCES

American Community Survey. 2018. "Subjects included in the survey." June 17. https://www.census.gov/programs-surveys/acs/guidance/subjects.html (Accessed July 1, 2018).
American National Election Studies. 2018. "About us." https://electionstudies .org/about-us/ (Accessed July 1, 2018).
Andreasen, Alan R., Philip Kotler, and David Parker. 2008. *Strategic marketing for nonprofit organizations*. Upper Saddle River, NJ: Pearson/Prentice Hall.
Barrow, Colin. 2016. *The 30 day MBA in marketing: The fast track guide to business success*. New York: Kogan Page Publishers.

Bias, Randolph G., Paul F. Marty, and Ian Douglas. 2012. "Usability/User-centered design in the iSchools: Justifying a teaching philosophy." *Journal of Education for Library & Information Science* 53, no. 4: 274–289.

Bordac, Sarah, and Jean Rainwater. 2008. "User-centered design in practice: The Brown University experience." *Journal of Web Librarianship* 2, no. 2/3: 109–138.

Boudway, Ira. 2012. "Right or wrong, Gallup always wins." *Bloomberg Businessweek* no. 4304: 49–50.

Bowler, Leanne, Sherry Koshman, Jung Sun Oh, Daqing He, Bernadette G. Gallery, Geoffrey C. Bowker, and Richard J. Cox. 2011. "Issues in user-centered design in US." *Library Trends* 59, no. 4: 721–752.

Claessens, Maximillian. 2018. "Difference between market research and marketing research—What is marketing research?" January 9. https://marketing-insider.eu/difference-between-market-research-and-marketing-research/ (Accessed July 1, 2018).

Comeaux, David J. 2008. "Usability studies and user-centered design in digital libraries." *Journal of Web Librarianship* 2, no. 2/3: 457–475.

Dempsey, Kathy. 2009. *The accidental library marketer*. Medford, NJ: Information Today.

Devault, Gigi. 2017. "How to analyze qualitative market research data." October 22. https://www.thebalancesmb.com/how-to-analyze-qualitative-market-research-data-2296916 (Accessed August 23, 2018).

Fernandez, Joe. 2009. "A SWOT analysis for social media in libraries." *Online* 33, no. 5: 35–37.

Gallup Corporation. 2018a. "About us." https://www.gallup.com/corporate/212381/pressing-problems-solved.aspx (Access July 1, 2018).

Gallup Corporation. 2018b. "How does the Gallup U.S. daily work?" https://www.gallup.com/174146/gallup-daily-methodology.aspx (Access July 1, 2018).

Gallup Corporation. 2018c. "How does the Gallup-Sharecare Well-Being Index work?" https://www.gallup.com/224870/gallup-sharecare-index-work.aspx (Access July 1, 2018).

Gil, Esther L.1. 2017. "Maximizing and assessing a one-shot information literacy session: A case study." *Journal of Business & Finance Librarianship* 22, no. 2: 97–110.

Good, Bill. 2018. "Worst cold-calling scripts: There are many reasons cold-calling isn't successful. The script you're using could be one of them." *Property & Casualty 360* 122, no. 2: 42–43.

Harris, Sasekea Yoneka. 2018. "SWOT analysis of Jamaican academic libraries in higher education." *Library Management* 39, no. 3/4: 246–278.

Hauser, Alexandra1. 2017. "User-centered design for first year library instruction programs." *College & Research Libraries* 78, no. 6: 867–868.

Hijji, Khalfan Al. 2012. "Strategic analysis process at academic libraries in Oman." *Library Management* 33, no. 4/5: 307–323.

Hill, Brian. 2018. "Why perform a SWOT analysis?" June 27. https://small business.chron.com/perform-swot-analysis-5050.html

Jones, Wilma L. 2011. "Re-engaging/engaging part-time librarians." *College & Undergraduate Libraries* 18, no. 1: 37–43.

Kinsman, Matt. 2010. "Telemarketing: The power user's guide to overhauling scripts." *Audience Development* 25, no. 2: 14–15.

Kumar, P. K. Suresh. 2012. "University Libraries in Kerala: A SWOT analysis for marketing." *Library Philosophy & Practice*: 1–12.

Levin, Roger P. 2016. "Using scripts to upgrade customer service." *Journal of The American Dental Association* (JADA) 147, no. 11: 911–912.

Madrigal, Demetrius, and Bryan McClain. 2012. "Strengths and weaknesses of quantitative and qualitative research." September 3. https://www.uxmat ters.com/mt/archives/2012/09/strengths-and-weaknesses-of-quantitative -and-qualitative-research.php (Accessed August 23, 2018).

Manzari, Laura, and Jeremiah Trinidad-Christensen. 2006. "User-centered design of a web site for library and information science students: Heuristic evaluation and usability testing." *Information Technology & Libraries* 25, no. 3: 163–169.

Mapulanga, Patrick. 2013. "SWOT analysis in the planning of information services and systems in university libraries: The case of the University of Malawi strategic plans." *Bottom Line: Managing Library Finances* 26, no. 2: 70–84.

"Marketing Research." 2009. In *Encyclopedia of Management, 6th ed.*, 561–564. Detroit: Gale. http://link.galegroup.com/apps/doc/CX3273100182/ GVRL?u=cuny_statenisle&sid=GVRL&xid=24d69251

Mersdorf, Sherrie. 2016. "Qualitative vs. quantitative research methods." September 26. https://blog.cvent.com/events/feedback-surveys/qualitative -vs-quantitative-research-methods/ (Accessed July 1, 2018).

Morgenstern, Jim, and Rebecca Jones. 2012. "Library strategic planning: Voyage of starship *Enterprise* or *Spruce Goose*?" *Feliciter* 58, no. 5: 12–14.

National Center for Education Statistics. 2018. "Surveys and programs." https://nces.ed.gov/surveys/ (Accessed July 1, 2018).

National Opinion Research Center. 2018. "About the general social survey." http://gss.norc.org/About-The-GSS (Accessed July 1, 2018).

Nielsen Company. 2018. "Nielsen top ten." http://www.nielsen.com/us/en/ top10s.html (Accessed August 23, 2018).

Paul, Prantosh K., Kalyan Kumar, and Dipak Chatterjee. 2014. "Cloud computing and information infrastructure: Emerging possibilities—A SWOT analysis." *SRELS Journal of Information Management* 51, no. 2: 129–134.

Polger, Mark Aaron. 2011. "Student preferences in library website vocabulary." *Library Philosophy and Practice.* 1–16. http://digitalcommons.unl.edu/libphilprac/618/

Polger, Mark Aaron. 2014. "Controlling our vocabulary: Language consistency in a library context." *The Indexer* 32, no. 1: 32–37.

Sharma, Aparna, Mindy Lanum, and Yolanda Suarez-Balcazar. 2000. "A community needs assessment guide: A brief guide on how to conduct a needs assessment." September. https://cyfar.org/sites/default/files/Sharma%202000.pdf

Shilpa Rani, N. R., and Lalitha, Aswath. 2016. "SWOT analysis of consortia in academic libraries." *KIIT Journal of Library & Information Management* 3, no. 2: 76–80.

Spradley, James P. 2016. *The ethnographic interview.* Long Grove, IL: Waveland Press.

Sonsteby, Alec, and Jennifer Dejonghe. 2013. "Usability testing, user-centered design, and LibGuides subject guides: A case study." *Journal of Web Librarianship* 7, no. 1: 83–94.

Steinberg, Brian. 2017. "Nielsen says it will measure audiences for TV episodes that stream via netflix." October 18. https://variety.com/2017/tv/news/nielsen-measurement-netflix-1202592985/ (Accessed July 1, 2018).

Victorino, Liana, and Alexander R. Bolinger. 2012. "Scripting employees: An exploratory analysis of customer perceptions." *Cornell Hospitality Quarterly* 53, no. 3: 196–206.

Victorino, Liana, Rohit Verma, and Don G. Wardell. 2013. "Script usage in standardized and customized service encounters: Implications for perceived service quality." *Production & Operations Management* 22, no. 3: 518–534.

Walsh, Gianfranco, and Eva Katharina Hammes. 2017. "Do service scripts exacerbate job demand-induced customer perceived discrimination?" *Journal of Services Marketing* 31, no. 4/5: 471–479.

Walters, Suzanne. 2004. *Library marketing that works.* New York: Neal-Schuman Publishers.

West, James. 2006. "Scripted . . . or from the heart?" *Service Management* 16–20.

CHAPTER 4

Creating Your Library Marketing Plan

IN THIS CHAPTER

- Why library marketing plans are useful
- Selecting the key members who will develop the plan
- Key elements of a library marketing plan
- Sample library marketing plans

REASONS FOR DEVELOPING A LIBRARY MARKETING PLAN

Libraries and librarians cannot successfully develop collections, programs, and services on the fly. Like any organization, they need a strategic plan. A strategic plan is a document that describes the goals and objectives of the organization over a specific period. For some libraries, the strategic plan may include a marketing plan. A marketing plan can be short—a few pages—or lengthy and exhaustive. This marketing plan is a roadmap (Fisher and Pride, 2006, p. 27) for successfully planning the library's marketing activities, and it provides a foundation for the library's future success and growth.

Marketing plans are living documents that should be continuously updated and tailored to specific services within the library (Duke and Tucker, 2007). They can cover a specific time frame (for example, the marketing plan for an academic year) or a particular service or resource (for example, a marketing plan to increase database usage). The process of creating the plan helps libraries and librarians understand their strengths and weaknesses, their competition, and their goals for future growth.

Although, unlike businesses, libraries are not selling products or services, they still need to market themselves—to connect their services and resources with potential customers. Successful marketing can improve customer satisfaction, increase participation, increase the number of users, and increase customers' usage of existing services and resources (Duke and Tucker, 2007, p. 58). Libraries need marketing plans in order to meet these goals; marketing plans connect specific marketing activities with various audiences and map out what success looks like (Duke and Tucker, 2007).

SELECTING THE KEY PLAYERS WHO WILL CREATE THE PLAN

A marketing plan should be created by a team of likeminded individuals who are passionate about marketing the library and raising awareness to their constituents (Duke and Tucker, 2007). For example, a hospital library marketing team might include an advisory committee of physicians, nurses, and other library users (Enyeart and Weaver, 2005; Bridges, 2005; Witman, 2012). In a university library, the marketing team should include the Outreach librarian and other Public Services staff, such as the Web Services Librarian, Reference and/or Instruction Librarians, and Electronic Resources/Services Librarians; faculty from the marketing or business departments; graphic designers; and library users (Duke and Tucker, 2007; Neuhaus and Snowden, 2003; Alire, 2007). Students who are majoring in business or marketing can also be valuable team members (Meulemans and Fiegen, 2006), providing help with market research. In all types of libraries, the group developing the marketing plan must consult regularly with the Chief Librarian (or library director). The plan cannot move forward without the support of the library director.

KEY ELEMENTS OF A MARKETING PLAN

Scholars differ about some specific elements of library marketing plans (see Kassel, 1999; Allen, 2015; Walters, 2004), but most agree that a library's marketing plan should contain the following basic components, which are described in detail below: information about the 4 Ps; a brand statement and tagline; background information about the library; target audience; positioning to ensure that marketing messages appeal to that target audience; tangible goals; brand elements; specifics about the marketing mix and communication tools; budget/R.O.I.; and evaluation tools.

The 4 Ps (Promotion, Price, Place, and Product)

A marketing plan should examine the 4Ps: promotion, place, product, and price (Allen, 2015; see chapter 1 for a detailed discussion of the 4 Ps). *Promotion* is the set of activities, behaviors, events, and materials produced to raise awareness about the library. The marketing plan should specify what types of promotion it will use and where it will use them. (Promotion is discussed in more detail in chapter 1.) *Place* refers to where these promotions take place: inside the library, outside the library (i.e., outreach), in print, online, or in person (Allen, 2015, p. 10). Print and online promotion are more than formats; the physical facility and the website both represent the library, and both need to be welcoming, user friendly, accessible, and intuitive. *Products* are the combination of services and resources that the library offers. Products may include print books and periodicals, electronic resources, and technology and equipment (Allen, 2015, p. 9). The marketing plan should specify which products the library is promoting and why. The *Price* section should break down how the library is funded and the costs of products and services (Allen, 2015, p. 9). Although libraries do not charge users for their services, the plan must document the actual cost of library services, which are primarily subsidized by taxes, grants, and donations, and what the library spends each year should balance with the total of the funding it receives (Allen, 2015, p. 9). The Price section, or cost analysis section, helps determine the value of the library's products and services, and it will help in calculating the marketing activities' return on investment (discussed in detail later in this chapter).

Brand Statement/Tagline

The marketing plan should include a brand message or statement, because library employees need a consistent message to relay to their users.

A brand statement should be succinct and emphasize the objectives of the organization. It should contain a consistent color scheme, font type, and logo. The brand message sums up the spirit of the organization; the message should inform users how the library is different from the competition. (Branding is discussed in further detail in chapter 6.)

Background Information

The background information section of the marketing plan expands on the library's mission and vision. It describes library services and resources that are provided to its users, it addresses some statistics, and it describes the staff and the library's goals. University libraries should examine the university's planning documents and use this section of the marketing plan to align itself with the larger institution's goals (Duke and Tucker, 2007, p. 62). Public libraries use this section to describe library services and resources and to show how they respond to the unique needs of the greater community. Some libraries provide a SWOT analysis (see chapter 3) in this section, and others include an environmental scan of their library here.

Target Audience

Marketers typically cluster potential customers by demographic data, such as age, gender, ethnicity, income, and educational level (Fisher and Pride, 2006, p. 44). These clusters, or "segments," make up your target audiences (Fisher and Pride, 2006, p. 43; Duke and Tucker, 2007, p. 55; Meulemans and Fiegen, 2006, p. 25; Walters, 2004, p. 33; Alman and Swanson, 2015, p. 112). Marketing needs to be tailored to appeal to these different audiences (Duke and Tucker, 2007, p. 55). Audience segmentation enables libraries to show how their services meet the needs of different groups of users, and allows them to direct marketing efforts for particular services at particular groups (see chapter 2 for a detailed discussion of segmentation).

An academic library's user segments might include:

- Students new to campus (first year students and transfer students)
- International students/English language learners
- Sophomores

- Juniors
- Seniors
- Honor students
- Alumni/Community members
- High school students /prospective students
- Staff
- Full-time faculty
- Adjunct faculty
- Administration

A public library might serve the following segments:

- Parents
- High school students
- Primary school students
- College students
- Seniors/retired persons
- Library trustees

Positioning

Libraries promote products or services to particular audience segments using positioning (Fisher and Pride, 2006, p. 57). Positioning is the strategy used to tailor your marketing efforts, promoting to each audience segment, who share similar values, beliefs, and lifestyle factors, the services that meet their particular needs (Fisher and Pride, 2006, p. 44). For example, a flyer promoting Library Workshops for First Year Students will be written differently if it is aimed at the students themselves than if it is aimed at faculty. Faculty need to know the learning outcomes and how the workshops satisfy their students' learning needs; students want to know how to register, what classroom the workshops are held in, how long the workshop will be, and what value the workshop will offer them.

Tangible Goals

Libraries do not have the staffing or resources to promote everything, and any large-scale marketing strategy is costly and time-consuming. Libraries must therefore focus on a few select services and/or resources to promote, and they must carefully research the marketing plan, justifying the cost. A marketing plan should contain one to two tangible, measurable goals that can be realistically achieved over the course of a specific time period (often a calendar or academic year).

One popular goal among public libraries is to increase the number of library card holders. Some libraries have partnered with other organizations to increase their success; for example, IDNYC provided a free ID card for all New Yorkers that also worked as a library card (Peet, 2015). This collaboration benefited both organizations. Other tangible goals a library may wish to accomplish in a year include

- Increasing the number of library card holders
- Increasing the number of reference desk transactions
- Increasing the number of circulating items in the collection
- Increasing the usage of select database subscriptions that might otherwise be canceled
- Increasing the number of students enrolled in library instruction workshops

Branding Elements

The marketing plan should be designed around the brand you want to convey to your users, and it should include your brand message, slogan, or tagline. The elements of your brand are memorable visual symbols that carry an emotional attachment and instant recognition (Fisher and Pride, 2006, p. 56). Your tagline should be brief and summarize the main goals and objectives of your service.

Marketing plans are often designed to re-brand libraries, transforming users' ideas about them from places that store dusty books to one-stop information centers that have books, computers, Internet access, and comfortable study spaces. The best way to discover your library's brand is by conducting a brand audit (brand audits are discussed in greater detail in chapter 6).

Communication Tools

The marketing plan should list the various tools that communicate marketing messages to your users. These tools may include in-person, online, and print tools; they may include traditional advertising messages or subtle branding in the library's products and services themselves. For example, in-person messages may include elevator speeches, meetings, and word of mouth. Online messages may include the library's website, with its mission, vision, brand statement, and logo; blog posts; social media posts; event photographs posted online; and email announcements. Print messages may include newsletters, press releases, signage, and brochures and flyers. Traditional ad campaigns may include print, radio, or television ads on local stations and branded swag, such as bookmarks or pens. Subtle branding can also be used in the library's displays, exhibits, and its repository of presentation materials.

In addition, the library should develop a list of media outlets that will help promote your libraries' services and resources. In an academic library, this list might include your university's communications department or the chairperson of each academic department. Some university libraries hire academic librarians in particular subject areas to work with relevant academic departments. This relationship was originally created to give the faculty liaison or chair of these departments a say in collection decisions (Rodwell and Fairbairn, 2008), but now, liaison librarians often serve as contact persons for promoting library services and resources to the relevant academic departments. Public libraries should cultivate relationships with local media outlets, including newspapers, radio stations, television stations, local websites and/or blogs, and local newsletters. Public libraries should cultivate local contacts, including specific reporters, politicians, and public figures (Alman and Swanson, 2015). Public libraries may also reach out to city councilors or library trustees or "friends of the library." Some public libraries collaborate with academic libraries, helping each other promote their programs and events.

Return on Investment (ROI)

The return on investment (ROI) is the measure of the net gain or loss compared to the cost of initiating an action or change (Crumpton, 2014). In the context of library marketing, ROI is the measurement of the benefit gained by promoting library services and resources compared to the cost of the promotion (Romero, 2011). For example, when promoting library instruction workshops in order to increase student enrollment, the investment—the time and cost involved in promoting the workshops, including producing promotional posters, social media postings, signage, brochures, promotional videos, and curated email messages—must be compared to the return on that investment, or the number of students enrolled. If the goal was to improve quiz grades, then the time and cost involved in developing the online quiz and rubric involved would be measured against the quiz grades; if the quiz grades improved, then the ROI is positive, and if they declined, then the ROI is negative and the organization has sustained a loss. Ordinarily, libraries do not think about ROI, since they are nonprofit (Romero, 2011), but libraries should consider the value and impact of their marketing efforts. By analyzing the time and costs of marketing, they can decide whether their efforts were worth the investment.

Libraries might also wish to think about non-financial returns on investment. Engagement is often a major goal of library marketing efforts; return on engagement has been called the new ROI (Fisher, 2009), and the more engaged the library's users become, the higher the ROI on the library's marketing (Polger and Sheidlower, 2017). For libraries, it is often more important to measure ROI for engagement than it is to determine the financial returns of the marketing plan; libraries need engaged users who use library services and resources and who support and advocate for them.

Evaluation Tools

Evaluation (discussed in more detail in chapter 3) is an important part of any marketing plan, and evaluation methods should be included in the research and planning phase, before the plan is implemented (Alman and Swanson, 2015, p. 24; Duke and Tucker, 2007, p. 58). These evaluation tools should aim to measure the success (or failure) of your marketing efforts. Evaluation tools can also provide information about resource usage, helping managers decide whether to renew or cancel particular subscriptions or purchase a specific product. Below are some metrics for evaluating library marketing efforts (Alman and Swanson, 2015; Duke and Tucker, 2007):

- Circulation Statistics
- Door/gate counts
- Student enrollment
- Number of new library card sign ups
- Website hits
- Social media metrics: Facebook likes, shares, comments, Twitter likes and retweets
- Number of library tours
- Database usage (downloads, searches)

These metrics all gather actual data about usage and are relatively easy to collect. This information can be used to advocate for funding.

There are also several ways that librarians can measure how their users *feel* about the library and its services. These methods (which are slightly more involved than the metrics above) can be used to test the success of branding campaigns or renovations of the library's physical facilities:

- Questionnaires
- Focus groups
- Interviews
- Surveys about awareness level (Likert scale)

Evaluation is part of the marketing cycle, and should be integrated into the marketing campaign from beginning to end (Fisher and Pride, 2006, p. 92). In the drafting phase of creating the marketing plan, evaluation is used to better understand the community and the target users; after all, marketing is really aimed at matching users' needs and wants with libraries' products and services. This type of evaluation begins long before marketing activities do. After the marketing plan is implemented, evaluation assesses whether the products and services have successfully met users' expectations. Evaluation done after the campaign might ask questions like these: What lessons did we learn? Did we meet our goals? What needs to be changed? What did we accomplish? How much did it cost? How long did it take? (Fisher and Pride, 2006, p. 92).

KEY POINTS

This chapter described the importance of developing a marketing plan, which is the roadmap that helps guide libraries' marketing of their services and resources. This plan should be an integral part of the library's broader strategic plan. It is a living document, so it needs to be regularly updated and adapted to fit each library's needs. Libraries can have multiple marketing plans promoting any services or resources within the library, but each marketing plan should be specific and targeted; one marketing plan can aim to increase social media engagement, while another can target an increase in reference desk transactions.

A library marketing plan should

- Include the library's mission and vision statement
- Have tangible goals and explicit target outcomes
- Be developed by a team of likeminded library advocates and stakeholders
- Include an environmental scan and SWOT analysis of the library to understand library users' needs and the library's strengths, weaknesses, competition, and opportunities for growth
- Include the Return on Investment (ROI), an important metric for measuring the impact of marketing efforts that is unique to each library. ROI = net outcome of marketing efforts − (time + cost of marketing efforts)
- Identify its audience segments
- Position marketing activities properly for these segments
- Include a list of evaluation tools to measure the impact of the marketing campaign

Sample Library Marketing Plans

The following four marketing plans were adapted from plans used by the Toronto Public Library, the Milner Library at Illinois State University, Yale University Medical Library, and Mount Mary University Library. The marketing plans are at the end of this chapter after the references.

REFERENCES

Alire, Camila A. 2007. "Word-of-mouth marketing: Abandoning the academic library ivory tower." *New Library World* 108, no. 11/12: 545–551.

Allen, Jeannie. 2015. "Building a foundation for marketing success." In *Creative library marketing and publicity: Best practices*, 1–16. Lanham, MD: Rowman & Littlefield.

Alman, Susan W., and Sara Gillespie Swanson. 2015. *Crash course in marketing for libraries*. Santa Barbara, CA: Libraries Unlimited.

Bridges, Jane. 2005. "Marketing the hospital library." *Medical reference services Quarterly* 24, no. 3: 81–92.

Crumpton, Michael. 2014. "Accounting for the cost of social media." *The Bottom Line* 27, no. 3: 96–100.

Duke, Lynda M., and Toni Tucker. 2007. "How to develop a marketing plan for an academic library." *Technical Services Quarterly* 25, no. 1: 51–68.

Enyeart, Amanda L., and Debbie Weaver. 2005. "Relationship marketing in a hospital library." *Medical reference services quarterly* 24, no. 4: 89–97.

Fisher, Patricia Holts, and Marseille Miles Pride. 2006. *Blueprint for your library marketing plan: A guide to help you survive and thrive*. Chicago: American Library Association.

Fisher, Tia. 2009. "ROI in social media: A look at the arguments." *Journal of Database Marketing & Customer Strategy Management* 16, no. 3: 189–195.

Kassel, Amelia. 1999. "How to write a marketing plan." *Marketing Library Services* 13, no. 5: 46.

Kotler, Philip. 2016. Dr. Philip Kotler answers your questions on marketing. http://www.kotlermarketing.com/phil_questions.shtml (Accessed June 3, 2018).

Meulemans, Yvonne Nalani, and Ann Manning Fiegen. 2006. "Using business student consultants to benchmark and develop a library marketing plan." *Journal of Business & Finance Librarianship* 11, no. 3: 19–31.

Neuhaus, Chris, and Kent Snowden. 2003. "Public relations for a university library: A marketing programme is born." *Library Management* 24, no. 4/5: 193–203.

Peet, Lisa. 2015. "Public: NYC ID doubles as library card." *Library Journal* 140, no. 2: 16. Library & Information Science Source, EBSCOhost (accessed July 18, 2017).

Polger, Mark Aaron, and Scott Sheidlower. 2017. *Engaging diverse learners: Teaching strategies for academic librarians*. Santa Barbara, CA: Libraries Unlimited.

Rodwell, John, and Linden Fairbairn. 2008. "Dangerous liaisons? Defining the faculty liaison librarian service model, its effectiveness and sustainability." *Library Management* 29, no. ½: 116–124.

Romero, Nuria Lloret. 2011. "ROI. Measuring the social media return on investment in a library." *The Bottom Line* 24, no. 2: 145–151.

Strand, Jill. 2012. "Creating and executing a marketing plan." *Information Outlook* 16, no. 1: 28–29.

Walters, Suzanne. 2004. *Library marketing that works.* New York: Neal-Schuman Publishers.

Witman, Lydia. 2012. "Hospital clinicians' iPad use: An interim report." *Medical Reference Services Quarterly* 31, no. 4: 433–438.

SAMPLE LIBRARY MARKETING PLANS
(USED WITH PERMISSION BY THE COPYRIGHT HOLDERS)

Mount Mary University
Haggerty Library & Learning Commons
2017–2018

Haggerty Library & Learning Commons (HLLC) strives to be a place that supports and enhances learning and scholarship at Mount Mary University. The HLLC wants a well-used book and serials collection and through marketing and outreach, aims to show who we are, what we do, and what it's worth to all our patrons.

Overall goals

➢ To raise and maintain the visibility and viability of Haggerty Library & Learning Commons among the Mount Mary community. This includes undergraduates, graduates, and doctoral students, all faculty, staff, and alumni. It also includes the wider community when appropriate.
➢ To support the mission and vision of the HLLC
➢ To continue branding the HLLC

  ○ The "Making your library work like you" slogan changed to "Uncover. Discover" in 2016
  ○ Cooper Hewitt font is used for library contact info and/or as a de facto logo
  ○ Other fonts are stored in the library's Canva account profile

➢ To communicate with library staff the importance of recognizing the marketing goals, plan, and brand

Marketing Strategies

➢ Always promote with benefits, not just service rundown in list form
➢ Continue to maintain the library home page and Haggerty Help Guides
➢ Continue rotating signage in and around the library, including the stacks, and around select campus locations
➢ Continue speaking and presenting at student and faculty orientations and seek out additional opportunities to engage the Mount Mary community
➢ Market library services to faculty of lagging disciplines

  ○ Identify those already "on board" to assist

➢ Create subject-specific flyers for all disciplines for IL instruction
➢ Create and publicize Mount Mary events in the library

Marketing Calendar and Forms of Publicity

In general, each semester begins anew and you should be prepared to market other services or products as needed. Also be prepared to repeat things as needed. Consider faculty and student marketing separately, although there is some overlap. And keep trying to get faculty to help promote the library via their flyers.

Beginning of the semester	**Faculty:** New stuff/newsletter, general service reminder, Liaison who's who, IL offers, department meetings, book requests **Students:** New stuff/initiatives, summer journals, Haggerty Help Guides, student group outreach, Start and continue any series
Midterms	**Faculty:** Faculty Guide, RSS, repeat IL and department meetings, new books **Students:** new books, chat, Opposing Viewpoints, Haggerty Help Guides specifics, I Need/other series
Nearing the end of the semester	**Students:** Finish series, survey ads
Finals Week (December)	**Students:** Bagel Study Break
Finals Week (both)	Emergency Chocolate

National Library Events

Please note that all have tabs in the General Web Resources Guide in LibGuides—plan to promote these!

Mid-September through mid-October: Hispanic Heritage Month
September/October: Banned Books Week
Dec. 1: World AIDS Day
February: Black History Month
March: Women's History Month
April: National Poetry Month
May: Asian-Pacific American Heritage Month
Plus election year promotion

Forms of publicity

We use a combination of general MMU announcements, all-campus student email account (for survey communications) faculty announcements, paper signs and flyers for faculty mailboxes, and the library blog. An online and paper Library Smart Guide was completed in 2015. PDF downloads are also available on our My Mount Mary page.

Assessment of Marketing Techniques

We will assess based upon attendance to events and daily patron counts, as well as online statistics, wherever possible, and overall surveys participation. More options to come.

Marketing Team Members

As of spring 2017, the team consists almost solely of the Coordinator of User Services and Library Assessment, with assistance from the Library Director and Reference staff.

\<Sample Marketing Plan for Program Name\>   *Version x*

Prepared by

\<Name\>, Marketing & Communications

---

1. **Program Goals and Objectives**

2. **\<Program Name\> Program Positioning**

   2.1 Key Benefits/Value Propositions

   2.2 Key Differentiators

   2.3 Key Messages

3. **Target Audience and User Profiles**

   3.1 Primary Target Audience

   3.2 Secondary Target Audience

   3.3 More Target Audiences

> This section is information that is gathered by the Comm. Officer from the program or service "owner". This information is necessary in order to understand what kinds of marketing strategies and tactics will be most effective.

4. **Marketing and Communications Programs and Initiatives**

   4.1 Program Packaging, Naming and Identity

   4.2 P.R. and Media Relations

   4.3 In-branch Materials/Merchandising

   4.4 "Beyond the Branch" Promotion & Advertising

> This section details the "marketing mix" that will most effectively deliver on the marketing and communications strategies identified above. Not all of these tactics will be used in every program initiative.

4.5 Events

4.6 Online Communications

4.7 Partnerships/Affiliations

4.8 Internal Marketing Communications Plan

5. Desired Outcomes and Metrics

This section describes what success looks like for the objectives, strategies and tactics identified, including measurable outcomes. Alternatively, these metrics could be incorporated into each section of the plan.

6. Timelines and Milestones

This section gives a high level outline of the timelines for the program and marketing plan rollout, and lists major project milestones.

1. Program Goals and Objectives

[This section describes the organizational goals and objectives of the program for which this marketing plan is designed.]

Example: Ready for Reading

Primary Goal:
To increase early literacy skills in children ages birth to five by providing resources, tools, programs, and supports to their parents and caregivers, childcare workers and other relevant stakeholders who support the healthy growth and development of children in this age group.

Secondary Goals:

- To raise the profile of TPL and position it as a leader in early literacy within the city and within the province;
- To expand the reach of programs and services being delivered by TPL by taking Ready for Reading and early literacy principles and program elements into the community through community training and outreach initiatives, and encourage community agencies and childcare providers to incorporate these principles in their programming;
- To improve the literacy of Toronto's children, especially those within newcomer and low income families;
- To educate and raise awareness of the value of early literacy principles.

2. [Program Name] Program Positioning

[This section describes the positioning of the program and/or of the library as the provider of the program.]

Example: Ready for Reading

Toronto Public Library introduces parents and caregivers to the importance of early literacy and teaches them how to develop pre-reading skills in their children. The emphasis is on providing an atmosphere that is fun, verbal and stimulating, full of opportunities to talk and be listened to, to read and be read to, and to sing and be sung to. Ready for Reading is not a program designed to teach reading, but rather to lay the groundwork for the development of early literacy skills.

With the quality of our material collections, our expertise in using these materials for early childhood literacy, our 98 accessible locations, and our experience in serving the diverse needs of the city's residents, the Toronto Public Library is the first and best source for early literacy programs, services, and education in Toronto.

2.1. Key Benefits/Value Propositions

[This section lists the key benefits and value propositions of the program or service being marketed.]

Example: Ready for Reading

- A broad variety of collections, programs and services that help prepare children for reading, developed and delivered by early literacy experts
- Free
- Universal reach and access: Available to all Torontonians, in multiple locations across the city, and designed for multiple constituencies (e.g., different levels of literacy, multi-language, etc.)
- The latest research and library expertise in early childhood literacy has been incorporated into all materials, programs, and services.

2.2. Key Messages

[This section lists the key benefits and value propositions of the program or service being marketed.]

Example: Ready for Reading

1. As parents and caregivers, you are your child's first and best teachers, and home is where your child begins to learn.

2. Through fun, easy, everyday activities you do with your child—like talking, reading, singing, playing, and writing—you are building important early literacy skills that help to get your child ready for reading.

3. These are the early literacy skills you build through these everyday activities:

Liking books: Children who enjoy books will want to learn to read

Hearing sounds in words: Being able to hear the smaller sounds in words help children sound out written words

Knowing lots of words: Knowing many words helps children recognize written words and understand what they read

Telling stories: Learning to tell a story helps children develop skills in thinking and understanding

Recognizing that words are words: Being familiar with printed language helps children feel comfortable with books and reading

Knowing letters: Knowing the names and sounds of letters helps children to sound out words

4. Toronto Public Library introduces parents and caregivers to the importance of early literacy and teaches them how to develop pre-reading skills in their children with:

—free *Ready for Reading* storytimes, literacy-rich interactive play spaces, and expert staff assistance **at library branches throughout the city**

—books, resource guides, brochures, and other reading and learning materials that parents and caregivers can use with their children **at home**

—online resources, videos, and library services **on the library's website** for children and their parents and caregivers

2.3. Key Differentiators

[This section describes how the library program/service and/or the library itself is different from others who offer the same or similar programs or services—or may be perceived to be the same. This information is helpful in understanding how to position the library program or service in relation to these other programs, services, or providers.]

Example: Ready for Reading

• *Compared to schools*—Toronto Public schools address a different age range of children (i.e., ages five and up), and therefore their focus is more on teaching children to read, rather than on preparing them to read.

- *Compared to early childhood educators*—Focused on all aspects of early childhood education. The library is very specifically focused on literacy and getting children ready to read. The library also has extensive expertise in the development and utilization of collections specifically designed for this purpose.
- *Compared to other city agencies* (e.g., Parks & Rec, Public Health)—although these agencies offer literacy services as part of their overall programming, these organizations do not have the experience or expertise to deliver these programs as effectively as the library.
- *Compared to other Ready for Reading programs*—In specific areas of experience and expertise, the TPL has the opportunity to develop value-add components to its Ready for Reading–focused programs that can then be shared among other academic and professional organizations who deliver Ready for Reading programs. For example, in the areas of multicultural language and integration support, TPL could incorporate its expertise and experience to improve and enhance the Ready for Reading programs.

3. Target Audience and User Profiles

[This section describes the target audience(s) for the program's marketing and communications initiatives, and provides detailed profiles of these audiences. This is not simply saying who we are communicating to, but providing an idea of who these people are. The more we understand our target audience, the better able we are to communicate effectively with them.]

Example: Ready for Reading

3.1. Parents and Caregivers (Primary Target Audience)

This is a diverse group of people which includes parents, grandparents, siblings, extended family members, friends, nannies, and babysitters. This group of users should be segmented further into library users and non-library users:

Current library users who are likely familiar with many aspects of TPL's programs and services, but are not necessarily familiar with our children's services and Ready for Reading.

Non-library users may not be frequent library users, for many reasons—lack of awareness of library services and their benefits, cultural resistance to participate in library programs (including just visiting the library), not being available to visit during branch hours because they are working, etc. Therefore, in-branch promotion alone will not be sufficient, and reaching out to these people outside of the library with marketing tactics will be necessary in order to inform them of the program and to encourage its use.

3.2. Providers of Early Literacy Services and Supports (Secondary)

This audience is comprised of individuals and organizations that deliver education and childcare services and supports directly to children ages birth to five and their parents. These include daycares, schools, literacy centers, Public Health, and postsecondary institutions that educate educators. The educators of preschoolers work directly with children from birth to five years, and have a broad Early Childhood Education background in a preschooler's various developmental areas (e.g., social, emotional, intellectual, creative, and emotional skills and development). These educators of preschoolers spend time with children on a regular basis in a classroom or daycare setting, sometimes with parents/caregiver present. The educators of educators subgroup is made up of highly educated ECE university and college professors and instructors, researchers and academics who have been, or are currently, ECE or literacy practitioners.

3.3. Library Staff (Secondary)

This audience is made up of people with varying amounts of early literacy experience and education; however, all deliver library programs and readers' advisory to both children and the parents/caregivers of children. Some library staff members are professional librarians, while some are library assistants and clericals. These people work in branches of various sizes, and in neighborhoods that range in size, character, and diversity.

4. Marketing and Communications Programs and Initiatives

[This section details the "marketing mix" that will most effectively deliver on the program, marketing, and communications strategies identified above. Only list those tactics that are appropriate for this particular initiative.]

The following are the marketing programs and initiatives proposed to launch and support the [program name] program

- Program Packaging, Naming, and Identity
- Press and Media Relations
- In-branch Materials/Merchandising
- "Beyond the Branch" Promotion & Advertising
- Events
- Online Communications

• Partnerships/Affiliations
• Internal Marketing Communications Plan

4.1. Program Packaging, Naming and Identity

Objective of marketing tactic: For users to easily and readily associate the benefits and value of the [program name] program with services delivered under that brand.

[Generally speaking, if a program is going to be packaged, an associated name and visual platform will need to be developed. If a brand or sub-brand is to be developed, a branding exercise should be undertaken.]

Example: Ready for Reading

Objectives of marketing tactic: For users to easily and readily associate the value of the Ready for Reading program with the various products, programs and services delivered under that brand (i.e., each time they see the name and associated branding/packaging, they will remember the messages associated with that brand and therefore understand the value).

The TPL Early Literacy program and the various programs and services delivered under the umbrella of this larger program will need to be named, and a logo, brand identity, and visual platform for these programs will need to be developed.

Umbrella Program (became Ready for Reading)

• Logo/brand identity
• Visual platform
• Positioning of program and of library brand within it
• Name

Some new programs will be developed and incorporated into the TPL Early Literacy suite of programs and services. In addition, existing programs will be repositioned, renamed and/or redeveloped to incorporate ECRR principles and practices. Depending on the program and intent, branding and naming of programs will need to be done.

4.2. P.R. and Media Relations

Objectives of marketing tactic:

[State objective(s) of the media plan to be developed]

Example: Ready for Reading

1. To raise awareness of the library's programs and services for early childhood literacy;

2. To raise the profile of the library as a leader of early childhood literacy in the community and to the city and province;

3. To educate the public on the value of early childhood literacy, of the principles of Ready for Reading, and on the library's value in delivering Ready for Reading programs and services.

[A detailed public relations and media plan should be developed and outlined here. It could include, but does not need to be limited to the following:]

- Press Release
- Listings
- Short and Long-lead stories (pre-launch for promotion or profile-building)
- Short and Long-lead stories (post-launch for profile-building)
- Interviews with TPL or guest spokespeople

Example: Ready for Reading

TPL will develop a detailed public relations and media plan to achieve the above-stated objectives. The plan will be designed to leverage the current interest and excitement in early childhood literacy and the studies that have been conducted, and position the library as a leader in early childhood literacy in Toronto and the province of Ontario.

The media plan will also incorporate a strategy to position and promote the library's Children and Youth Advocate as the evangelist and spokesperson for the library's Ready for Reading programs and services. The goal of this strategy is to personify the Ready for Reading brand by attaching a recognizable and credible personality and expertise to it.

4.3. In-Branch Materials/Merchandising

Objectives of marketing tactic:

1. To communicate to in-branch users information about the [program name] program.
2. To cross-promote related library services, collections, and programs to library users.

Example: Ready for Reading

1. To communicate a variety of information about Ready for Reading programs and services to a number of different audiences. Information will include the value of Ready for Reading programs and services, when and where they're available, the value of the role of the library in delivering these programs and services, etc.

2. To unify and provide consistency of message across all children's birth-to-five (i.e., Ready for Reading) communications materials.
3. To support the training of TPL staff who will be delivering Ready for Reading programs and services to library customers.

[Note that these materials communicate with only a subset of potential audiences (i.e., existing TPL, in-branch users). Therefore, some thought should be given to how extensively these materials should be made available, in which branches, and whether they need to be customized to this particular audience. Some thought must also be given to how these materials will be merchandized within the branches to ensure they are as effective as they can be. In-branch materials may include, but are not limited to, the following:]

- Posters and/or display material
- Promotional/informational postcard or bookmark
- Brochures/flyers
- Buttons, stickers, etc.
- Booklists

4.4. "Beyond the Branch" Promotion and Advertising

Objectives of marketing tactic:

[Describe the objectives this marketing tactic is designed to achieve.]

Example: Ready for Reading

1. To raise awareness of the library's programs and services for early childhood literacy;
2. To raise the profile of the library as a leader of early childhood literacy in the community and to the city and province;
3. To educate the public on the value of early childhood literacy, of the principles of Ready for Reading, and on the library's value in delivering Ready for Reading programs and services.

[When developing the list of "beyond the branch" promotion and advertising tactics, be creative. This can be an expensive tactic, but through partnerships, innovative outreach and "guerrilla marketing" strategies, reaching your audiences beyond the branch can be cost-effective and compelling (beyond traditional advertising channels).]

4.5. Events

Objectives of marketing tactic:

[Describe the objectives this marketing tactic is designed to achieve.]

Example: Ready for Reading

1. To raise awareness of Ready for Reading programs and services. It is unlikely that any events would be specifically designed and executed to launch the Ready for Reading program. However, depending on the timing of the launch of the program, we may want to leverage existing events to promote the program. In addition, on an ongoing basis, we may want to ensure that Ready for Reading programs are highlighted and consistently promoted at TPL events. Possible TPL-initiated and community events that could be leveraged include:

- Word on the Street
- Keep Toronto Reading.

TPL could also participate in events put on by partners or other organizations that present synergies with the Ready for Reading program—for example, local and International Literacy Day events.

4.6. Online Communications

Objectives of marketing tactic:

[Describe the objectives this marketing tactic is designed to achieve.]

[Note that, when developing online communications strategies, consideration of multiple online tactics should be explored, beyond just promotion on TPL website properties and cross-promotion on partner sites. This can include social media and different web technologies, marketing techniques, and properties.]

Example: Ready for Reading

1. To raise awareness of Ready for Reading programs and services to existing and potential library users
2. To provide education material to parents on how to apply Ready for Reading principles to improve readiness for their child's reading
3. To help library customers find out information about Ready for Reading programs including program details, locations, and times.

Existing TPL online vehicles will be utilized, including the TPL main website, as well as the KidsSpace website. A dedicated Ready for Reading web presence may also be developed, if necessary, which would be linked to from the other TPL websites.

The online medium could also be used to promote Ready for Reading programs and services by offering "virtual samples" to existing and potential library users. These would be especially well-suited for those users who may either prefer to receive content electronically, or are unwilling or unable to receive content through their physical branch. Some examples of this would be video clips of staff demonstrating storytelling with hand-play, or a brief description by staff of one of the Ready for Reading principles, a download of a song or booklist that would support that principle, and some instruction to the parent/caregiver on how to use that resource.

We will also explore non-TPL online communications vehicles which could be well-suited to deliver TPL/Ready for Reading messaging, information, and educational material to our target audiences.

4.7. Partnerships/Affiliations

Objectives of marketing tactic:

[Describe the objectives this marketing tactic is designed to achieve.]

Example: Ready for Reading

1. To raise awareness of Ready for Reading programs and services to existing and potential library users
2. To provide education material to parents on how to apply early literacy principles to improve readiness for their child's reading
3. To align the library brand with a complementary or high-profile brand to elevate the library brand and/or raise awareness of the library brand
4. Leverage the marketing/communications machines of other partners to reduce costs and/or improve reach to target audiences of Ready for Reading messages.

These could include:

- Family Literacy Day
- Today's Parent
- TVO
- Help! We've Got Kids (get a listing there, at least)
- Canadian Living
- School Boards.

4.8. Internal Marketing Communications Plan

Objectives of marketing tactic:

1. To educate internal TPL staff on [program name] program.
2. To support the training of TPL staff who will be delivering the [program name] program.

[Materials and communications channels could include, but are not limited to, the following:]

- Communication Packages: email/intranet to all staff and hard copy sent to branches
- @TPL
- Formatting/packaging of training materials
- Road shows
- Launch Package—The intent of such a package would be to generate some excitement about the program, while also raising awareness and understanding. It would also provide staff with key facts and information about the program. Examples of package contents could include a small giveaway branded with the program logo and a laminated "Quick Guide to [program name]."

5. Desired Outcomes and Metrics

[This section describes what success looks like for the objectives, strategies, and tactics identified, including measurable outcomes. Alternatively, these metrics could be incorporated into each section of the plan.]

Timelines and Milestones

[This section gives a high level outline of the timelines for the program and marketing plan rollout, and lists major project milestones.]

CUSHING/WHITNEY MEDICAL LIBRARY MARKETING PLAN

YALE UNIVERSITY

Last revised 2.27.17

Marketing Committee Charge

The committee is charged with the following responsibilities, as laid out by Medical Library leadership in 2014:

1. Oversee library marketing and communication to ensure that the library's message is clearly presented in a timely, synchronized, and vibrant manner, with a positive and suitable tone via a variety of communication channels.
2. Strategize how best to promote and market library collections, resources, services, and initiatives, so as to help the library accomplish its overall mission.
3. Help individual library staff increase awareness among specific users and targeted groups of the expertise and services that the staff member can provide these users.
4. Preparing and distributing promotional materials, e.g., announcements, news items, monthly liaison emails, flyers, posters, postcards, etc.
5. Scheduling and synchronizing promotion and communications through a variety of methods, e.g., social media, Yale Medicine, YNHH Bulletin, YSM and YUL event calendars.
6. Compiling content and materials for the library's annual report.
7. Other marketing and communications activities beyond those enumerated above.

The committee's work is also informed by the Medical Library's 2012–2015 strategic plan, available at [redacted URL]. The broad objectives of the strategic plan include:

1. Expand clinical information services to support the university, hospital, and health system.
2. Support the education programs of the communities we serve.
3. Develop programs and services that anticipate and engage the full research cycle.
4. Build, disseminate, and preserve our world-class collections.
5. Provide inviting physical and virtual spaces for learning, collaboration, research, and creativity.

The committee's activities support these objectives by promoting and marketing the library's programs, services, and collections through targeted advertising, publications, events, social media channels, the library website, and seasonal mailings. The committee also helps document and assess the efforts of library staff toward these objectives. A large component of effective marketing is ensuring a consistent brand identity. The committee oversees branding and ensures a consistent brand identity by:

- Drafting and editing major library publications including:
  - Library's quarterly newsletter
  - "A message from your librarian" emails
  - Annual Report
- Working with the library's webmaster on the design and content of the library's website, with a focus on updating web content with news, events and exhibits
- Approving any printed or web-based material that is "outward facing" (e.g., posters, postcards, mailings)
- Ensuring consistency with YUL branding guidelines for all public facing materials
  - See the guidelines here: http://www.yale.edu/printer/library-id/index.html

Committee Membership

To help attain a holistic perspective on the diverse activities of the library, the committee includes representation from several library departments:

Chair:	[redacted]
Committee Support:	[redacted]
ADMIN:	[redacted]
CDM:	[redacted]
REED:	[redacted]
Cushing Center:	[redacted]
HIST:	[redacted]
YUL:	[redacted] (ex officio)

Audience analysis

To help inform this marketing plan, the committee has conducted an informal audience analysis:

Activities/Items	Audience
Lectures, Associates Day	Associates, alumni, donors, current students, and faculty
Alumni/Reunion Weekend	Alumni
Orientations	First year students, new faculty, and staff
Exhibits	All of the above; also visiting families, scholars, and student groups

Outlet	Potential Audience
Annual Report	Donors, associates, higher-level administrators (YSM, YNHH, YSN)
Services	New and old beneficiaries
Social Media (primarily Facebook)	Followers
Website	Not specific, but namely Yale folks who use the site
Calendar (both CWML and YSM)	YSM, YNHH, YSN
The monitor in the hallway	Visitors to the library
Blog	Visitors to the website
"Finn Fridays"	Visitors to the library
Coffee hours, learning "bashes"	Visitors to the library, students, affiliates with YNHH

Matrix of Library Marketing Outlets

The committee has ensured that this marketing plan is aligned with the library's overall strategic communication plan by conducting a thorough survey of all existing library marketing outlets (see Matrix below).

Library Outlets	Specifications
YUL publicity	Specific documentation provided by [YUL Director of Communications], including a request form, and available on the Marketing Committee's Box folder. Send to [Sr Admin Asst], then she will send to [DirComm] and [YUL Admin Asst]
Monitor slide	draft slide using PPT template, send to [webmaster]
Blog (http://library.medicine.yale.edu/blog, Cushing Center, Historical)	Draft and post the blog. Ask [webmaster] for help if needed.

Library Outlets	Specifications
Featured News block on library homepage	Send [webmaster] link to blog post and a mockup of what you want (can be hand-drawn, PPT slide) including any image/ graphic that could be used and the text you want. Dimensions are 960x190px
Facebook: http://facebook .com/yalemedlibrary	Post to Facebook—everyone is an admin. [Sr Admin Asst] or [webmaster] can show you how to post if you need help. YUL Facebook guidelines: http://www.yale .edu/printer/library-id/custom-social -media.html
Photos	Contact [Cushing Center Coordinator]
YSM Calendar (http://tools .medicine.yale.edu/ library/calendar/)	Post event to the YML calendar; Marketing Committee Chair will approve

(Note: the following contacts have been redacted for institutional privacy; unredacted plan includes names and contact information)

YSM Outlets:	Sr Administrative Assistant* is responsible for contacting the following partners:
YSM—general publicity	[redacted]
YSM Facebook (https://www .facebook.com/YaleMed)	[redacted]
YSM Instagram, Yale Medicine, & weekly news digest	[redacted] Images for posting on YSM homepage need to be at least 720x494px
YSM Twitter	[redacted]
Med@Yale	[redacted]
OPAC	[redacted]
YNHH	[redacted] For tabling at YNHH, contact Assistant Director of Clinical Information Services
YSN	Go through Nursing Librarian
YSPH	[redacted]

*YUL Director of Communications also has established relationships with many of these partners.

Appropriateness Guidelines

The committee has developed criteria to evaluate the appropriateness of content for each outlet (see table below).

Outlet	Guidelines	Notes (audience, tone, etc.)
Blog	Pretty much anything that might be of interest to any segment of our audience/ users, BUT must be somehow connected to the library or to library services, and that connection made explicit to the reader.	General audience (users of library website) Informal
Homepage slideshow	Only items that are of interest to a significant part of our audience. Not department-specific, generally speaking. Preference given to upcoming events/ announcements/news, or to marketing valuable services or resources. At least 1–2 slides should always be allocated to current exhibits.	General audience (users of library website) Formal
Lobby monitor	Stuff that is of interest to a significant part of audience, particularly those that enter the physical library. Needs to lend itself to succinct "at a glance" description.	General audience (visitors to library) Formal
YSM Calendar	Event/announcement needs to be coordinated by someone who works at the library and somehow library-related.	Formal

Outlet	Guidelines	Notes (audience, tone, etc.)
Newsletter	Sent to Medical Center Departments and Students. Includes items of broad interest because it is edited by liaisons. Can feature one or more resources to promote. Includes trials of databases, exhibits, classes, interfaces changes and updates, technology updates, information about events.	Monthly. Sent to over 10,000 people. Mostly clinical and basic science faculty plus students, residents, fellows, researchers and staff. Requires utmost attention to proofreading and accuracy. Formal in terms of content, but has an informative tone. Can use "you" construction. Succinct with table of contents to save readers' time and keep their attention. Currently plain text with no formatting.
Yale Library Calendar	Details for events and exhibits sponsored by the Medical Library. These are sometimes put into the YUL weekly email.	Local Audience, Formal
Facebook	Informal, but hopefully fun and informative. Not necessarily directly related to our library or services, but can be of related interest to our users.	General Audience, Informal

Marketing Materials Policy and Inventory

Policy re: printing, June 2016: Design and print costs represent a significant expense. In light of budget constraints, our policy is that printing by YPPS, University Printer, or other external vendors is a development tool and should be reserved for that (e.g., targeted mailing to select donors). Routine publicity should be designed in house and the final product should be digital-only.

Item	Location	Cost	Notes
Persian cards	Admin office supply closet	For sale	For sale
Digital Collections postcards	Historical	Free	Free. [Historical Library Assistant] has these
Cushing Center postcards	[Cushing Center Coordinator]	Free	Free
Retractable badge holders	Circulation Desk	For sale	
Library brochures	Admin office supply closet	Free	For development purposes
Bookmarks	Admin office supply closet	Free	For development purposes, old fashioned
Class photos	Digital images on Box	Free	Check with [Sr Admin Asst] or [Historical Library Assistant]
Paper weights	Director's office closet	Free	For development purposes
Watercolor Historical Library Prints	Director's office closet	Free	For development purposes

Exhibitions Marketing Checklist

[Sr Admin Asst]: YUL Calendar

[Committee Support]: YSM calendar—both exhibitions AND events. Make sure to check off the box for the event to be included in the Weekly Digest.

[Sr Admin Asst]/[Committee Support]: Facebook

[webmaster]: Website—including homepage, blog post, update Current and Past exhibitions pages (http://library.medicine.yale.edu/historical/explore/behind and http://library.medicine.yale.edu/historical/explore/exhibits respectively)

Signage Policy

The Marketing Committee oversees the temporary signage at CWML. Temporary signage should follow the YUL identity guidelines for temporary signage (http://library.identity.yale.edu/templated-signage.html) which are as follows: "Temporary signs should be set in the Yale typeface, either in sentence case or small caps (letterspaced or 'tracked' open about 10 percent). Type should be arranged to adhere to one axis—either all centered or all flush-left ragged right."

Staff members who find the need to create a new sign should send the committee chair a copy of the new sign along with details of where it will be posted.

Digital copies (e.g., MS Word or InDesign files) of new signage will be kept in a subfolder of the Marketing Committee folder on Box.

MARKETING PLAN FROM A UNIVERSITY

Library, Sample 1
Milner Library, Illinois State University
2012–2014 Marketing Plan

INTRODUCTION

While plans are not usually followed to the letter, the planning process is indispensable as it enables us to answer basic questions about what we do and why we do it.

One doesn't often hear marketing and library in the same sentence. Many see marketing as a process of for-profit organizations. This document is written to enable the University Libraries (hereafter library or Milner Library) to pursue a certain process in the promotion of its activities; to complement the Library's Strategic Plan; and to assist the library's and university's faculty and staff in understanding the tactics, strategy, and procedures related to the marketing of cultural events and intellectual resources.

Milner Library plays an integral role in the university teaching, learning, and research. The library's vision and mission statements enforce the library's increasing leadership role in the life and culture of the campus and community.

In its vision statement, the library aspires "to be the preeminent center of learning, information, culture, and technology in higher education" (Vision Statement, http://library.illinoisstate.edu/library-information/about/strategicplan.php).

It also aims to "create and sustain an intuitive and trusted information environment that enables learning and the advancement of knowledge in a culturally and technologically superior setting. ISU Libraries' staff is committed to developing innovative services, programs, space, strategies, and systems that promote discovery, dialogue, learning, and the human spirit" (Mission Statement, http://library.illinoisstate.edu/library-information/about/strategic-plan.php).

OBJECTIVES

The University Libraries Marketing Plan aims to:

1. increase the visibility of the library and its value in our society;
2. increase the awareness of the community of the added value of the library activities and services;

3. increase the level of participation of ISU alums and community members in the life of the university and stimulate the donation and gifting process;
4. increase the level of satisfaction among our patrons; and
5. facilitate the branding of the library activities.

MARKETING STRATEGIES

To promote the Milner Library's services, resources, and activities, the library will undertake the following strategies:

- Increase the visibility of library resources through the library's homepage, brochures, social networking tools, and other appropriate channels.
- Identify services and collections to highlight through a program or a course with one of the teaching faculty.
- Publicize special events in coordination with other colleges and programs as well as community partners.
- Seek out opportunities to work with the University Library Committee as representative of the faculty and student body.
- Work with the board of the Friends of the Library on community events.
- Sponsor and support external speakers, exhibits, and programs that highlight Milner's cultural role on campus and in central Illinois.
- Seek input from the community in relation to cultural needs.
- Establish new community partnerships to support speakers, strengthening relationships between the university and local businesses and not-for-profit organizations (i.e., bookstores, museums, and public libraries).
- Highlight Milner faculty and staff research and service contributions to the profession through professional circles as well as national media.

FORMS OF PUBLICITY

ASSESSMENT/EVALUATION

All marketing strategies will be evaluated through a number of methods. These include but are not limited to surveys, focus groups, and event evaluation forms. The PR staff will use the Activity Planning Feedback and the Speaker Assessment Form (Appendixes 2 and 3) for quick feedback.

TARGET AUDIENCES

Primary audiences of Milner Library are members of the Illinois State University community. This includes students, faculty, staff, and alumni. Secondary audiences include but are not limited to the Bloomington/ Normal community, other institutions of higher education, families of Illinois State University students, library organizations, and elected officials (Appendix 4).

MEDIA CONTACTS

The Dean of University Libraries or the dean's designee is the official spokesperson for the library and partnership organizations stated in the library's mission. The dean may ask the head of the Public Relations Unit to respond to media questions or to provide information as appropriate. The unit head will be responsible for providing current, accurate information or identifying the appropriate source of information to the media. The unit head will act as liaison to campus and external publications (Appendix 5).

Although the president's office serves as the ultimate spokesperson for the university, a crisis communication plan is expected to be developed through the spring of 2012.

Public Relations and Marketing Unit Team Members
Toni Tucker (Unit Head and Assistant Dean)
ttucker@ilstu.edu
309-438-7402

Sarah Dick
sdick@ilstu.edu
309-438-2680

Jan Johnson
jrjohnso@ilstu.edu
309-438-3897

APPENDIX 1

MILNER LIBRARY LOGO

(To be used on all publications)

AVAILABLE AT

P:\Library Coordination Groups\Public Relations Committee\FINAL (read- only)\Graphics_Logos\milner- logos

Illinois State University Libraries adhere to the university's graphic and editorial standards developed by the University Market- ing and Communications Department. Standards can be found at http://universitymarketing.illinoisstate.edu/identity.

APPENDIX 2

Activity Planning Feedback

	Date:	
Event:		
Event date:		
Location:		
Message:		

AUDIENCE(S)
1.
2.
3.
4.
5.
6.
7.
8.

MEDIA
1.
2.
3.
4.
5.
6.
7.
8.

CONTACTS
1.
2.
3.
4.
5.

REPORT INCLUDED

_____

_____

APPENDIX 3

Speaker Assessment

Form

Today's Event

Your responses help us improve our events and give us ideas for others.

How did you hear about this event?

☐ Newspaper   ☐ Radio   ☐ Flyer/Poster   ☐ Website   ☐ Other

Are you a student?   ☐ NO   ☐ YES   ☐ High School   ☐

College

How would you rate the event/speaker?

☐ Excellent   ☐ Just OK   ☐ Below expectations

How far (miles) did you travel to this event?

Will you attend future Milner Library events?   ☐ YES   ☐ NO

We love your ideas! Suggestions:

Speakers _____

Programs _____

Exhibits _____

Other _____

Please use the back for any additional comments you would like to share.

Printed on recycled paper.

APPENDIX 4

Target Audience/Specific Media

Media è / Audience ê	Vidette	Campus Connections	Signcades	Flyers	Brochures	Newsletters	Bulletin Boards	Electronic Signs	Posters	TV 10	Radio	College & Main	Lib Web Site	ISU Web Site	ISU Report	Social Media	Pantagraph	E-mail
Internal																		
Students	X	X	X	X	X	X	X	X	X	X	X	X	X	X		X	X	
Faculty	X		X	X	X	X	X	X	X	X	X	X	X	X	X	X	X	X
Library Personnel	X		X	X		X	X	X	X	X	X	X	X	X	X	X	X	X
ISU Staff and Admin.	X		X	X		X	X	X	X	X	X	X	X	X	X	X	X	X
External																		
Alumni						X						X	X	X	X		X	X
Friends of Milner					X	X						X	X	X	X		X	X
Parents					X	X						X	X	X			X	X
Community Inst.			X			X		X	X	X	X	X	X			X	X	X
Library Consortia			X			X		X				X	X	X		X	X	
Citizens of Illinois												X	X	X				
Media												X	X	X	X		X	X	X
Elected Officials													X	X		X	X	X
Vendors																		X

APPENDIX 5

Media Contacts

Illinois State University Marketing and Communications
438-5091

PRINT

Daily Vidette

Contact changes year to year 438-5931
Broadcast E-mail Illinois State University
See campus policy at www.ctsg.ilstu.edu/policies_faq/broadcasts.shtml

Pantagraph (Local Newspaper)

Higher Education Reporter: 820-3232

MEDIA (RADIO AND TV)
WGLT NPR Radio Station
Charlie Schlenker, News, ceschle@ilsu.edu
438-7353
Willis Kern, News Director, wekern@ilstu.edu
438-5426 Development 438-2257
WJBC Radio Station
News 821-1000, Ext. 205, newsroom@wjbc.com
HOI Television News
(309) 698-1950

Campus Connections

Closed circuit TV in resident halls, www.uhs.ilstu.edu/forms/campus_conn
.shtml

COLLEGE & MAIN
Deb Wylie, Coordinator of Public Service and Outreach, dkwylie@ilstu
.edu, 438-2937

ELECTRONIC MESSAGE BOARD
Prairie Room—Contact a PR committee member.
Milner—Contact a PR committee member or Jan Johnson.

SIGNCADES
Contact a PR committee member.

APPENDIX 6

Marketing Timeline for Standing Annual Activities

FALL SEMESTER
New Faculty
Orientation
Banned Books
Week
Homecoming
Honored Alum Parade
Visiting Author Program
Illinois School Library Media
Association Reception Study Breaks
Commencement

SPRING SEMESTER
Founders Day
Bryant Jackson Lectureship Children's Author Visit Lincoln Speaker
Edible Book Festival National Library Week
Science & Technology Week Speaker (partnering w/CAST) Campus
Theme (when available)
Study Breaks Commencement
SUMMER
Preview Expo

ADDITIONAL EVENTS
Exhibits
    National Endowment for the Humanities
    Traveling Exhibits Museum Traveling Exhibits
    ISU University Galleries Exhibits Curriculum-Based Exhibits
    Exhibits from the Library's Special Collections Student Organization
        Exhibits
    Community Exhibits

APPENDIX 7

Public Relations/Marketing Request

Send to any member of the Public Relations and Marketing Unit—Sarah Dick, Jan Johnson, or Toni Tucker.

			Today's date:
Project name:			
Project contact(s):			
Project/event date:			
Estimated marketing period: Start date: End date:			
Describe service, program etc. to be publicized: Include attachment(s), if necessary:			
Select text and delete. Field will expand as you type.			
Intended target audience(s): Select all that apply.			
◦ All			
◦ ISU students	◦ ISU faculty	◦ ISU staff	◦ ISU administration
◦ Library personnel	◦ Alumni	◦ Parents	◦ Friends of Milner
◦ Courtesy Card users	◦ Local community	◦ Media	◦ Elected officials
◦ Other:			

Suggested media: Select all that apply.

PRINT	ELECTRONIC	MEDIA (RADIO AND TV)
○ Flyer ○ color	○ B/W	○ Milner website	☐ Press release
☐ Bookmark	○ Electronic sign (Milner)	☐ ISU Report
☐ Brochure	○ Electronic sign (campus)	☐ *Daily Vidette*
☐ Newsletters		☐ WJBC
☐ Table tents	○ Campus Connections	☐ WGLT
☐ Invitations	○ E-mail	☐ Channel 10
☐ Signcades	○ Bulletin boards	☐ Press conference
	○ University calendar	☐ *College & Main*
○ Other:		

Additional information that could be helpful in promoting this event:

Select text and delete. Field will expand as you type.

APPENDIX 8

FLIER POSTING INFORMATION; MAILBOX STUFFING INFORMATION

Flier Posting Information 2012–2013

University Housing Services (UHS) allows registered student organizations and University departments to post fliers in designated public areas with the following stipulations:

1. The flier relates to events, announcements, services, or activities sponsored and sanctioned by Illinois State University or one of its departments or registered student organizations.
2. The flier does not contain references to alcohol, tobacco, or illicit drugs, or to any event, activity, program, or sponsor whose purpose or activity is the sale, use, or promotion of alcohol, tobacco, or other drugs.
3. The flier does not contain profanity.
4. The flier is printed on recycled paper and contains the recycling logo along with the statement "Printed on recycled paper."
5. The flier contains the following statement for an event: "If you need a special accommodation to fully participate in this program/event, please contact Toni Tucker, Milner Library at 438-7402. Please allow sufficient time to arrange the accommodation."
6. The flier does not exceed 400 square inches.
7. Fliers will be posted for one (1) week.
8. UHS is not responsible for items that get torn down or removed prematurely.

POSTING PROCESS
Fliers are to be taken to the reception desk of each hall for approval by a UHS staff person prior to posting. The numbers of copies needed for distribution are as follows.

POSTING NUMBERS FOR 2012–2013
Hamilton-Whitten	2
Hewett	1
Atkin-Colby	2
Manchester	1
Wilkins	1
Watterson	3

Mailbox Stuffing Information

University Housing Services (UHS) allows registered student organizations and University departments to submit stuffings for the residence hall mailboxes. The items to be stuffed must follow the same stipulations as stated for flier postings.

APPENDIX 9

Table Tent Guidelines for Campus Dining Halls

Unfolded dimensions 4¼ by 11 inches printed on card stock
Must have the statement:
"If you need a special accommodation to fully participate in this program/
event, please contact Toni Tucker Milner Library at 438-7402."

Approval at the John Green Building (take a draft for approval before printing) Fill out application form One week request/distribute and take down
on Saturdays May fill out a form for up to three weeks of display Watterson
175/Southside 77/Linkins 84

CHAPTER 5

Campaigns

Developing Activities, Events, and Materials to Promote Your Library

IN THIS CHAPTER

- What a campaign is
- Types of campaigns
- Components of a campaign
- Examples of campaigns from libraries and the corporate sector

DEFINING A CAMPAIGN

A campaign is a systematic, large-scale set of marketing activities designed to achieve a specific goal over a specific period of time. Campaigns center on a consistent theme, and may express this theme though different types of media, events, and promotional material. This chapter gives an overview of the components of a campaign and offers examples of campaigns from both libraries and the corporate sector.

TYPES OF CAMPAIGNS

This chapter illustrates the differences, similarities, and overlaps between the following types of campaigns: public awareness campaigns, advocacy campaigns, advertising and marketing campaigns, and rebranding campaigns. Public awareness campaigns aim to raise awareness; they are not necessarily selling anything, and there is no immediate call to action. Advocacy campaigns seek funding; they use persuasive techniques to reach decision makers and convince them to fund a particular cause. Advertising campaigns (which are just one subset of a larger marketing campaign) use a variety of communication channels in order to sell a specific product.

COMPONENTS OF A CAMPAIGN

Operations

Campaigns are usually overseen by a single project manager. They can be short or extend over several years, but they have specific start and end dates.

Goals and Objectives

A successful advocacy, marketing, or public awareness campaign must have clear, straightforward, tangible, realistic goals and objectives, and these objectives and the desired outcomes should be laid out in the campaign's marketing plan. Examples of specific library campaign goals include increasing circulating book transactions by 50 percent, increasing the number of library instruction sessions by 75 percent, increasing the number of attendees at library events by 200 percent, or reducing the number of library fines by 50 percent. Objectives need not be quantified, but when they are, the campaign's objectives are more tangible and specific.

Theme

Memorable, unique campaigns have a unifying theme connecting all promotional elements. This theme should be connected to the library's brand, but should stand on its own. Most example campaigns described in this chapter have a theme that shapes the campaign's development.

Targeted Audience

The campaign needs to focus its promotion to a specific target audience, which is a specific subgroup of users. Target audiences and market segmentation are discussed in more detail in chapter 2.

Community Needs Assessment

Before designing a campaign, a needs assessment must be conducted, for understanding user needs is an important part of the planning process. Campaigns are time-consuming and expensive, and the theme of the campaign must address a knowledge gap or needs gap in the user community—the difference between the community's needs or expectations and their current condition. Needs can be assessed by examining census data from the community or collecting data using assessment instruments (usually focus groups, surveys, and questionnaires) to learn about your users. Chapter 3 lays out and describes in detail the four steps of a community needs assessment: the assessment plan, the data collection, the summary and analysis of the data, and the action plan (which is used to plan your campaign). Assessing community needs helps libraries and librarians make better decisions about how to run a successful marketing, advertising, or public awareness campaign.

Messaging Tools

To be successful, a campaign needs to spread its message. It does so using tools and such as word of mouth, print advertisements, email marketing, signage, and publicity, which may be delivered via the media, your website, or social media. Advocacy campaigns and advertising campaigns include with their message a "call to action" (CTA), which encourages users to immediately take some action, such as making a phone call, following a link to a website, or clicking a "share on social media" button. The CTA can be as simple as "call this number now to get your 50 percent discount." For example, Netflix uses persuasive text to promote its free trial. According to Egan (2017), a CTA should contain active language and strong visuals and should convey a sense of urgency (Egan, 2017).

Events/Activities

Campaigns must identify events and activities to promote its message. Below are some examples of events and activities in a library campaign to promote a 50 percent increase in circulation of its new K–12 collection in an academic library:

- Tabling event at an open house for new education majors
- Social media posting using campaign hashtag (Facebook, Twitter, Instagram, YouTube)
- Article in the student newspaper
- Slideshow on the front page of the library website
- Partnership with the local public library branch to promote the collection to public library users
- In-person presentation(s) to the university's education department at a department meeting
- Library tours or a formal presentation during new student orientation before the semester begins
- Article in the library newsletter
- Launch party in the library, inviting the chair and faculty of the education department
- Faculty author lecture about their related research or publications
- Signage and large-scale posters promoting the new collection
- Contest asking students to write a book review of their favorite K–12 book, with an Amazon gift card prize
- Swag promoting the K–12 collection (stickers, magnets, bookmarks, postcards, notepads, USB sticks)
- Blog post

Media Relations

Establishing a relationship with local news media (print, radio, or television) may increase and improve user awareness of and exposure to your campaign. News reporting on any advertising campaign can help increase sales and customer interest. To generate media interest, write a press release and send it to local newspapers and TV or radio news agencies, or invite a reporter to visit your library and interview staff and students. Academic libraries may use their connection to their university's external relations/communications department, which may report on their activities. These departments may also have direct connections to a local reporter or TV station who may report on your campaign activities.

Campaign Website and Online Marketing

Online marketing can reach a global audience and engage directly with its target audience (Viemisto, 2018). Online marketing also enables much more precise tracking of each message's effect than traditional marketing methods, for there is no way to know whether traditional methods are successfully reaching their target audiences. Website traffic can be assessed using Google analytics, and social media marketing provides metrics on demographic reach, likes, comments, and engagement. Chapter 9 offers more detail about social media metrics.

Campaign information can also be conveyed through websites, which are often the best marketing tools to communicate campaign messages. Compared to newspaper ads, television and radio interviews, flyers, postcards, billboards, and telemarketing, websites are extremely cost-efficient, and are both more flexible and more environmentally friendly than print; websites can be updated nearly instantly, and without incurring reprinting costs.

Some smaller campaigns may use existing organization websites; for example, permanent library websites may publicize particular library campaigns. Other campaigns may have campaign-specific websites. For example, politicians running for office usually have a website communicating their political platform. Campaign websites should reflect the themes of your campaign, which should remain consistent across different media: flyers, mailings, postcards, TV, radio, and social media advertisements all share the same "look and feel," and campaign websites should also be visually aligned with the rest of these materials. Websites that are not updated daily (as news sites or blogs are) should contain all important basic information and should act as a springboard, linking out to social media posts and news articles. A library-specific example of an independent campaign website is the site of the Libraries Transform campaign, an initiative of the American Library Association. The campaign has its own identity and a website independent of the ALA's site, with its own URL (www.librariestransform.org).

Evaluation and Assessment

A campaign's success—its tangible outcomes—must be measured to see whether it met its goals and objectives. For example, if a library campaign's goal was to increase reference desk transactions within a given year, an ideal metric would compare the number of reference desk transactions from the first year with the number from the second year. If a library campaign aimed to increase awareness of a particular resource, such as liaison librarians, its success might be best measured by conducting a pre- and post-campaign assessment; a significant increase in awareness of the liaison librarian program between the pre-campaign and the post-campaign assessment would indicate that the campaign had successfully achieved its purpose.

Throughout the campaign, there should be built-in assessment via feedback forms, printed surveys, email surveys, and web polls, as well as interviews with volunteers after campaign events. This ongoing assessment gathers data for the final analysis, which informs future marketing decisions. Campaign team postmortem meetings, in which the marketing team discusses the campaign timeline, the planning, the community analysis, the costs, the activities, the outcomes, and the community needs that should be addressed in the future, are critical in identifying gaps and errors and in planning future marketing campaigns.

TYPES OF CAMPAIGNS

Public Awareness Campaigns

Public awareness campaigns are usually run by nonprofit organizations, though they may involve partnerships with the government and nongovernmental organizations (NGOs). They usually involve community outreach, celebrity endorsements, and PSAs (public service announcements) and are conveyed by television commercials, newspaper and magazine ads, YouTube videos, and social media. These campaigns aim to raise awareness on a specific issue. These campaigns have a strong central message and themes that support that message, but they do not have an immediate call to action. These campaigns are often very successfully conducted on social media. Every campaign should have its own unique hashtag, a unified label or keyword that enables users to easily find all posts tagged with it. Hashtags are a powerful way to make social media posts discoverable and to enable users to engage with each other online about shared topics of interest (Jacobson and Mascaro, 2016).

A memorable example of a public awareness campaign was the 1987 anti-drug campaign from the Partnership for a *Drug*-Free America (now called the Partnership for Drug-Free Kids). The campaign's spots conveyed the central campaign message about the harmfulness of drugs in a striking way: they showed an image of an egg being fried, accompanied by the tagline, "This is your brain on drugs" (Shapiro, 2017). The public service announcements, which were run on television and in newspapers and magazines in the late 1980s, were reissued in the late 1990s and in 2016 and 2018, and it continues today (despite objections from the egg industry, which felt that the ads would make children afraid to consume eggs; Blistein, 2014).

A library-specific example of a public awareness campaign is Banned Books Week, which is an annual awareness campaign sponsored by many nonprofit advocacy groups, including the American Library Association, the American Booksellers Association, the Association of University Presses, the Freedom to Read Foundation, People for the American Way, Index on Censorship, the National Coalition against Censorship, the Dramatists Legal Defense Fund, the Comic Book Legal Defense Fund, and the National Council of Teachers of English. It was inspired by a 1982 exhibit of 500 books that were challenged at the American Booksellers Association convention (Macrae, 2011). The campaign offers libraries and librarians an opportunity to fight censorship and to celebrate the freedom to read and the First Amendment. During this campaign, libraries are encouraged to promote and display challenged books, since 85 percent of challenges receive no media attention (Long, 2006). The campaign is always controversial; in 2006, for example, the campaign received 547 complaints, up from 459 the previous year (Long, 2006).

Libraries that participate in Banned Books Week create displays, buttons, t-shirts, special web pages, social media posts, and posters, and they often send targeted email messages to their users to inform them about the campaign. Some libraries may coordinate special events, such as book talks where scholars discuss challenged books. Macrae describes an event at the Boulder Public Library where the community created a paper chain of banned book titles they had read, cutting book titles into strips and connecting them together into a 6,000-link chain that spanned the entire building. This activity made a strong impact on the community, engaging and empowering them (Macrae, 2011). The Banned Books Week website offers resources and promotional materials such as posters, banners, shelf talkers, and free artwork and logos by the American Library Association.

Another library awareness campaign is ALA's READ poster campaign. This campaign is one of the oldest library awareness campaigns in the United States. According to Peggy Barber (2003), the Children's Book Council used posters to promote reading and libraries as early as 1919, but it was not until 1975, when the American Library Association took over the National Book Council's poster campaigns, that the familiar modern-day campaign was designed. The first READ poster, printed in 1980, featured Mickey Mouse; the first celebrity READ poster, printed in 1985, featured Bill Cosby. Since then, READ posters have included all kinds of public figures, including television and film celebrities, professional athletes, scientists, politicians, authors, and artists, all of whom volunteer their participation. The campaign promotes a love of reading and helps to change public perceptions of libraries and librarians.

Advocacy Campaigns

Advocacy campaigns use politics, lobbying, and persuasion to influence people to take a particular action—often, that action is to fund a certain project. There is a sense of urgency to an advocacy campaign. These campaigns go beyond raising awareness to include a "call to action." Advocacy campaigns are more assertive than public awareness campaigns and require more strategic planning and political savvy (Siess, 2003).

Advocacy campaign examples

SaveIMLS. An example of an advocacy campaign is the Save the Institute of Museum and Library Services (SaveIMLS) campaign. The IMLS is the primary source of federal funding for the nation's approximately 120,000 libraries and 35,000 museums. When the Trump administration announced that IMLS funding would be eliminated (Neal, 2017), the Save IMLS campaign was started by concerned individual citizens and, later, joined by the American Library Association and vendors such as Gale and other publishers (see http://learn

.cengage.com/GWP17213297 for more information). The ALA created campaign web pages on the ALA site, which publishes an advocacy guide: a list of senators and representatives who have committed to signing legislation for IMLS funding in the future, ways to contact local and state representatives to advocate for IMLA funding, and links to other resources. The campaign is also carried through on the website of EveryLibrary, a national nonprofit that works on local library ballot initiatives to ensure that libraries continue to receive funding. EveryLibrary provides boilerplate emails that can be sent to politicians (EveryLibrary, 2018). The campaign also used social media to get the word out. Using the hashtag #saveIMLS, the campaign encouraged people to contact their state senators and congressional representatives to support IMLS funding.

Campaign for America's Libraries. The Campaign for America's Libraries (2000–2015), sponsored by the ALA, aimed to promote the value of libraries and librarians. It used the @your library trademark to create a consistent set of promotional materials and communications across the United States (the campaign was adapted for global use by IFLA for their Campaign for the World's Libraries). The @your library trademark could be freely used (with credit) by any library to promote its services and resources, and thousands of libraries across the country used it. The @your library trademark used the "@" symbol to showcase libraries' dynamism and ability to change with changing needs. The campaign framed libraries as a "third place" for community, collaboration, and socialization (Montgomery and Miller, 2011).

The campaign's aim was to communicate the following messages:

- Libraries are changing and dynamic places
- Libraries are places of opportunity
- Libraries change lives
- Libraries change communities (ALA, 2015)

The campaign aimed to raise awareness and support for libraries by emphasizing libraries' value, dispelling stereotypes and promoting libraries as places of innovation, discovery, curiosity, possibility, and growth. In 2015, the @your library trademark ended, and the Campaign for America's Libraries became the Libraries Transform Campaign, which similarly aims to raise awareness of the value provided by libraries and library employees. This campaign centers on the theme of transformation, and it focuses on literacy, lifelong learning, critical thinking, collaboration, open mindedness, librarians as research experts, information privacy, and individual empowerment (ALA, 2015).

National Library Week. National Library Week, founded in 1958, is sponsored by the American Library Association and is a campaign to honor and promote our nation's libraries and librarians. According to the ALA, during the 1950s, Americans were spending less time reading and more time using television and radio. In 1954, the nonprofit National Book Committee was formed by the ALA and American book publishers to promote reading. The theme for the inaugural year was "Wake Up and Read" (ALA, 2018). National Library Week is celebrated by all libraries—school, public, academic, and special.

Advertising Campaigns

Advertising campaigns, or ad campaigns, are a series of advertisement messages that contain a common theme. The theme's message is broadcast through different communication outlets, which are created to achieve a particular set of objectives: to establish a brand, to raise awareness, and to seek new and returning customers. Advertising campaigns usually have defined start and end dates and use communication outlets such as television, newspapers, magazines, billboards, radio, and video. More recently, advertising campaigns have begun using websites, social media, and email to spread their message. When these tools are used in a cohesive, integrated plan, the strategic approach is called integrated marketing communications (IMC). IMC unifies all communications across platforms and channels so that consumers recognize the products and/or services being promoted (Kitchen and Burgmann, 2015).

Libraries can learn from the corporate sector when they plan their campaigns, gathering ideas and inspiration from big-budget campaigns. The following section describes the themes and goals of several corporate advertising campaigns. The examples show the importance of spokespersons, who are key influencers in the campaign, as well as campaign themes that are topical, relatable, humorous, and compelling.

Campaigns from the Corporate Sector

Dove Campaign for Real Beauty. The goal of the Dove Campaign for Real Beauty was to celebrate the natural beauty of women of all physical types. The campaign included advertisements, TV ads, billboards, interactive websites, a book, and a play. It featured portrayals of women of all ages, sizes, and shapes. The campaign grew out of an early-2000s study conducted by Dove's PR agency, Edelman. The study asked more than 3,000 women from 10 countries if they saw themselves as beautiful. Very few women (2 percent) did (Bahadur, 2014). In response, Dove and British marketing firm Ogilvy & Mather launched a photography exhibit titled, "Women Photographers on Real Beauty." The exhibit, which featured the work of 67 female photographers, began a larger conversation that became the "Campaign for Real Beauty" in September of 2004 (Neff, 2014).

The campaign had many components. Dove commissioned a multinational survey and hired scholars like Nancy Etcoff, Susie Orbach, and Naomi Wolf to contribute to an anthology titled *The Real Truth about Beauty: A Global Report* (Johnston and Taylor, 2008). On the Dove website, women were invited to post photos of themselves and interact on the discussion boards. Sections of the website had titles like "let's dare to love our hair" and "let's make peace with our bodies" (Johnston and Taylor, 2008). Dove partnered with the American Girl Scouts; they also created the Dove Self-Esteem Fund and programs like "Uniquely ME!" and "Body Talk" (Johnston and Taylor, 2008). The campaign also included a photo exhibition, Beyond Compare, featuring the work of female photographers from 22 countries (Johnston and Taylor, 2008). Of course, the campaign themes of female empowerment, self-confidence, and celebration of our bodies were being used to promote the sales of Dove products, and as critics have noted, Dove's parent company, Unilever, sells products that oppose the messages of the "Real Beauty" campaign: Slimfast, Axe cologne, and Fair and Lovely skin lightening cream (Bahadur, 2014). But since the campaign's inception in 2004, Dove's sales have increased from $2.5 billion to $4 billion (Neff, 2014).

Progressive Insurance. In 2008, Progressive Insurance began a large advertising campaign featuring the character "Flo, the Progressive Girl." The campaign was so successful that Flo, a quirky character with quick wit, an energetic personality, retro hair, and a sparkling white uniform, became a regular representative of the company. Flo has appeared in 100 Progressive TV ads thus far. Over the years, Flo's and her family's storylines were threaded through a series of TV commercials, and this helped customers develop an ongoing personal connection to Flo and, by extension, to the Progressive brand. Flo's fan base is so strong that they even dress up as her for Halloween, with a retro wig, apron, nametag, and insurance box (Rodriguez, 2014). In 2010, the company broadened its focus to Flo's family and circle of friends, introducing other characters (different family members, Flo's sidekick Jamie, and Pickles the dog) and revamping the look of the spots, with new sets and alternate worlds (Rodriguez, 2014).

Farmers Insurance. Farmers Insurance uses storytelling in its TV, print, and web ads to showcase the outrageous claims it receives. Their spokesperson, Professor Nathaniel Burke (played by J. K. Simmons), was introduced in 2011 giving tours at the fictional University of Farmers (Pasquerelli, 2017), telling outrageous stories based on actual insurance claims, all supporting their message: "At Farmers, we've seen almost everything, so we know how to cover anything" (Farmers, 2018). This integrated marketing campaign runs on TV, radio, videos (hosted on the Farmers website), social media, and direct marketing. The Farmers Hall of Claims interactive website (www.farmers.com/hallofclaims) offers visitors an opportunity to explore real claims depicted in short video vignettes. One video shows a reenactment of a badly installed hot water tank that skyrocketed from the basement through three floors of a house and out the roof before smashing down onto a car on the street. Another video showed several dogs swimming in a living room, looking like they were at a pool party; one dog had accidentally turned on the kitchen faucet and flooded the home.

Wendy's. Wendy's famous 1984 "Where's the Beef" advertising campaign featured 81-year-old Clara Peller in a series of TV, radio, and print advertisements. Originally, the ad was titled "Fluffy Bun," and featured three elderly women examining the lack of beef on a squishy white bun. The ad became famous when Peller, one of the three, repeatedly asked the other two in bewilderment, "Where's the beef?" (Nemetz, 2017), implicitly criticizing competitors McDonald's and Burger King for their burgers' lack of beef. The campaign resulted in a 31 percent increase in Wendy's annual revenue, and the expression became a part of popular culture, even being used in a campaign for the Democratic presidential nomination; Walter Mondale used the expression to challenge rival Gary Hart in the 1984 Democratic primaries (Walsh, 2012). The campaign, which made Peller famous, spawned merchandise such as t-shirts, bumper stickers, Frisbees, mugs, beach towels, and a board game (Nemetz, 2017). After Peller used the same phrase in a Prego commercial, she was terminated for violating a non-compete clause (Nudd, 2003). Wendy's replacement campaign starred Wendy's founder Dave Thomas, but in 2011, they revamped the original Peller campaign, this time titling it, "Here's the Beef" (Nemetz, 2017).

Rebranding Campaigns

A very specific type of advertising campaign is the rebranding campaign. This type of campaign is used when an organization needs to redefine itself. Some rebranding campaigns remind a company's customers of their mission, vision, goals, and objectives; others help change negative perceptions by providing an updated message, new design, and perhaps even a new name (Sullivan, 2017). Libraries may need to rebrand because their parent organization (city or college) is undergoing a rebranding that the library needs to align themselves with. Rebranding also provides an opportunity for a makeover or a revitalization, or it can serve as a self-reflective inventory of an organization's visual identity (Singh, 2011; Kenneway, 2006).

Below are some examples of some rebranding campaigns from the corporate sector.

Charter Communications. Charter Communications began to rebrand Time Warner Cable (TWC), a cable, voice, and Internet company that they purchased for $60 billion as Spectrum in mid 2016. Charter used a rebranding campaign that aimed to convince people that the change would be for the better (Shayon, 2016). A young man with a friendly demeanor and a non-threatening boy-next-door look became the new face of TWC, and he reassured viewers that the rebranding would be seamless and effortless. Other Spectrum ads showed the dedication of Spectrum employees to excellent customer service, depicting a repair person waking up very early in the morning and driving a great distance to meet the first customer of the day before the sun rises. As the rebranding campaign progressed, Spectrum shifted to the next phase of the campaign; ads narrated by Ellen De-

Generes and carrying the new tagline "Think Forward" contain upbeat music and feature innovative technologies (see https://www.ispot.tv/ad/w3TA/spectrum-think-forward-coming-fast).

McDonald's. Over the last decade, McDonald's has rebranded itself in response to its negative portrayal in Morgan Spurlock's 2004 documentary *Supersize Me*. The documentary vividly illustrated the negative health impacts of consuming McDonald's food for every meal of the day (Young and Nestle, 2007). In response to the sensation created by the documentary, McDonald's and many other fast food giants began offering healthier food options and smaller portion sizes. McDonald's did not change its iconic logo (see chapter 6 on branding), but it made changes to the menu and to the physical stores to make it seem more upscale, modern, and environmentally conscious and to appeal to a more upscale clientele. Some stores have updated their interiors to be more chic, changing the lighting and offering more comfortable seating (Nieva, 2016; Gasca, 2014; ALA, 2017), and some have added self-serve kiosks (ALA, 2017). To offset the stigma of having a McDonald's in the neighborhood, some stores are replacing the iconic bright red and yellow exterior color scheme with more understated, darker exterior colors. To be more environmentally conscious, some U.K. stores have turned their used cooking oil into biodiesel fuel to power their vans (Barriaux, 2007). And through its McCafé coffee shop, which was piloted in Australia in 1993 (Wright, Frazer, and Merrilees, 2007) and came to the United States in 2001 (Lacsamana, 2016), the restaurant has begun to offer more upscale products.

Library Marketing Campaigns

A library marketing campaign may combine elements of awareness, advocacy, and advertising campaigns: these types of campaigns aim to raise user awareness of various library services, to increase library funding, and to promote library usage. Like all campaigns, a library marketing campaign is a planned series of activities and messages, delivered using various communication channels (television, radio, video, newspapers, magazines, billboards, the internet, and social media) to raise awareness, sell a product or service, or simply connect with its target audiences.

Each year, the best library marketing campaigns are recognized by the annual John Cotton Dana Library Public Relations Award, which is named after the librarian who pioneered library public relations.[1] The award, which is sponsored by the Library Leadership and Management Association (LLAMA) and funded by EBSCO and the H. W. Wilson Foundation, is the most prestigious honor conferred by the ALA. Each year, eight recipients are awarded $10,000 each for their library's campaigns. The initial award, which spanned two years, from 1940 to 1942, was sponsored by the H. W. Wilson Company and the ALA Public Relations Committee. In 1942, the PR Committee proposed that the award be made permanent, and the first John Cotton Dana Award was given in 1946 (Eldredge, 1992). Below are descriptions of four winning campaigns.

University of Tennessee Knoxville, 2017. Bedenbaugh (2016) gives an account of how her library at the University of Tennessee Knoxville developed their 2017 John Cotton Dana–award winning marketing campaign. Their three-year campaign aimed at raising awareness of libraries and liaison librarians; it depicted librarians engaged in their favorite sports in order to reduce library anxiety and to humanize librarians. They saw the need for the campaign after a 2013 LibQUAL+ survey revealed that their community generally lacked awareness of the library or had anxiety about using the library. The Marketing and Communications team decided to adapt the ALA's celebrity READ advertising campaign and create photographs of the librarians engaged in sports on campus, since sports is an important part of the university's culture (Bedenbaugh, 2016). The campaign connected librarians to the campus community's interests, in the process humanizing the librarians and dispelling negative stereotypes about them by portraying them as athletic. Each liaison (subject) librarian who wished to participate was photographed at sports venues across campus. Posters, flyers, sports cards (like baseball cards), and YouTube videos were created. The campaign tagline was "Information Is Our Game"; individual photos of librarians had taglines with variations on this theme, such as "Music Is My Game," "Journalism Is My Game," and "Agriculture Is My Game." Accompanying the tagline was the statement, "Big Ideas Demand Reliable Information" and a short narrative explaining each librarian's job responsibilities. The campaign put a face to the subject librarians, helping patrons feel comfortable with them; it showed the dynamism of the modern library profession and promoted the campus libraries; and it showed the diversity, approachability, and expertise of the librarians (see https://www.youtube.com/watch?v=c2HWR9AajfE). Images of the sportscards from this campaign appear in figures 5.1 through 5.4, with permission from the copyright owner.

Figure 5.1.   Information is Our Game—Music is My Game. Front of sports card.
Robin A. Bedenbaugh, University of Tennessee Knoxville

CHRIS DURMAN
Music Library Coordinator
cdurman@utk.edu | 865-974-7542

Subject librarian for:
MUSIC

BIG IDEAS demand reliable information.

The University Libraries supports scholarship, research, and learning at UT by acquiring, organizing, preserving, and facilitating access to the world's knowledge. The wide-ranging expertise of our librarians might surprise you.

As Music Library coordinator, Chris Durman is responsible for public services in the George F. DeVine Music Library. He supervises the staff, offers help on the reference desk, provides information literacy instruction to students in the School of Music, supports Music faculty research and teaching, and works to build the Music Library collection.

Chris's position has allowed him to bring his work and hobbies together and to further his research into the roots of current American popular and folk music, the musical traditions of East Tennessee, and issues associated with the digital delivery of music. Chris is a semi-professional singer/songwriter/folk and rock musician. He has performed for local audiences for more than 30 years.

Chris holds a bachelor's degree in English literature and a master's degree in information sciences from UT.

Figure 5.2. *Information is Our Game—Biography of Music Librarian Chris Durman. Back of sports card.*
Robin A. Bedenbaugh, University of Tennessee Knoxville

COMMUNICATION
IS YOUR GAME
INFORMATION
IS MINE

Figure 5.3. *Information is Our Game—Communication is your Game, Information is Mine. Front of sports card.*
Robin A. Bedenbaugh, University of Tennessee Knoxville

ROBIN A. BEDENBAUGH
Coordinator of Library Marketing and Communication
rbedenbaugh@utk.edu | 865-974-0430

Subject librarian for:
COMMUNICATION STUDIES AND
PUBLIC RELATIONS

BIG IDEAS demand reliable information.

The University Libraries supports scholarship, research, and learning at UT by acquiring, organizing, preserving, and facilitating access to the world's knowledge. The wide-ranging expertise of our librarians might surprise you.

As coordinator of Library Marketing and Communication, Robin Bedenbaugh leads our efforts to publicize the Libraries' services and resources. She is also the librarian for communication studies and public relations, providing research consultations, information literacy instruction, and collection development in those disciplines.

Robin is the creative genius behind recent library marketing campaigns. Printed collateral with lots of eye-appeal and a nod to the Volunteer spirit—like our READ posters and this Information Is Our Game trading card - entertain while delivering a serious message.

Robin holds master's degrees in library and information science and in communication studies and is pursuing her PhD in communication from Texas A&M University. She is currently finishing a dissertation on changes in scholarly communication and publishing.

Figure 5.4. Information is Our Game: biography of Coordinator of Library Marketing and Communication Robin A. Bedenbaugh. Back of sports card.
Robin A. Bedenbaugh, University of Tennessee Knoxville

The San Francisco Public Library, 2017. The San Francisco Public Library (SFPL) won a 2017 John Cotton Dana Award for their three-month Summer Stride campaign, a collaboration with the National Park Service (Jardine, 2017). This campaign encouraged reading both inside the library and outside, in the region's national parks. Its goal was to help combat "summer slide"—the loss over summer break of academic skills attained during the school year—by increasing summer reading participation. The library, which also partnered with local publisher Chronicle Books, used artwork from Lizi Boyd, an award-winning author and illustrator who worked with SFPL and the NPS to create illustrations to promote reading and learning about the surrounding national parks. All promotions had a consistent design and used the tagline, "Read. Explore. Connect." Weekly programs for children, teens, and adults promoted reading and national parks; these activities included crafts, hip hop classes, reading programs, LEGO robotics, engineering, magic classes, free film screenings, and free community shuttles from library locations to partnering national parks. There were weekly raffles and a finishing prize for all participants, a library tote bag designed by Shawn Harris, illustrator of the new Dave Eggers picture book *Her Right Foot* (San Francisco Public Library, 2018). This campaign promoted youth success in the community and fostered a positive image of the SFPL.

The campaign implemented assessment tools that captured important data about library usage. During Summer Stride 2016, 18,644 people participated in the program and 26,266 youth participated in the weekly free reading programs; 822 teens volunteered 8,805 hours during Summer Stride. In their user surveys, they learned that 59 percent of all participants were first-time participants, 84 percent reported learning something new, and 84 percent of participants visited a national park during the campaign (San Francisco Public Library, 2018).

Figure 5.5. *Summer Stride—Read, Create, Explore*

Figure 5.6. Poster—Find Your Park—Summer Stride

Rochester Public Library, 2018. The Rochester Public Library (RPL) in Rochester, Minnesota, won a 2018 John Cotton Dana Award for their campaign Summer Playlist. The campaign's goal was to promote early literacy to local residents. It used integrated marketing communications such as word-of-mouth, social media, and advertisements

Figure 5.7. Book Bag—Summer Playlist

Figure 5.8.   Promotional Video—Summer Playlist

in the library's summer program. The campaign featured a Summer Playlist postcard that also promoted local attractions. The postcards were mailed to local schools and community events and were available at library branches. The library created promotional YouTube videos showing library users giving testimonials. It also offered branded swag that carried through the unified campaign message. This swag included t-shirts and custom prizes, such as free books, a Bookmobile party at your home or school, Target gift cards, and Bowlocity Entertainment Center gift certificates. The campaign was sponsored by the Friends of the Rochester Public Library, the Rochester Public Library Foundation, Bremer Bank, the History Center of Olmsted County, and the Bowlocity Entertainment Center. According to assessment data, 82 percent of participants gained a new skill, learned a new fact, or tried something new; 96 percent of participants reported a positive experience; and 53 percent reported learning more about their community.

District of Columbia Public Library, 2018. The District of Columbia (DC) Public Library, another 2018 John Cotton Dana Award Winner, implemented a goDigital campaign to help increase patron awareness and usage of their library's electronic resources. A team of library staff worked with a team of web development consultants to plan and implement the campaign. During the market research phase of their campaign, they carried out the following tasks:

- Testing digital services and reporting on individual experiences via the Digital Scorecard
- Curating digital content
- Conducting surveys to gather research data
- Reorganizing website content, mainly digital content, to make it easier to find
- Developing a new digital landing page
- Holding internal and external focus groups to test patron reactions to the prototype of the library's portal (Kandace Foreman, email message to author, July 23, 2018.)

The data from the surveys was used to inform how the group executed the campaign, targeted at DC residents ages 18 to 64. The campaign's theme ("Watch. Read. Listen. Learn.") divides the campaign into four action verbs. These verbs name the actions that users can take with the library's more than one hundred online resources: patrons can Watch (videos and DVDs), Read (print books and periodicals), Listen (audiobooks and live programming), and Learn (carry out research). These verbs help users quickly find what they seek on the library website.

Figure 5.9.   goDigital Bus advertisement
Kandace Foreman, District of Columbia Public Library

Figure 5.10. goDigital Landing page on District of Columbia Public Library Website
Kandace Foreman, District of Columbia Public Library

Figure 5.11. goDigital promotion on mobile devices
Kandace Foreman, District of Columbia Public Library

Figure 5.12. goDigital Flat Screen Monitor Promotional Display
Kandace Foreman, District of Columbia Public Library

CONCLUSION

This chapter describes and offers examples of different types of campaigns: awareness campaigns, advocacy campaigns, advertising and marketing campaigns, and rebranding campaigns, as well as information about specific library marketing campaigns. This chapter also offers an overview of the components of any campaign, which include a specific set of tangible goals and objectives; an overarching theme; a target audience; an integrated marketing communications strategy used to convey a compelling, consistent message across various communication channels; and evaluation and assessment tools to measure campaign effectiveness.

NOTE

1. See chapter 1 for an in-depth explanation of the term public relations.

REFERENCES

American Library Association. 2015. "Libraries transform campaign." http://
www.ilovelibraries.org/librariestransform/ (Accessed July 1, 2018).

American Library Association. 2018. "National library week history." http://
www.ala.org/aboutala/1958/national-library-week-history (Accessed July
1, 2018).

Bahadur, Nina. 2014. "Dove 'Real Beauty' campaign turns 10: How a brand
tried to change the conversation about female beauty." January 21. https://
www.huffingtonpost.com/2014/01/21/dove-real-beauty-campaign-turns
-10_n_4575940.html (Accessed July 1, 2018).

Barber, Peggy. 2003. "Mickey Mouse, Miss Piggy, and the birth of ALA
graphics." *American Libraries* 34, no. 5: 60–63.

Barriaux, Marianne. 2007. "Rebranding: McDonald's goes green—but not all
customers are lovin' it: The global fast food chain, tired of being vilified, is
hitting back with revamps, recycling and new menus." *The Guardian*, July 5.

Bedenbaugh, Robin A. 2016. "Marketing is our game: Tackling the library
awareness gap." *Public Services Quarterly* 12, no. 4: 321–328.

Blistein, David. 2014. "This is your brain on drugs." Feb 26. https://www
.huffingtonpost.com/david-blistein/this-is-your-brain-on-dru_1_b_4832929
.html (Accessed July 1, 2018).

Bobo, Lawrence D. 2017. "Racism in Trump's America: Reflections on culture, sociology, and the 2016 US presidential election." *The British Journal
of Sociology* 68: S85–S104.

Bravo, Caroline, and Laurie Hoffman-Goetz. 2016. "Tweeting about prostate
and testicular cancers: What are individuals saying in their discussions
about the 2013 Movember Canada campaign?" *Journal of Cancer Education* 31, no. 3: 559–566.

Brizek, Michael G. 2012. "Coffee wars: The big three: Starbucks, McDonald's
and Dunkin Donuts." *Journal of Case Research in Business & Economics*
5: 1–12.

Dijkstra, Majorie, Heidi E. J. J. M. Buijtels, and W. Fred Van Raaij. 2005.
"Separate and joint effects of medium type on consumer responses: a comparison of television, print, and the Internet." *Journal of Business Research*
58, no. 3: 377–386.

Egan, Karisa. 2017. "Call-to-action examples: 15 designed to REALLY
generate leads." July 11. www.impactbnd.com/blog/examples-of-calls-to
-action-for-lead-generation (Accessed July 1, 2018).

Eldredge, Jonathan. 1992. "The John Cotton Dana legacy: Promoting libraries
for users." *Wilson Library Bulletin* 66, no. 8: 46.

EveryLibrary. 2018. About us. http://everylibrary.org/about-everylibrary/ (Accessed July 1, 2018).

Farmers Insurance: Hall of Claims. 2018. www.farmers.com/hall-of-claims/ (Accessed July 1, 2018).

Gasca, Peter. 2014. "McDonalds' rebranding strategy: Why the world's biggest restaurant thinks it's time to tweak its recipe." July 29. https://www.inc.com/peter-gasca/mcdonalds-rebranding-strategy-why-the-world-s-biggest-restaurant-thinks-it-s-tim.html(Accessed July 1, 2018).

Gazdik, Tanya. 2015. "Farmers uses real claims for creative inspiration." December 28. https://www.mediapost.com/publications/article/265552/farmers-uses-real-claims-for-creative-inspiration.html (Accessed July 1, 2018).

Huber, Lindsay Perez. 2016. "Make America great again: Donald Trump, racist nativism and the virulent adherence to white supremacy amid US demographic change." *Charleston L. Rev.* 10: 215–243.

IFLA. 2015. "IFLA—About the campaign for the world's libraries." October 10. https://www.ifla.org/about-the-campaign-for-the-worlds-libraries (Accessed July 1, 2018).

Jacobson, Jenna, and Christopher Mascaro. 2016. "Movember: Twitter conversations of a hairy social movement." *Social Media+ Society* 2, no. 2: 1–12.

Jardine, Katherine. 2017. "Combatting summer slide with summer stride." May 12. https://sfpl.org/releases/2017/05/12/combatting-summer-slide-with-summer-stride/ (Accessed July 1, 2018).

Johnston, Josée, and Judith Taylor. 2008. "Feminist consumerism and fat activists: A comparative study of grassroots activism and the Dove Real Beauty campaign." *Signs: Journal of Women in Culture and Society* 33, no. 4: 941–966.

Kenneway, Melinda. 2006. "Branding for libraries: Communicating your value to increase reader awareness and usage of the library service." *Serials* 19, no. 2: 120–126.

Kitchen, Philip J., and Inga Burgmann. 2015. "Integrated marketing communication: Making it work at a strategic level." *Journal of Business Strategy* 36, no. 4: 34–39.

Lacsamana, Pauline. 2016. "McDonald's challenges Starbucks and Dunkin' Donuts with major McCafé upgrades." December 7. https://www.thedailymeal.com/news/eat/mcdonald-s-challenges-starbucks-and-dunkin-donuts-major-mccaf-upgrades/120716 (Accessed July 1, 2018).

Long, Sarah Ann. 2006. "Banned books week: A celebration of intellectual freedom." *New Library World* 107, no. 1/2: 73–75.

Macrae, Cathi Dunn. 2011. "Banned books week basics (the first freedom)." *Voice of Youth Advocates* 34, no. 3: 247.

Montgomery, Susan E., and Jonathan Miller. 2011. "The third place: The library as collaborative and community space in a time of fiscal restraint." *College & Undergraduate Libraries* 18, no. 2–3: 228–238.

Neal, Jim. 2017. "House approves full federal funding of library programs." September 20. https://americanlibrariesmagazine.org/blogs/the-scoop/ef forts-helping-saveimls/ (Accessed July 1, 2018).

Neff, Jack. 2014. "Ten years in, Dove's 'Real Beauty' seems to be aging well." January 22. http://adage.com/article/news/ten-years-dove-s-real -beauty-aging/291216/ (Accessed July 1, 2018).

Nemetz, Dave. 2017. "The inside story of Wendy's 'Where's the Beef?' ad." February 1. https://www.yahoo.com/entertainment/the-inside-story -of-wendys-wheres-the-beef-ad-140051010.html (Accessed July 1, 2018).

Niemisto, Katrina. 2018. "Why Digital Marketing Is Crucial—No Matter the Size of Your Business." February 2018. https://blog.marketo.com/2018/02/ digital-marketing-crucial-no-matter-size-business.html

Nieva, Rene. 2016. "How McDonald's in US is rebranding to stay on top." *Business Mirror*, September 11.

Nudd, Tim. 2003. "When good spokespeople go bad. (The best and worst of Shoptalk) (Brief Article)." *ADWEEK* 44, no. 45: 103.

Pasquarelli, Adrianne. 2017. "Forget the Oscars, Farmers Insurance is running their own awards." February 20. http://adage.com/article/cmo-strategy/ forget-oscars-farmers-running-awards/308031/ (Accessed July 1, 2018).

Robinson, Michael. 2010. "Pink ribbons give way to mustaches as 'Movember' raises awareness of cancer in men." *L.A. Times.* November 4. http://articles .latimes.com/2010/nov/04/news/la-heb-moustache-cancer-men-20101104

Rodriguez, Ashley. 2014. "Flo's Progressive Revolution." November 12. http://adage.com/article/cmo-strategy/flo-s-progressive-evolution/295734/ (Accessed July 1, 2018).

San Francisco Public Library. 2018. "Summer Stride 2018." http://sfpl.org/ summerstride (Accessed July 1, 2018).

Schultz, E. J. 2017. "Coca-Cola's corporate brand campaign moves beyond soda." September 17. http://adage.com/article/cmo-strategy/coca-cola-s-cor porate-brand-campaign-moves-soda/310490/ (Accessed July 1, 2018).

Shapiro, Ari. 2017. "A look at the effectiveness of anti-drug advertising campaigns." November 1. https://www.npr.org/2017/11/01/561427918/a -look-at-the-effectiveness-anti-drug-ad-campaigns (Accessed July 1, 2018).

Shayon, Sheila. 2016. "Time Warner Cable starts rebranding markets to Charter Spectrum." September 20. https://www.brandchannel.com/2016/09/20/ charter-spectrum-092016/ (Accessed July 1, 2018).

Sheehan, Kim Bartel, and Caitlin Doherty. 2001. "Re-weaving the web: Integrating print and online communications." *Journal of Interactive Marketing* 15, no. 2: 47–59.

Siess, Judith A. 2003. *The visible librarian: Asserting your value with marketing and advocacy.* American Library Association.

Singh, Rajesh. 2011. "Re-branding academic libraries in an experience culture." *Kansas Library Association College and University Libraries Section Proceedings* 1, no. 1: 91–95.

Sinha, Mridu. 2016. "Online marketing vs. print advertising: Which is best media to achieve maximum ROI?" July 1. https://www.linkedin.com/pulse/ online-marketing-vs-print-advertising-which-best-max-mridu-sinha-/ (Accessed July 1, 2018).

Sullivan, Brian. 2017. "Thinking about rebranding? First consider the 5 Rs of the branding spectrum." *Forbes.* March 21. https://www.forbes.com/sites/ forbesagencycouncil/2017/03/21/thinking-about-rebranding-first-consider -the-5-rs-of-the-branding-spectrum/

Sundar, S. Shyam, Sunetra Narayan, Rafael Obregon, and Charu Uppal. 1998. "Does web advertising work? Memory for print vs. online media." *Journalism & Mass Communication Quarterly* 75, no. 4: 822–835.

Szala, Joseph. 2017. "McDonald's of the future—How the brand is stepping up its game" April 3. https://gritsandgrids.com/2017/04/mcdonalds-inte rior-design-branding/ (Accessed July 1, 2018).

Walsh, Kenneth T. 2012. "6 best 'zingers' from past presidential debates." *U.S. News and World Report.* October 1. https://www.usnews.com/ news/blogs/ken-walshs-washington/2012/10/01/6-best-zingers-from-past -presidential-debates (Accessed July 1, 2018).

Wassersug, Richard, John Oliffe, and Christina Han. 2015. "On manhood and Movember . . . or why the moustache works." *Global Health Promotion* 22, no. 2: 65–70.

Wohl, Jessica. 2018. "Dunkin Donuts gets a brand update, but the orange and pink logo isn't going anywhere." July 6. http://adage.com/article/cmo -strategy/dunkin-donuts-a-brand-update/314128/ (Accessed July 1, 2018).

Wright, Owen, Lorelle Frazer, and Bill Merrilees. 2007. "McCafe: The McDonald's co-branding experience." *Journal of Brand Management* 14, no. 6: 442–457.

Young, Lisa R., and Marion Nestle. 2007. "Portion sizes and obesity: Responses of fast-food companies." *Journal of Public Health Policy* 28, no. 2: 238–248.

Zenitsky, Ben. 2016. "Library Foundation announces goal reached in Great Libraries Create campaign." November 7. https://www.columbuslibrary .org/press/library-foundation-announces-goal-reached-great-libraries-cre ate-campaign (Accessed July 1, 2018).

CHAPTER 6

Creating Your Own Library Brand

IN THIS CHAPTER

- Defining "brand" and "branding"
- Identifying the key elements of a library brand
- Conducting a brand audit to learn your library's story
- Creating your library's unique brand
- Creating your own personal brand

UNDERSTANDING "BRAND" AND "BRANDING"

A brand is the collection of mental images a person has in their mind when they think of a particular product or service or company; it represents the feelings and experiences that occur when they have used or interacted with this product or service. Brands are perceived and experienced and are considered a living entity (Walters and Jackson, 2013), as opposed to a static label for a company or product. Brands are powerful because they influence peoples' decisions and they affect consumer behavior. A brand is a unique way to distinguish one company or product from another. It is more symbolic and conceptual, rather than simply a name. In corporate terms, branding is a key component of the company's marketing strategy. A brand expresses the ideals and beliefs of a company and its products.

Uber is an example of a brand that people either love or hate. Some people may prefer it because it represents individual choice, anti-regulation, flexibility, and youth (Posen, 2015). Others may use the traditional taxi (or yellow cab, in New York City) because they prefer regulation, price consistency, stability, and the comfort of a traditional service that has been around for a long time (Cramer and Krueger, 2016).

Brand names are words or slogans that identify products or services. McDonald's and Burger King both sell large hamburgers, but one is known as the Big Mac and the other, the Whopper. Essentially, they are large hamburgers with cheese and a variety of condiments but their brand names are different. Brand names usually refer to words, expressions, symbols, logos, colors, and design elements such as fonts types or font colors.

One of the origins of the word "branding" refers to stamping a specific identity onto a cow so that it belongs to a particular farmer (Moggy et al., 2017). Branding allows someone to recognize the product (e.g., dairy cow) as belonging to a particular person (e.g., a farmer), and it establishes itself as unique.

A trademark is also an important term to define but it's not very applicable to libraries. It refers to the process of legally protecting a brand. Trademarks protect the integrity of the company's valued assets—its products or services. Since the main goal of a library is not to generate large amounts of profit, this chapter will focus on brand development and how to develop a brand audit.

A brand can be a powerful asset. Sometimes, the brand is more powerful than the product. This is known as brand strength. For example, many people use the term "Kleenex" (the brand name) instead of the actual product (tissue). This is because the brand is so strong and recognizable, that people no longer refer to the product. Many have referred to Xeroxing a copy (referring to the Xerox brand) rather than making a photocopy. When brand names become strong, the company will usually trademark them so they retain exclusive rights, and competitors are not allowed to use the brand name.

Many people may confuse a brand with a logo, but they are different. A logo is one of the many ways a brand can be represented (Chiaravalle and Schenck, 2015). The brand should extend beyond its logo as it embodies the essence and spirit of the company; a brand represents the symbolic foundation of the company's core values and mission. Effective brands are recognizable, and they should be able to tell a story. A brand should be consistent throughout the marketing process and must not change its shape or color or size. Very often a brand is coupled with a slogan or statement that quickly summarizes the company's intent.

The Three Dimensions of Branding

According to the book *Breakthrough Branding: Positioning Your Library to Survive and Thrive*, Walters and Jackson argue that branding can be explained in three dimensions. Two out of three dimensions are experiential and one is physical; they are creating (1) a unique personality, (2) a recognized image, and (3) a distinctive identity (Walters and Jackson, 2013). In order to establish a consistent identity, the authors recommend that library employees take a moment to get together and discuss the mission and vision of their organization. This helps them define their library's identity. Everyone must be on the same page and understand the "who we are," "what we do," and "who benefits."

The *personality* of the brand embodies the characteristics of the organization—its unique qualities and features. A library's personality may be the various touchpoints that library users will remember. This may be the grand entrance or a unique feature like a large skylight. The *personality* may be embodied by the open-concept floor plan or futuristic architecture or furniture. It may be the playfulness of the staff and librarians or the forward-thinking improvements implemented by the library. The *personality* characterizes the selling points that employees may promote.

The *image* illustrates a recognizable visual such as a logo or photograph or caricature that library users can connect with the library. Too often the library's image is books on a shelf, which frequently leads to stereotypes about libraries and librarians. Library employees should get together and brainstorm an appropriate image that typifies their library. It is recommended to avoid using stereotypical images like books and to think about how library services and resources are represented visually.

The *identity* is how a company wishes to be perceived by its customers. In order to forge an identity, the company needs to conduct a self-assessment with a SWOT analysis. In addition, identifying their target audience and their business goals is critical for success. An established brand identity will be able to exhibit the brand's personality so that it will attract customers and build loyalty. For example, when someone thinks of Apple computers and its products (Macbook, iPod, iPad, iPhone), its identity is slick, innovative, user friendly, hip, and sophisticated. The Apple store is minimalist, with clean lines, approachable and knowledge-able staff, and the *genius bar* exemplifies an identity of a creative work-ing space that is inventive and forward thinking (Payne, 2017).

WHY BRANDING IS IMPORTANT

In order to be successful, a company must connect with its customers. In an economy where customers have choices, the company must stand out as unique. Branding helps define a company's vision and long-term goals. It also motivates employees to discuss the exceptional qualities of their organization, their products, and services. Branding also pro-vides a unified vision that illustrates the persona of their organization. A strong brand has a life of its own, regardless of the company and its products. If a corporation only sells one product and the product dies, then the business dies with it. The brand must be strong enough to out-live its products (Weintraub, 2013). Applying a branding strategy will lead to brand strength and brand loyalty.

A strong brand must develop a compelling story to attract custom-ers. Branding embodies the visual summation of the company's key messages. In order to be successful, the message must be consistent with what customers want, and employees must fully understand the company goals.

For example, the Starbucks mascot is the famous green mermaid. Part of Starbucks original branding from 1971 stemmed from the idea that the company wanted to convey an exotic and robust coffee, so they developed the image of the bare-breasted, twin-tailed mermaid (Klara, 2014). The mascot's image has changed over the years, and her origi-nal full body is now cropped to her face and flowing hair. The brand remains consistent—robust and exotic coffee blends (Klara, 2014).

Part of Trader Joe's brand strategy is illustrated in cashiers engaging in conversations about their products. Although it may feel somewhat scripted, Trader Joe's staff are trained to be energetic and helpful, and are adorned in Hawaiian short-sleeve button-down shirts (Allaway et al., 2011), conveying a tropical, laid-back image.

Branding involves remembering a product or service by connecting experiences with a particular image, slogan, or expression. The Nike "swoosh" may resemble action or movement, and the slogan of "just do it" is automatically understood (Weil, 2011).

In the commercial world, branding helps sell products and services. When a brand has strength, it is easier to gain trust and acceptance. In the world of academia, some private schools have built a solid brand solely based on their name. Harvard Business School and the *Harvard Business Review* are strong entities because they are based on the Harvard University brand. Television shows on the HBO network are known for being innovative, sometimes controversial, and forward thinking (Nygaard, 2013).

Brand Strength

Brand strength allows customers to recognize your brand just by seeing an element of the entire brand. The three black stripes on a shoe denote the Adidas brand. Independent of the shoe type, the Nike brand is globally recognized by its iconic stripes and the "swoosh" (Jiang, Gorn, Galli, and Chattopadhyay, 2016; Ruihley and Pate, 2017). The Apple brand is a simple, sleek image of a bite of an apple in silhouette form. Brands help build status. A decade ago, Apple computers used to be the alternative for artists and graphic designers who were seeking a more robust system to help with developing graphics. Now Apple products have entered the mainstream with the iPhone, iPod, iPad, iMac, and Macintosh computers.

A library's brand strength depends on the positive experiences library users have with that brand. In terms of a library's brand strength, it may be related to the level of services provided, the fact that libraries are free, and the overall perceptions of users. To develop a strong brand, libraries need to conduct a brand audit (which will be discussed later in this chapter). Further, they need to develop a unique identity that sets them apart from the competition.

In order to develop brand strength, a library must conduct a self-assessment of its strengths and weaknesses. The goal in attaining brand strength is ultimately brand loyalty. A library must identify its unique strengths. For a public library, it may be its free movies, newspapers, and magazines, and unlimited access to the Internet. For a college library, it may be free textbooks, or lending laptops, iPads, and calculators.

A library can also take advantage of its natural strengths and further develop them. So many students in a college already think of the library as the place for printing. If the library has the most computers on campus and does the most printing, then it should promote printing as part of its brand. If the library develops its brand strength to showcase itself as the ideal place for printing, students will think of the library as their first place for printing and not their departmental computer lab. Of course, a college library offers many more services than printing, but identifying just a few unique characteristics helps beat the competition. Another strength of libraries is that most or all services and resources are free. Targeting the "free" component is another strength that Amazon or Barnes & Noble cannot beat.

The Aaker model (2012) discusses brand strength by focusing on three factors: awareness, attitude, and beliefs. For libraries, determining brand strength primarily involves understanding user awareness. Some questions for academic librarians to ask themselves are:

1. Are students aware that we have a college library?
2. Are students aware that our services are free?
3. What are students' and faculty's attitude toward college libraries?
4. How do faculty understand the support of libraries and librarians?
5. What are students' and faculty's beliefs about libraries?

Further in this chapter, there is a list of sample questions that can be incorporated into a brand audit. One set of questions is directed at library employees and the other set of questions focuses on library users.

Brand Loyalty

Brand loyalty can be defined as the level of trust and commitment a customer has toward that specific brand. Brand loyalty leads to greater brand strength. Customers who have brand loyalty to a company will purchase products or services from that company despite the competition. Brand loyalty involves the repetitive purchasing habits of customers, regardless of competition or price increases. It can take a long time for a brand to develop loyal customers.

When the Samsung Galaxy phones became faulty and some devices exploded in the hands of customers, Samsung used public relations to help remedy their product. Those customers who continued to use Samsung Galaxy products exhibited a degree of loyalty toward the Samsung brand (Burlacu, 2016). Loyalty is very individual and can be measured by the small details. For example, local coffee shop employees may remember a customer's particular order and the personal touch may affect a customer such that they will go the extra distance and pay the extra price for that cup of coffee.

Companies can develop loyalty with their brand by having rewards programs. Popular stores such as Walgreens, Kmart, Staples, Starbucks, and many other stores have point cards that offer discounts, coupons, rebates, and free items to repeat customers who reach a certain reward level (Filipe, Marques, and Salgueiro, 2017). Airlines also offer loyalty programs that relate to earning points in order to gain free airfare or discounts (Kang, Alejandro, and Groza, 2015).

Brand loyalty leads to returning customers, new customers, and long-term committed customers; it is influenced by two key factors: attitudes and beliefs (Sasmita and Suki, 2015). Marketers have an easier time changing beliefs than attitudes, so they tend to promote products that are aligned with a specific attitude of a potential customer. They promote products by persuading people to change their belief system. Marketers also wish to target highly involved customers who are committed and deeply engaged with the brand. Low-involvement customers may use that brand, but they tend to purchase many brands and are not committed to one brand.

Brand loyalty in libraries is directly related to library advocacy. A loyal library user is an advocate who can convince others to support the library. Advocacy can be achieved through public relations and marketing (Albert, 2017). If users consistently use the library as their first stop in conducting research, studying, or simply typing up their paper, they possess greater brand loyalty than going to the bookstore, computer lab, or renting/buying a book via Amazon. Brand loyalty shows that despite the competition, patrons who prefer to use the library as opposed to other similar services represent the prototype of the valued customer who is committed to the library. In many cases, these users are not only loyal, but they become library advocates by passing on their loyalties through "word of mouth marketing." Libraries attempt to gain loyal users by offering programs such as fine forgiveness and amnesty programs (Hockenberry and Blackburn, 2016).

Co-Branding

Sometimes two companies work in tandem by partnering together in selling a product or service. Co-branding is also known as a branding partnership (Seno and Lukas, 2007). An example of a promotion and loyalty program that benefited both brands was the JetBlue airlines and American Express co-branded relationship where customers received reward points for travel (Sidel, 2015). Very often food brands are coupled together when promoting a finished product like a cake or dessert. In this example, the Dairy Queen Blizzard will often co-brand with other companies to cross-promote each other's products. The Blizzard is a separate sub-brand of Dairy Queen and one flavor in particular is the Oreo Blizzard. The Blizzard is a brand in itself, but it is a trademark of Dairy Queen (McCarthy and Van Hoene, 2014).

There are advantages and disadvantages to co-branding. Co-branding is more affordable than having the separate companies do their own marketing. It also reaches a wider audience and perhaps may gain more customer loyalty. Company partnerships provide more resources and avoid competition, especially if both companies sell different products. Both companies benefit if their products go well together such as Dell computers with Intel processors.

Co-branding may have some disadvantages. If two brands are selling their products, it may dilute the brand strength of one of them and the other brand may benefit. Some co-branding ventures have been terribly planned and resulted in disaster. The Susan G. Komen Walk for a Cure (for cancer) branded with Kentucky Fried Chicken was one of the most inappropriate co-branding partnerships because the public felt that a fast food chain was not an appropriate sponsor for breast cancer (Freedhoff, 2014). Co-branding also may confuse customers, since there are two companies (or more) that are trying to promote and sell their products.

In a library setting, a co-branding opportunity may consist of a program or event co-sponsored by the college library and the local public library. Both libraries offer different resources, and they are using their brand identity to promote each other. They are not competing against each other since they are different. Sometimes a large corporation may donate swag (such as EBSCO or Elsevier); if the college library puts out an information fair and couples their own stationary (with the library logo) and the corporate identity of EBSCO or Elsevier, that may be a successful partnership. It is easier to co-brand in a library setting because competition is less likely.

Very often commercial database providers such as EBSCO or Gale allow libraries to co-brand their logos on their databases to give it a "local" feeling. It is still very clearly an EBSCO or Gale database, but since the library can add their visual identity to the database, it gives a more familiar interface for the library user.

Sometimes libraries wish to promote their services by co-branding their event or contest through sponsorship opportunities or by using the library brand to promote a cause or another company. Some libraries may have contests and reward Amazon or Starbucks gift cards (Courtier and DeLooper, 2017). Gift cards or free food are often used as incentives to promote programs and events. In this case, it is not equal co-branding, but a way for a library to promote itself and another brand. Co-branding is supposed to benefit both entities, but it often may benefit one over another. Libraries may not always want to promote Starbucks coffee or store gift cards, but it may be a way to draw potential users into the library.

LIBRARY BRANDING

A library brand should involve all the things that come to mind when customers think of your library (Rowley, 2013), including perceptions and expectations of services and programs as well as the employees who work in the library. The library brand extends to the website, the building, the collection, the services, and even the cleanliness of the restrooms. Brands enable libraries to create their own identity and to allow customers to make choices amongst the competition. In the late 1990s, large book retailers such as Barnes & Noble (in the United States) and Chapters-Indigo (in Canada) began to have cafés and comfortable seating. These bookstores starting showcasing public online book catalogs that resembled the OPAC (Online Public Access Catalog), and customer service associates started answering questions on readers' advisory, providing a service that librarians offer. Librarians realized they needed to be proactive and not simply reactive, and started embedding cafés into their libraries to change the perceptions of how users saw libraries (Harris, 2007). In responding to the competition between libraries and big box bookstores, librarians began to transform their spaces into information (or learning) commons with comfortable seating and flexible workspaces.

With the advent of the information commons, libraries are starting to brand themselves as innovative spaces that foster community, creativity, and collaboration. An information commons (or learning commons) is an open space with a mixture of hardware, advanced level software, computers, and collaborative furniture placed in an open area. Each institution may interpret their information commons differently, depending on their mission, budget, space, and resources. Renovating a library and adding an information commons may improve the library's image (Andrews, Wright, and Raskin, 2016; Hay, 2010).

Although many libraries cannot afford to revise one of their floors into an information commons, doing so may change the brand image of their library. Of course, the library will need to conduct market research (this was discussed in chapter 3) and a brand audit to understand whether a library makeover and the construction of an information commons would improve its brand.

Steps Involved in Conducting an Audit

A successful branding audit involves analyzing your marketing plan and assessing your users. This includes reaching out and asking questions. Typically, a SWOT analysis is implemented, in addition to conducting market research (Phillips, 2012). Market research may be executed through in-depth interviews, focus groups, and question-naires. You should conduct these assessments on an ongoing basis to get a sense of the expectations of your users. Since branding is not tangible, it is important to think about the emotions and feelings your users experience when they come to the library (Szilagyi, 2015). It is also important to identify your competition and to try to develop a unique identity for your brand. What can the library do to help change people's perceptions so that they change their consumer behavior?

Another aspect of a brand audit comprises examining analytics. This might involve circulation statistics, database usage, gate counts, textbook and/or technology loans, and reviewing feedback forms. For a brand audit to be successful, the library must respond to user feedback. In addition, libraries should recognize a consistent and uniform identity, and all employees should be made aware of it. The brand must reflect the library's mission statement and its core values. Further, the library must recognize its gaps so that it can address them in order to keep current. For example, if a nearby public library starts lending out iPad and iPhone chargers, then it may be a good idea for the college library to ask its users if this additional service might be beneficial to them. A brand audit should provide a roadmap to best understand your library's mission, your users' expectations, and compare your services against your competition.

The way a library develops its brand is by reflecting on the messages it is trying to convey to its users. These messages are known as the library "story." In order to collect this important data, the library must assess its employees and users to best understand their expectations of what their library should be.

The library must be strategic in asking key questions such as "what makes us unique?" and "how are we different from the bookstore or Google or the public library?" Conducting a SWOT analysis (discussed in detail in chapter 3) will uncover some of these answers. In brief, a SWOT analysis is short for: strengths, weaknesses, opportunities, and threats. This type of assessment is an important exercise in understanding your organization.

These questions should be given to library employees as a form of self-reflection and self-assessment. See http://aidiamarketing.com/technique-brand-audit-survey-employees/ for an example of a brand audit questionnaire directed at employees.

The textbox contains some questions directed to library employees when creating a brand audit questionnaire.

QUESTIONS TO ASK LIBRARY EMPLOYEES FOR A BRAND AUDIT

1. What words come to mind when you think of our library?
2. What makes our library unique?
3. List our library's unique strengths.
4. What are some of our library's weaknesses or shortcomings?
5. How do you think our library is perceived by the public?
6. Who is our library's competition?
7. What are the expectations your users may have of our library? List some.
8. Why do you think they visit our library?
9. What do you think your users like most about our library?
10. What do you think your users like least about our library?
11. What are some images that best represent our library?

In addition to obtaining feedback from staff, it is critical to implement a brand audit questionnaire to library users. The questions will be slightly different. The textbox suggests some questions that originate from a corporate brand audit that have been adapted to libraries (Marsh, 2015).

QUESTIONS TO ASK PATRONS FOR A LIBRARY BRAND AUDIT

1. What words best describe the library?
2. What services do you use at the library?
3. Why do you use the library?
4. How do you feel when you use the library?
5. What do you use when the library is closed?
6. Where did you learn about the library?

7. What are some valuable qualities about the library?
8. Would you recommend the library to your friends?
9. What is an appropriate image or logo for the library?
10. What do you think of when you see the logo of the library?
11. Describe your experiences with the library staff and librarians at the library.
12. How can we improve your experience at the library?

Another way of conducting a brand audit is known as the "3 circle approach," where you examine points of differences from the competition, focusing on customer needs and having a clear understanding of your competition (Phillips, 2012). The brand audit needs to accomplish the following:

1. measure how aligned its brand is in relation to its mission
2. identify customer goals, needs, and desires
3. provide a breakdown of the different components of the brand (brand statement, mission, logo, font face, slogan, colors)
4. provide any information on the competition
5. evaluate the strengths and weaknesses of the organization (Phillips and Hopelain, 2015).

In order to understand conducting a brand audit, assessment tools must be used to collect data from the questions above.

Reflecting on these questions as part of a brand audit helps libraries develop their own brand. Since a brand is much more than a logo, the library needs to develop a tagline or brand message. A brand statement is similar to an organization's mission statement. Nike's "Just Do It" emphasizes spontaneity, freedom, choices, hope, and opportunity. The "swoosh" emphasizes movement and action (Batey, 2015). If a college library supports the learning, research, and teaching for students, faculty, and staff, then perhaps a college library's brand statement might be "helping you succeed" or "promoting life-long learning." Brand statements emphasize the essence of the library in a brief succinct phrase. The statement should include action words such as helping, finding, promoting, and fostering. It should emphasize the core values of the library and be memorable. Brand messages should be consistently displayed across all promotional material and must convey the mission of the library. Library employees must be made aware of the brand message, and there must be buy-in.

EXAMPLES OF LIBRARY BRANDING

Incorporating branding into the library is not limited to promotional materials, signage, posters, and the library website. Branding can be part of your library's services and resources. This section consists of examples of how libraries can create a brand identity for various library services.

Web-Based Database Subscriptions

Vendors such as EBSCO allow libraries to personalize their database subscriptions by adding their local logo and color schemes to their various database subscriptions. Librarians know that each database subscription is different and may have a different look and feel, but many vendors will help libraries adapt the user interfaces to integrate the databases into the library website. One such example is State University of New York's University at Buffalo where they have branded Blackboard as "UB Learns." This is consistent with the University's branding as "UB" (https://ublearns.buffalo.edu/). Another example is Columbia University Libraries where they state in their staff web pages that the university's brand identity is more important than the corporate vendor's (https://library.columbia.edu/bts/cerm/e-resource-branding.html).

Google Apps

The Google apps suite of different cloud-based software is offered for free for nonprofit organizations and is also offered for businesses and academic institutions. Their Google email (Gmail) interface can be adapted so that the organization can brand its own email service. Obviously, the user interface will resemble the Gmail interface, but the company or academic institution can tailor the color scheme and the mascot/logo of its organization so that its email service does not

resemble Gmail. Columbia University (https://cuit.columbia.edu/lion
mail-apps), Stanford University (see https://uit.stanford.edu/service/
googleapps), and New York University (NYU) (http://www.nyu.edu/
life/information-technology/communication-and-conferencing/nyu
-email.html) use Google apps to manage their email and files in the
cloud. They do not brand their email as "Gmail," but they use branding elements of their schools, which include the school colors, mascot/
logo, and the associated fonts.

Library Catalogs and Discovery Services

Upon examining a directory of library catalogs, it became evident that
in the mid 1990s, it was fashionable to name library catalogs as part
of the branding process. Some library catalogs began having cute and
funny names that were somehow linked to their institution (St. George
and Larsen, 1992). Some colleges and universities named their catalog
based on their school's mascot or used a reference to its historic past,
while others named their catalog based on an important person who
helped found the institution. New York University (NYU) uses Bobcat
to identify its catalog, named after its main library (Bobst); Oskicat is
the name for University of California at Berkeley (Oski the bear is the
UC Berkeley mascot); and Hollis is the acronym for Harvard Online
Library Information System, but it also refers to Thomas Hollis, a historic figure in Harvard's history (Harvard University Archives, 2017).
Sometimes libraries label their catalogs for simplicity, rather than for
branding reasons. Kupersmith (2012) argues that branding library catalogs provides more confusion for users, and the trend is to unbrand the
catalog. The City University of New York (CUNY) recently stopped
using its catalog name (CUNY+) and simply labeled its catalog "The
Library Catalog."

More recently, branding has become more evident with assigning
simple names to the library's discovery services. EBSCO already has
branded their discovery service "OneSearch," while Primo has not
given its system a consistent brand name. Many libraries have adopted
simple names with the word "search" to denote that their discovery
service is a complete, comprehensive, and easy way to search all materials in a library.

Reference Services

The University of Texas at San Antonio Library experienced a decline in reference questions from 2010 to 2012 (Peters and Kemp, 2014). The librarians decided to brainstorm a creative way to increase the number of questions. As part of this process, they developed a marketing campaign, branded the "Blue Crew" with the brand statement "Ask Us Anything." Named for its school's colors, the "Blue Crew" campaign involved library staff wearing blue t-shirts, who made themselves available to answer any type of question. To make things more seamless, the circulation and reference desks were consolidated into one service desk. This one-service desk model allowed staff to answer questions in a more streamlined fashion. The librarians conducted

Figure 6.1.   Stress Loves Company—Ask Us Anything—Blue Crew
Anne Peters and Carolyn L. Ellis, University of Texas at San Antonio Libraries

Figure 6.2.   Asking the Blue Crew for Help isn't a sign of Weakness—it's a sign of Wisdom—Ask Us Anything
Anne Peters and Carolyn L. Ellis, University of Texas at San Antonio Libraries

preliminary market research the year before to test the effectiveness of their plans. The Blue Crew campaign ran from January to December of the 2013 calendar year with several mini campaigns held during the year that coincided with Valentine's Day, National Library Week, and New Student Orientation in the summer. Smaller campaigns also focused on trends such as memes on social media and held contests to generate more interest. Over the next year, reference questions increased by 48 percent. Their "Ask Us Anything" marketing campaign were one of the eight winning entries in the annual 2014 John Cotton Dana Awards (Schoensee, 2014).

Interlibrary Loan Service

Texas Tech University Library started branding their interlibrary loan and document delivery service to increase usage (Litsey and Daniel, 2013). When brainstorming their brand image and statement, the librarians met with the marketing communications department (of their university) to brainstorm the rational and emotional importance of their interlibrary loan and document delivery service. Working alongside a graphic designer, the librarians created a series of humorous videos that promoted the interlibrary loan and documentary delivery service. Finally, through a campaign of email communications, graphics, YouTube videos, posters, QR codes, computer terminal background wallpaper, brochures, and social media postings, a unified message was developed that promoted document delivery with simple images and short messages such as "the earth is flat?," "she's unsinkable," and "best gift ever" [and] "let document delivery help you dig a little deeper" (2013: 27). The goals of branding document delivery emphasized ease of use, lightning fast speed, a sense of relief, and quick gratification. Branding represents a way for an organization to set itself apart by creating a unique identity for itself. In this case, the marketing campaign raised the profile of a rather invisible service by providing a collection of different media with a consistent message across all platforms.

Library Service Delivery Models

Humber River Hospital Library branded their research requests to hospital staff and physicians as "Information Takeout and Delivery" service (Polger, 2010). Traditionally, medical staff and physicians rarely visited the health sciences library because it was hidden in the basement in a very inaccessible part of the hospital. In order to raise the profile of the hospital library's article delivery and medical research service, the librarian implemented a new model for delivering library services. It was promoted in monthly new staff orientation, and promotional materials were created and distributed to different hospital units. In the hospital's education calendar, the information takeout and delivery service was promoted with a set of online web-based request forms. In addition, it was promoted on the library website. The intent was to align something simple like pizza delivery with information delivery by having medical librarians leave the library and offer delivery services in the clinical units. The hospital library staff needed to raise awareness of its services and resources targeted to staff and physicians.

Re-Branding the Library's Overall Image

The University of East London collaborated with a corporate marketing firm to help develop a campaign that promoted library services. Working with a marketing team and a graphic designer, librarians brainstormed a short and simple brand message using brochures with the slogan "It's More than Just Books" (Williams and Preece, 2005: 21). The librarians felt that the message was overly simplistic, but after debate with the graphic designer, they agreed that the message was memorable and carried a unified theme. Throughout the process, it was articulated that for their campaign to be successful, their branding must send a clear message to their users and must not contain library jargon.

PERSONAL BRANDING

Negative stereotypes about libraries and librarians abound (Seale, 2008; Erickson, Harris, and Seidl, 2014; White, 2012; Steffy, 2015; Pagowsky and Rigsby, 2014). The literature mostly focuses on how libraries are viewed as outdated, extinct, and irrelevant. Librarians are perceived negatively, especially in popular culture, because many people are unaware of what librarians do. The collective conscience of librarianship is characterized by spinster women, uptight people with control issues, and people who are seen as bookish (Branin, 2010; Wells, 2013; White, 2012). Librarianship is truly a profession without a concrete identity. There are many types of libraries, and librarians have different roles and responsibilities (Walter, 2008). Academic librarians now have specialized titles such as instructional design librarian, scholarly communications librarian, web/systems librarian, research data librarian, electronic resources librarian, and outreach librarian. In public libraries, a children's or young adult librarian may serve a different clientele than an adult services librarian.

When deciding to brand yourself, it is important to think about how to present yourself to your colleagues and to other professionals in your field. Developing a professional brand allows you to present the best version of yourself. Professional brands should be curated and should reflect the following questions:

1. What image are you trying to convey?
2. How does it complement your place of employment?
3. How is it unique?
4. What makes it memorable?
5. How do you develop trust with your audience and colleagues?

Some celebrities have developed their own brand using a nontraditional route. They become engaged on social media as a hobby and get discovered and then get promoted to celebrity status. Some have popular YouTube channels, Facebook pages, or blogs. Jazz Jennings may be the new face of transgendered youth in the United States, and she became famous through social media (McInroy and Craig, 2017). Justin Bieber and David Archuleta, both young singer/songwriters became famous through YouTube. All have curated a brand for themselves in a more organic and informal way (Marwick, 2013).

As an example, a children's librarian may wish to brand themselves by acting playful at the reference desk or during storytime. They may dress in colorful clothing or wear a different colored bowtie every day. They may start out a library program with a particular greeting or song that kids like. They may offer stickers to all children who come to the reference desk for help. A professional brand creates a memorable image of that person that makes them stand out from others. Other aspects of personal branding include incorporating one's individual style into their professional role, as well as other elements such as makeup, hairstyle, clothing, behavior, and nonverbal communication (Quast, 2013).

Assessing your personal brand requires self-reflection and involves conducting a personal SWOT analysis (Quast, 2013). It is important to identify your professional vision and your future goals, and to define your professional goals and objectives, like developing a personal mission statement. When developing your own professional brand, you need to research the competition and learn from others. Starting points for exploring brand attributes include listing a set of adjectives that describe yourself and selecting a specific segment of the market to target. Conducting a self-assessment to determine how you are perceived by colleagues and users is important to better understand how to develop your professional brand. Your branding plan may involve creating a consistent image of yourself using different tools such as maintaining a professional website; joining and using LinkedIn, Facebook, and Twitter; creating a professional blog; and designing business cards. Cultivating a distinctive professional identity by developing a uniqueness that sets yourself apart from others is paramount; it will require self-reflection and crafting a memorable (and positive) image of yourself that you want people to remember. This can be achieved in how you present yourself to others, your handshake, your behavior, mannerisms, teaching style, personality, website, and social media presence. Your overall professional brand should present a consistent "professional story" of your life and should be directed to a specific audience that you wish to target.

KEY POINTS

This chapter defined branding as the non-tangible experiences associated with a company, product, or service. Brand components may incorporate a logo, slogan, and a set of colors and fonts. The concepts of brand strength, brand loyalty, brand audit, and co-branding were illustrated. Lastly, branding concepts were applied to libraries with the steps involved in conducting a brand audit.

- Branding represents much more than a logo. It signifies the "personality" of a business. It illustrates the essence of a particular company, product, or service.
- Branding is necessary in building a unique identity for an organization. It helps set the product or service apart from the competition.
- Brand loyalty is the tendency for customers to continue purchasing (or using) products or services, despite a price increase, or a decline of quality.

- Brand strength is the value a company generates from a product with a recognizable name. The twin-tailed mermaid is so recognizable, for example, that the Starbucks coffee cup no longer has the words "Starbucks" written on it.
- A brand audit is an important assessment method to survey both employees and customers. It helps the organization understand how their employees and their customers perceive them.
- Librarians may wish to cultivate their own personal brand by conducting a self-reflective assessment of their personal and professional aspirations.

Chapter 9 will review best practice guidelines when promoting library services and resources on social media, specifically Facebook, Google+, Twitter, and Instagram. The chapter will examine the features of "likes," "shares," and "comments" as engagement metrics. Lastly, a discussion of social media assessment will be addressed.

REFERENCES

Aaker, David A. 2012. *Building strong brands*. New York: Simon & Schuster.

Albert, Amanda B.1. 2017. "Building brand love and gaining the advocacy you crave by communicating your library's value." *Journal of Library & Information Services in Distance Learning* 11, no. 1/2: 237–250.

Allaway, Arthur W., Patricia Huddleston, Judith Whipple, and Alexander E. Ellinger. 2011. "Customer-based brand equity, equity drivers, and customer loyalty in the supermarket industry." *Journal of Product & Brand Management* 20, no. 3: 190–204.

Andrews, Camille, Sara E. Wright, and Howard Raskin. 2016. "Library learning spaces: Investigating libraries and investing in student feedback." *Journal of Library Administration* 56, no. 6: 647–672.

Batey, Mark. 2015. *Brand meaning: Meaning, myth and mystique in today's brands*. New York: Routledge.

Branin, Joseph. 2010. "Bookish librarians." *College & Research Libraries* 71, no. 6: 508–509.

Burlacu, Alexandra. 2016. "Samsung will pay customers to stay loyal to its brand despite second Galaxy Note 7 recall." *Tech Times*, October 13. http://www.techtimes.com/articles/182183/20161013/samsung-will-pay-customers-to-stay-loyal-to-its-brand-despite-second-galaxy-note-7-recall.htm

Chiaravalle, Bill, and Barbara Findlay Schenck. 2015. *Branding for dummies.* Hoboken, NJ: John Wiley & Sons.

Courtier, Thomas, and John DeLooper. 2017. "Hosting a Super Smash Bros. tournament at the Hudson County Community College Library." *Library Hi Tech News* 34, no. 1: 11–16.

Cramer, Judd, and Alan B. Krueger. 2016. "Disruptive change in the taxi business: The case of Uber." *American Economic Review* 106, no. 5: 177–182.

Doucett, Elisabeth. 2008. *Creating your library brand.* Chicago: American Library Association.

Erickson, Lynne Martin, Aaron Harris, and Ann Seidl. 2014. *The Hollywood librarian: A look at librarians through film.* Media Education Foundation Collection. http://www.kanopystreaming.com/node/41609

Filipe, Sandra, Susana Henriques Marques, and Maria de Fátima Salgueiro. 2017. "Customers' relationship with their grocery store: Direct and moderating effects from store format and loyalty programs." *Journal of Retailing and Consumer Services* 37: 78–88.

Freedhoff, Yoni. 2014. "The food industry is neither friend, nor foe, nor partner." *Obesity Reviews* 15, no. 1: 6–8.

Harris, Cathryn. 2007. "Libraries with lattes: The new third place." *Australasian Public Libraries and Information Services* 20, no. 4: 145–152.

Harvard University Archives. 2017. Thomas Hollis letters. http://library.harvard.edu/university-archives/featured-item/15_ThomasHollisLetters (Accessed May 2, 2017).

Hay, Lyn. 2010. "Shift happens. It's time to rethink, rebuild and rebrand." *Access* 24, no. 4: 5–10.

Hockenberry, Benjamin, and Kourtney Blackburn. 2016. "Get out of fines free: Recruiting student usability testers via fine waivers." *Journal of Access Services* 13, no. 1: 24–34.

Jiang, Yuwei, Gerald J. Gorn, Maria Galli, and Amitava Chattopadhyay. 2016. "Does your company have the right logo? How and why circular and angular logo shapes influence brand attribute judgments." *Journal of Consumer Research* 42, no. 5: 709–726.

Kang, Jun, Thomas Brashear Alejandro, and Mark D. Groza. 2015. "Customer–company identification and the effectiveness of loyalty programs." *Journal of Business Research* 68, no. 2: 464–471.

Klara, Robert. 2014. "How a topless mermaid made the Starbucks cup an icon." *Ad Week.* September 14. http://www.adweek.com/brand-marketing/how-topless-mermaid-made-starbucks-cup-icon-160396/

Kupersmith, John. 2012. "Library terms that users understand." *EScholarship.* February 29. http://escholarship.org/uc/item/3qq499w7# (Accessed April 7, 2017).

Litsey, Ryan, and Kaley Daniel. 2013. "Resources—Anytime, anywhere: Branding library services, a case study of Texas tech's document delivery department." *Journal of Interlibrary Loan, Document Delivery & Electronic Reserve* 23, no. 1: 19–34.

MacDonald, Karen I., Wyoma Vanduinkerken, and Jane Stephens. 2008. "It's all in the marketing: The impact of a virtual reference marketing campaign at Texas A&M University." *Reference & User Services Quarterly* 47, no. 4: 375–385.

Marwick, A. E. 2013. *Status update: Celebrity, publicity, and branding in the social media age.* New Haven, CT: Yale University Press.

Marsh, Rob. 2015. "130 questions to ask when conducting a brand audit." *Brandstory* (blog). May 4. http://www.brandstoryonline.com/130-questions -to-ask-when-conducting-a-brand-audit/

McCarthy, Kelly, and S. Von Hoene. 2014. "Co-branding: A sweet business strategy?" *Westlaw Journal Computer & Internet* 31, no. 18: 3–6.

McInroy, L. B., and S. L. Craig. 2017. "Perspectives of LGBTQ emerging adults on the depiction and impact of LGBTQ media representation." *Journal of Youth Studies* 20, no. 1: 32–46.

Moggy, M. A., E. A. Pajor, W. E. Thurston, et al. 2017. "Management practices associated with pain in cattle on western Canadian cow–calf operations: A mixed methods study." *Journal of Animal Science* 95, no. 2: 958–969.

Nygaard, Taylor. 2013. "Girls just want to be 'quality': HBO, Lena Dunham, and girls' conflicting brand identity." *Feminist Media Studies* 13, no. 2: 370–374.

Pagowsky, Nicole, and Miriam E. Rigsby. 2014. *The librarian stereotype: Deconstructing perceptions and presentations of information work.* Chicago: American Library Association.

Payne, B. 2017. "Brand positioning and its usefulness for brand management: The case of Apple Inc." *Newcastle Business School Student Journal* 1, no. 1: 51–57.

Peters, Anne, and Jan Kemp. 2014. "Ask us anything: Communicating the value of reference services through branding." *Public Services Quarterly* 10, no. 1: 48–53.

Phillips, Carol. 2012. "Brand audits: Three powerful rings." November 12. https://www.brandingstrategyinsider.com/2012/11/brand-audits-three-pow erfulrings.html#.WNF9iTvyvcs

Phillips, Carol, and Judy Hopelain. 2015. "How to conduct a brand audit." August. http://brandamplitude.com/resources?task=callelement&format=raw&item_id=232&element=61fb63d0-acd7-4578-9744-e0d88150b9f8 &method=download

Polger, Mark Aaron. 2010. "Information takeout and delivery: A case study exploring different library service delivery models." *Journal of Hospital Librarianship* 10, no. 1: 3–22.

Posen, Hannah A. 2015. "Ridesharing in the sharing economy: Should regulators impose Uber regulations on Uber?" *Iowa Law Review* 101, no. 1: 405–433.

Quast, Lisa. 2013. "Personal branding 101." *Forbes Magazine Online*. April 22. https://www.forbes.com/sites/lisaquast/2013/04/22/personal-branding 101/#4f9681e5297c

Rowley, Jennifer. 2013. "Branding libraries: The challenges and opportunities." *Marketing Library and Information Services II, München: KG Saur*: 55–68.

Ruihley, Brody J., and Joshua R. Pate. 2017. "For the love of sport: Examining sport emotion through a lovemarks lens." *Communication & Sport* 5, no. 2: 135–159.

Sasmita, Jumiati, and Norazah Mohd Suki. 2015. "Young consumers' insights on brand equity: Effects of brand association, brand loyalty, brand awareness, and brand image." *International Journal of Retail & Distribution Management* 43, no. 3: 276–292.

Schoensee, Ryan. 2014. "Called 'the most prestigious award of the American Library Association,' the honor recognizes UTSA's 'Ask Us Anything' library marketing campaign." April 25. https://lib.utsa.edu/news/utsa-libraries -receives-john-cotton-dana-award (Accessed July 1, 2018).

Seale, Maura. 2008. "Old maids, policeman, and social rejects: Mass media representations and public perceptions of librarians." *Electronic Journal of Academic and Special Librarianship* 9, no. 1: 1–8.

Seno, Diana, and Bryan A. Lukas. 2007. "The equity effect of product endorsement by celebrities: A conceptual framework from a co-branding perspective." *European Journal of Marketing* 41, no. 1/2: 121–134.

Sidel, Robin. 2015. "AmEx, JetBlue end co-branded credit-card deal." *Wall Street Journal Online*, February 13. https://www.wsj.com/articles/amex -jetblue-end-co-branded-credit-card-deal-1423867653

St. George, Art, and Ron Larsen. 1992. "Internet-accessible library catalogs & databases." The Public's Library and Digital Archive. January 6. http:// www.ibiblio.org/pub/docs/lib-catalogs.online/library.list (Accessed April 5, 2017).

Steffy, Christina J. 2015. *Librarians & stereotypes: So, now what?* Berks County, PA: Crave Press.

Szilagyi, Sarah. 2015. "Know your brand: Conduct a thorough brand audit in 4 easy steps." Feb 10. http://elevatoragency.com/conduct-a-thorough-brand -audit-in-4easy-steps/

Walter, Scott. 2008. "Librarians as teachers: A qualitative inquiry into professional identity." *College & Research Libraries* 69, no. 1: 51–71.

Walters, Suzanne, and Kent Jackson. 2013. *Breakthrough branding: Positioning your library to survive and thrive.* Chicago: American Library Association.

Weil, Dan. 2011. "Just do it: Nike profits off and running." *Newsmax*, April 26. http://go.galegroup.com/ps/i.do?p=ITOF&sw=w&u=cuny_statenisle&v=2.1&it=r&id=GALE%7CA256023956&asid=596502b723cd51159ac85eb266cce6dc

Weintraub, Lindsey. 2013. "10 reasons why you need a brand strategy." October 10. https://www.parkerwhite.com/insights/brand-strategy-for-success/

Wells, Julia A. 2013. "The female librarian in film: Has the image changed in 60 years?" *SLIS Student Research Journal* 3, no. 2: 1–14.

White, Ashanti. 2012. *Not your ordinary librarian: Debunking the popular perceptions of librarians.* Oxford [England]: Chandos Publishing. http://public.eblib.com/choice/publicfullrecord.aspx?p=1575069

Williams, Peter, and Judith Preece. 2005. "It's more than just books: Working with a corporate marketing team to promote library services." *SCONUL Focus* 36 (Winter). 19–22.

CHAPTER 7

Identifying Library Spaces as Marketing Opportunities

IN THIS CHAPTER

- Marketing library spaces
- Promoting the library as a "third place"
- Designing user-centered library spaces
- Marketing the library's technological resources
- Using merchandising techniques for library spaces
- Identifying library touchpoints
- Using best practices for signage

LIBRARIES: THE THIRD PLACE

More and more people are working outside of office settings. Increasingly, people work in coffee shops and other places that indirectly charge for use of the space (users must buy food and/or drink to use the wireless Internet, power outlets, and table space). Public, shared, freely accessible work and study space is increasingly rare. In this environment, libraries are now marketing themselves as a *third place* (Harris, 2007; Montgomery and Miller, 2011; Waxman, Clemons, Banning, and McKelfresh, 2007; Elmborg, 2011; Demas and Scherer, 2002). The idea of the third place is based on the work of sociologist Ray Oldenburg (1993), who researches the spaces where people interact with each other. Shared public space—third places—are increasingly important, since 77 percent of Americans go online daily, and 26 percent of them are online constantly (Perrin and Jiang, 2018). The third place is a community space other than home or work, and libraries have always been a natural third place. The library is an emblem of democracy, a noncommercial space where people interact, freely access information (including the Internet), read, learn, and communicate with others.

The library should thus promote its space as welcoming, comfortable, accessible, and free. Many libraries are reinventing their physical spaces as community spaces, information commons, and makerspaces; they are adding cafés and larger workspaces to foster collaboration, community interaction, and creation (Montgomery and Miller, 2011; Harris, 2007) and "genius bars," inspired by Apple stores—raised tables where library users can socialize and interact with others (Sarwari, 2015; Smith, 2017; Koon, 2015; Johnson, 2017). Libraries are using principles of user-centered design to ensure that physical spaces meet user needs—a change that helps libraries compete with big box bookstores like Barnes & Noble in the United States and Chapters Indigo in Canada (Sannwald, 1998). Libraries proactively create a welcoming user experience with more comfortable seating, more electrical outlets for cell phone and laptop charging, and modular furniture that fosters flexible learning (Brown-Sica, 2012; Kate, 2003; Asher, 2017; Berman, 2014; Kollie, 2008).

User Experience (UX) Design

Libraries are designing these flexible spaces with user experience in mind. User experience (UX) is the intersection of the user's emotional experience and the usability of a particular interface (Schmidt and Etches, 2014). The discipline originated in computer science, but designing for UX now goes far beyond website design, extending to physical spaces (UX for web design will be discussed in chapter 8). User experience describes the sum of the feelings users have when they interact with the physical and virtual touchpoints of the organization: the employees and their level of customer service, the design of the building, the furniture design, the cleanliness of the restrooms, the usability of the signage, the brochure stands, the wayfinding, the display cases, whether the garbage containers are full or empty—all of these things affect the user's experience of the library (Brugnoli, 2009). Library marketing is organically connected with user experience (Potter 2012).

This chapter explains how libraries can promote their physical spaces, including the entrance, book displays, exhibits, brochures, signage, and touchpoints. It discusses how libraries that can afford to renovate can use the information commons, the learning commons, and the makerspace to market their spaces. Although most scholarly literature on marketing library spaces is related to promoting new or renovated facilities rather than existing facilities (Weare, Moffett, and Cooper, 2016; Fontane, 2016; Lance and Dorfman, 1999; Black and Kilzer, 2008; Doyle, 1998), not having the budget for renovation or a total rebuild should not keep you from marketing your space; older library buildings can and should be promoted, and this chapter will show you how.

MARKETING THE LIBRARY'S TECHNOLOGY

Physical library facilities reflect libraries' focus, and in the last thirty years, libraries have begun to focus less on print collections, reference material, and in-person interactions and more on technological offerings, virtual holdings, and remote interactions. Libraries often focus their marketing on their technological and digital offerings, perhaps in order to show that that libraries are still relevant, or perhaps in an attempt to offset the difficult library funding climate; in other words, libraries may be embracing technology—positioning themselves as innovative—in order to survive (Saunders, 2015; Van Scoyoc and Cason, 2006; Liu, 2006). In the Internet age, libraries attempt to prove their value by providing access to expensive databases, amassing robust and expensive digital collections (Herring, 2014; Herring, 2001; Ross and Sennyey, 2008), designing professional websites, creating beautifully curated LibGuides (that few access), performing countless usability studies, creating specialized librarian roles for websites and electronic resource management, and developing best practices for their presence on social media.

Libraries' recent focus on technological relevance is reflected in research trends. A literature search on "libraries and technology" in EBSCO's Library and Information Science source retrieved 5,500 scholarly articles on the subject published between 1980 and 1999 and 25,000 scholarly articles published between 2000 and 2018. The 45 percent spike in research into libraries and technology after 2000 indicates the intellectual and fiscal investment in getting technology into libraries. As libraries began to prioritize technology and electronic resources, they reduced their focus on print collections and physical space,[1] as the model of library acquisitions shifted from an ownership model to an access model (Kyrillidou, 2000). Annual library budgets now spend more than half of their funding on electronic resources (Kyrillidou, 2002; Miller, 2000). Collection patterns now focus less on monographs and more on serials, and electronic resources (periodical databases) now represent the majority of library expenditures.

These changes in collection patterns and in library focus directly shape libraries' physical spaces. Many old library buildings have limited space for physical books, and that limited physical space is often now given over to information or learning commons (Miller, 2016). But as libraries lease or purchase electronic books and reference titles and reduce reference collections to save space, they actually reduce some in-person interactions between librarians and patrons: there is an inverse relationship between the expenditures on electronic resources and the number of in-person reference transactions (Hughes, 2013; Dubnjakovic, 2012).

However, libraries must also market and optimize their physical spaces. This does not mean every library needs an expensive new building or an expensive renovation of the existing building; sometimes all that is needed to promote the library's physical facilities is a few inexpensive upgrades and a bit of thought about user experience to make the library's physical space more inviting and welcoming to users, and to make it better meet users' needs.

Information/Learning Commons

Renovating a library and transforming the space into a "commons"—an information commons or a learning commons—provides a marketing opportunity, especially if the library acquires new furniture and technology. Many library renovation projects take parts of their former reference collection or circulating space and convert it to an information or learning commons. The commons, as the name suggests, is an open concept space where collaboration, learning, access to library resources, and information technology come together. Beagle (1999) defines the information commons as a collection of access points and IT tools in the context of information resources that support learning.

Some information commons are part of library infrastructure, some are administered by other campus departments such as information technology, and some are separate entities. Every commons is conceptualized differently, according to the local needs and budget allocations of the institution. Some information commons may resemble computer labs, with large, collaborative group tables; some may incorporate sophisticated computer software and hardware; some may have modular furniture for flexible student learning. All information commons should support student learning and academic success (Beagle, 2012; Whitchurch, 2010; Beagle, 1999; Accardi, Cordova, and Leeder, 2010).

A learning commons is an extension of the information commons (Bennett, 2008). It combines the resources of an information commons with collaboration with other campus departments who share common learning goals. According to Bennett (2008), "the difference is that the information commons supports the institutional mission while the learning commons enacts it" (p. 183). The learning commons leverages the combined resources of various student support services and the library, removing silos between departments and enabling partnerships between libraries and campus departments such as the learning center, academic support, public libraries, student advising, student government, and information technology—partnerships that provide library marketing opportunities. Libraries can promote many aspects of the commons to their users: hardware such as scanners and audio-visual production equipment; specialized software not normally offered in computer labs; ergonomic furniture that supports flexible learning; and whiteboards, smartboards, and other collaborative workspaces.

The commons offer other promotional prospects also, including charitable naming opportunities. Naming rights have long been used to garner funding for other organizations, such as hospitals. For example, the NYU Medical Center was renamed the NYU Langone Center in 2008 after a $200 million gift from Kenneth and Elaine Langone (Beckman, 2008). Naming rights for information commons offer both promotional and funding opportunities: library development departments or foundation offices can solicit donations to renovate and rename information commons. For example, the University of Toronto received a large donation from Scotiabank, a large Canadian bank, for their information commons. The resulting Scotiabank Information Commons is a separate entity from the library that is located in the same building and provides both library and technical support (Beatty and Mountifield, 2006). Typically, donors receive naming rights for the period of time that they commit to funding, and contracts often spell out the terms of agreement. Naming rights can end (once funding ends) or be transferred (if another donor provides a larger donation); for example, the New York City marathon used to be sponsored by ING Bank, but the naming rights have now been transferred to Tata Consultancy Services Limited (Freeze, 2013). Naming rights serve as marketing opportunities for sponsors, but they also open up marketing opportunities for the library as well.

Makerspaces

A makerspace is any type of physical space where users can create and build physical and digital items (Alverson, 2015; Moorefield-Lang, 2015; Burke, 2015; Slatter and Howard, 2013). They can be situated in any type of library, and, like the commons model, they differ depending on physical size, funding, and the types of resources offered. Some makerspaces provide access to crafting and art supplies, like sewing machines, easels, and painting supplies. Others focus on technology, offering 3-D printers, laser cutters, highly specialized computer software, professional equipment for recording and editing audio and video, and equipment for scanning, photo editing, VHS conversion, game creation, and video animation (Burke, 2015). Makerspaces foster creativity, experiential learning, self-directed learning, community, investigation, curiosity, and collaboration (Colegrove, 2017).

Library makerspaces offer many marketing possibilities. Libraries can partner with different community groups, co-sponsor events with local area public schools, and collaborate with different academic departments, often STEM departments. They could create themed maker days and set up the makerspace for users to create particular items—a winter scarf, a video contest for incoming students, or innovative new tools for a specific college course. Promoting makerspaces highlights the library as a place that celebrates and supports creativity and innovation. Makerspaces help show the library's relevance in the digital age.

MARKETING THE LIBRARY BUILDING: FOCUS ON TOUCHPOINTS

In the library's physical space, touchpoints are the places where users make decisions: the bottom of a stairwell, the entrance to the elevator, the pathway to the service desk, the natural hallways that are created by library shelving, the entrance to the restrooms. Touchpoints map the customer journey (Bell, 2014; Marquez, Downey, and Clement, 2015). These natural pathways that users take when navigating through the building are crucial to the user experience, and evaluating library touchpoints enables researchers to better understand how users interact with both physical and virtual interfaces. Touchpoints should be clean, organized, and lack clutter; they should also have friendly and knowledgeable staff nearby who make the user feel welcome. The rest of this chapter examines several touchpoints that should be audited for user friendliness in order to make the library building as appealing and usable as possible.

The Building Entrance

A great way to promote the library space is by having an attractive and accessible entrance. The library's physical entrance is as important as the front page of the library website (as discussed in chapter 8). The area around the entrance should be clean, free of clutter, accessible by all patrons, welcoming, and easy to find (Schmidt and Etches, 2014). Appropriate, clear signage should be displayed so that users can easily find their way inside.

Unfortunately, some library entrances are difficult to find, and are not designed with user experience in mind. For example, in Montreal, Canada, the entrance to Concordia University's Webster Library is on the second floor of the J. W. McConnell Building (Concordia University Libraries, 2016); in Toronto, Canada, the Ryerson University

Library and Archives entrance is on the second floor of the library building (Ryerson University Library and Archives, 2017); and in Brooklyn, New York, the Ursula C. Schwerin Library of the New York City College of Technology (part of the City University of New York) is on the fourth floor of the Atrium building (Ursula C. Schwerin Library, 2017). These three academic institutions do not have traditional campuses with acres of land and many buildings; both Webster Library and Ryerson Library share their space with other administrative departments and classrooms. Many urban academic campus building look like office towers; urban colleges and universities (most of which were founded after the early twentieth century) often did not have the luxury of acquiring land, and their physical space is limited. Older college campuses with more abundant space usually have separate library buildings that have more attractive and user-friendly entrances, although many older buildings' entrances are not ADA compliant. From a UX design perspective, the library's entrance should be on the main floor at the center of the building (Latimer, 2011).

Hospital libraries, too, are often difficult to access and therefore difficult to market to users. There are usually two types of libraries for the hospital community: a consumer health information library (CHI) for patients and families, and a health sciences library for staff and physicians. Many hospitals have made an effort to promote their CHI libraries by placing them at the entrance or in the lobby of the hospital (Egeland 2015; Brawn, 2005; Nicholas, Huntington, and Williams, 2002; Forsberg, 2010; Oelschlegel, Gonzalez, and Frakes, 2014). However, health sciences libraries, which are primarily used by staff and physicians, are often hidden away in areas not accessible to the public. Health sciences libraries must often compete for real estate with other clinical units, and libraries (which support patient care but do not provide direct patient care) are often not prioritized. Many health sciences libraries are thus in basements or in obscure areas of hospitals—places that were not designed for libraries (Thibodeau, 2010; Lynn, Fitzsimmons, and Robinson, 2011). From a marketing standpoint, it is more challenging to promote health sciences library spaces to hospital employees when the libraries are tucked away out of sight.

Generally, academic and public libraries (with the exception of some libraries on urban college campuses, as mentioned) are usually well positioned. Some public libraries have their own buildings, with pleasing entrances that have curbside appeal. Some smaller public library branches in neighborhoods are adjacent to or attached to shopping malls or community centers. Evidence collected beginning in the 1960s shows that building public library branches in shopping centers or adjacent to community centers provides great public relations and a built-in audience (Henderson, 1967; Kim, 2006; Blankinship, 2005; Alverson, 2015).

Many academic libraries have their own buildings, often at the center of campus. In this situation, marketing messages should be aligned with their central location: the library is the heart of the campus, and it should be marketed as such (Kranich, Reid, and Willingham, 2004; Schopfel, Roche, and Hubert, 2015; Shill and Tonner, 2003).

Merchandising: Displays and Exhibits

Merchandising is the retail technique of displaying products in an attractive manner for customers to purchase. While most libraries are not in the business of selling books, they do wish to increase the circulation of materials, and book displays and exhibits can help promote circulation.

Book *displays* sort print materials into themes or topical groups, often with an artistic or aesthetic component. Displays provide an easy way to promote a particular collection by showcasing the library's offerings (Fiscus, 2017; Sullivan, 2010). For example, a topical book display might include all publications by faculty in a particular field. Displays might also promote seasonal events, cultural festivals, and holidays; for example, displays and exhibits can highlight special dates like Martin Luther King Day, Banned Books Week, National Library Week, Presidents' Day, 4th of July, Labor Day, Memorial Day, Black History Month, Pride Month, and Thanksgiving. Displays should not contain too many books, as that would overload the user with information; think *curation* and *selection* (not aggregation) when it comes to displays. Displays should be updated frequently and should invite patrons to borrow displayed items.

Library *exhibits* inform and educate patrons while promoting library services and resources to the community. Exhibits are promotional displays of multimedia materials on a specific topic. Both public and academic library spaces can be used to showcase exhibits that promote their general collection, their archives and special collections, or other unique collections, including traveling exhibits, which may promote other works in the community or across the country. Library exhibits can foster community engagement through partnerships with other cultural organizations. Exhibits can contain art, photographs, books, primary source materials, sculpture, digital materials, and other artifacts. They should be highly visual and attractive, and they should generate intellectual curiosity, engage library users, attract new library users, and spark interest in the community (Brown and Power, 2005). Some libraries have written exhibition policies that clearly articulate the types of exhibitions that the library supports. Exhibits may change monthly, and some libraries therefore have exhibit committees where the library and archives and special collections departments collaborate when planning their exhibition calendar. Exhibits create an opportunity to spotlight the library, inviting the larger institution or community to pay attention.

Signage

Signage, a vital part of physical library facilities, is an important communications tool. Signs are usually the first visuals that users interact with. Signage provides information; supports wayfinding, informs users about library policies, and promotes services, resources, and events. Signage should always be user friendly, use jargon-free language that is simple and straightforward, and be welcoming to the user (Stempler and Polger, 2013; Polger and Stempler, 2014; Potter, 2012; Serfass, 2011; Bosman and Rusinek, 1997). Many libraries have too many signs, and sometimes they are unfriendly, contradictory, passive-aggressive, outdated, or confusing. Policy signs, in particular, can seem unfriendly, because they are often prohibitive: cell phone, food, and noise policies are often communicated with signs that are perceived as hostile and unwelcoming. Signs (like all library communication channels, including the website and promotional materials) should therefore be welcoming, user-friendly, current, and as simple as possible (Polger, 2011; Hutcherson, 2004; Jurkowski, 2007; Kupersmith, 2012; Spivey, 2000).

Sign designers must consider the following criteria:

- Message
- Branding and design
- User friendliness (including clarity and simplicity)
- Placement
- ADA compliance
- Currency/timeliness

Polger and Stempler (2014) recommend that libraries create signage locator maps to enable regular audits of all signage. The signage locator map helps keep a running inventory of the number of signs and their locations. One element that should be regularly audited is ADA compliance. ADA-compliant signs should be high contrast (black font on white background), should avoid glare, and should use serif fonts, which are easier to read than sans serif fonts (ADA, 2010).

Polger and Stempler (2014) also offer a set of best practices for library signage. Signs should be mounted strategically at library touchpoints, or decision points, to guide users. They should be free of clutter and should not compete with other signs. They should follow a consistent design and align their branding with that of their parent institution. Instead of using all caps for emphasis (all caps can sometimes be interpreted as yelling), signs should emphasize text using bold fonts. Signs should avoid clip art, which looks unprofessional; instead, they should use original photographs that authentically convey the message in a clear and compelling way. Signs should be welcoming, and policy signs, in particular, should avoid using prohibitive language like "no." Instead, signs should convey what users *can* do (Matczak, 2018; Schmidt, 2015). For example, instead of a sign saying "No talking," emphasize what users can do, like "please converse in the lobby coffee shop."

CONCLUSION

This chapter examined how the physical spaces of the library building can be used to promote and market the library. This chapter's recommendations are grounded in the idea of designing for user experience (UX), a methodology that will be further discussed in chapter 8. UX considers users' emotions when they interact with a physical or virtual interface, and it can be applied to both virtual and physical spaces.

In fact, designing with UX in mind works on the same user-centered principles as market research: you must know what your users want and need in order to try to meet those wants and needs. This principle governs both collection and subscription and small physical decisions such as signage.

This chapter has argued that the library facility should serve as the "third place" for users: a noncommercial community space for interaction, learning, and collaboration. Library information or learning commons can help to make the library a third place for patrons, as can makerspaces. Some libraries have the budget for physical renovations to create these open-concept commons spaces and makerspaces and some do not. Even older library facilities and those that have no budget for renovations can make their physical spaces inviting in order to promote library use. Library buildings can be inexpensively promoted by having a welcoming entrance, clean and uncluttered displays, and pleasant, user-friendly signage that provides wayfinding, promotes events, and informs users about library policies.

NOTE

1. There has, however, been a slow and steady increase in the research into libraries' physical spaces. When I conducted the same literature search on "libraries and space," I found only 137 scholarly articles written about library spaces between 1980 and 1990 and 231 articles between 1990 and 2000. However, 1,790 articles were published between 2000 and 2010, and 2,400 between 2010 and 2018, indicating a renewed interest in libraries' physical spaces.

REFERENCES

Accardi, Maria T., Memo Cordova, and Kim Leeder. 2010. "Reviewing the library learning commons: History, models, and perspectives." *College & Undergraduate Libraries* 17, no. 2/3: 310–329.
Alverson, Brigid. 2015. "Library maker space in a mall." *School Library Journal* 61, no. 11: 14–15.

Americans with Disabilities Act. 2010. "2010 ADA standards for accessible design." September 15. https://www.ada.gov/regs2010/2010ADAStandards/2010ADAstandards.htm (Accessed August 15, 2018).

Asher, Andrew D. 2017. "Space use in the commons: Evaluating a flexible library environment." *Evidence Based Library & Information Practice* 12, no. 2: 68–89.

Beagle, Donald. 1999. "Conceptualizing an information commons." *Journal of Academic Librarianship* 25, no. 2: 82–89.

Beagle, Donald. 2012. "The emergent information commons: Philosophy, models, and 21st century learning paradigms." *Journal of Library Administration* 52, no. 6–7: 518–537.

Beatty, Susan, and Hester Mountifield. 2006. "Collaboration in an information commons: Key elements for successful support of e-literacy." *Innovation in Teaching and Learning in Information and Computer Sciences* 5, no. 4: 232–248.

Beatty, Susan. 2008. "Academic libraries in transformation to learning centers: information commons or learning commons?" *International Journal of Learning* 15, no. 8: 9–14.

Beckman, John. 2008. "NYU Medical Center changes name to honor chairman of board & wife." April 16. http://www.nyu.edu/about/news-publications/news/2008/april/nyu_medical_center_changes.html (Accessed August 23, 2018).

Bell, Steven J. 2014. "Staying true to the core: Designing the future academic library experience." *portal: Libraries and the Academy* 14, no. 3: 369–382.

Bennett, Scott. 2008. "The information or the learning commons: Which will we have?" *Journal of Academic Librarianship* 34, no. 3: 183–185.

Berman, Scott. 2014. "Furnishing for Flexibility." *College Planning & Management* 17, no. 6: 42–48.

Black, Elizabeth L., and Rebekah Kilzer. 2008. "Web 2.0 tools ease renovation service disruptions at the Ohio State University libraries." *Public Services Quarterly* 4, no. 2: 93–109.

Blankinship, Donna Gordon. 2005. "Let's go to the mall: Thinking outside the neighborhood branch, libraries in malls make for happy partnerships and patrons." *Library Journal* 130, no. 2: 44.

Bosman, Ellen, and Carol Rusinek. 1997. "Creating the user-friendly library by evaluating patron perception of signage." *Reference Services Review* 25, no. 1: 71–82.

Brawn, Tammy S. 2005. "Consumer health libraries: What do patrons really want?" *Journal of the Medical Library Association* 93, no. 4: 495–496.

Brown, Mary E., and Rebecca Power. 2005. *Exhibits in libraries: A practical guide.* Jefferson, NC: McFarland.

Brown-Sica, Margaret S. 2012. "Library spaces for urban, diverse commuter students: A participatory action research project." *College & Research Libraries* 73, no. 3: 217–231.

Brugnoli, Gianluca. 2009. "Connecting the dots of user experience." *Journal of Information Architecture* 1, no. 1: 6–15.

Burke, John. 2015. "Making sense: Can makerspaces work in academic libraries?" Proceedings of the ACRL National Conference. https://sc.lib.miamioh.edu/xmlui/bitstream/handle/2374.MIA/5212/Burke.pdf (Accessed August 23, 2018).

Colegrove, Patrick Tod. 2017. "Makerspaces in libraries: Technology as catalyst for better learning, better teaching." *Journal of Engineering and Education* 13, no. 21: 19–26.

Concordia University Libraries. 2016. "Webster Library floor plans." February 24. https://library.concordia.ca/locations/floor-plans/webster-library.php

Demas, Sam, and Jeffrey A. Scherer. 2002. "Esprit de place: Maintaining and designing library buildings to provide transcendent spaces." *American Libraries* 33, no. 4: 65–68.

Doyle, Christine. 1998. "New equipment, new building, new image: A marketing success story." *Computers in Libraries* 18, no. 8: 28–32.

Dubnjakovic, Ana. 2012. "Electronic resource expenditure and the decline in reference transaction statistics in academic libraries." *Journal of Academic Librarianship* 38, no. 2: 94–100.

Egeland, Mindwell. 2015. "Hospital librarians: From consumer health to patient education and beyond." *Journal of Hospital Librarianship* 15, no. 1: 65–76.

Fiscus, Allison Marie. 2017. "Visual merchandising: Applying bookstore insights to public library collections." *Public Libraries* 56, no. 6: 35–37.

Fontane, Walter M. 2016. "Assessing library services during a renovation." *Journal of Access Services* 13, no. 4: 223–236.

Forsberg, Nancy. 2010. "Family friendly space for research, reflection, and respite: A family resource center and library in a pediatric hospital setting." *Journal of Hospital Librarianship* 10, no. 1: 82–87.

Freeze, Amy. 2013. "Name change coming for the NYC marathon." October 2. https://abc7ny.com/archive/9271095/ (Accessed August 23, 2018).

Harris, Cathryn. 2007. "Libraries with lattes: The new third place." *Australasian Public Libraries and Information Services* 20, no. 4: 145–152.

Henderson, Winston R. 1967. "Plant a library in a shopping center." *Arizona Librarian* 24, 7–9.

Herring, M. Y. 2001. Why the Internet can't replace the library. *The Education Digest* 67, no. 1: 46–49.

Herring, Mark Y. 2014. *Are libraries obsolete?: An argument for relevance in the digital age.* Jefferson, NC: McFarland.

Hughes, Annie M. 2013. "There is a relationship between resource expenditures and reference transactions in academic libraries." *Evidence Based Library & Information Practice* 8, no. 1: 87–89.

Hutcherson, Norman B. 2004. "Library jargon: Student recognition of terms and concepts commonly used by librarians in the classroom." *College & Research Libraries* 65, no. 4: 349–354.

Johnson, Melanie. 2017. "Knowledge center brings 'genius bar' concept to library." February 9. http://polycentric.cpp.edu/2017/02/knowledge-center -brings-genius-bar-concept-to-library/ (Accessed August 15, 2018).

Jurkowski, Odin L. 2007. "School library website terminology." *Library Hi Tech* 25, no. 3: 387–395.

Kate, Sandy. 2003. "Flexible furniture for school libraries, media centers & computer labs." *Media & Methods* 39, no. 4: 28–29.

Kim, Young-seok. 2006. "Opening small public libraries in quiet shopping malls could boost local businesses in Goyang, Korea." IFLA Conference Proceedings, 1–13.

Kollie, Ellen. 2008. "The transformation of the library." *School Planning & Management* 47, no. 7: 32–34.

Koon, Mike. 2015. "Grainger Engineering Library being transformed into entrepreneurship hub." November 5. https://engineering.illinois.edu/news/article/12317 (Accessed August 15, 2018).

Kranich, Nancy, Michele Reid, and Taylor Willingham. 2004. "Civic engagement in academic libraries: Encouraging active citizenship." *College & Research Libraries news* 65, no. 7: 380–384.

Kupersmith, John. 2012. "Library terms that users understand." https://cloud front.escholarship.org/dist/prd/content/qt3qq499w7/qt3qq499w7.pdf (Accessed August 15, 2018).

Kyrillidou, Martha. 2002. "Research library spending on electronic scholarly information is on the rise." *Journal of Library Administration* 35, no. 4: 89–91.

Kyrillidou, Martha. 2000. "Research library trends: ARL statistics." *Journal of Academic Librarianship* 26, no. 6: 427–436.

Lance, Kathleen, and Andrew Dorfman. 1999. "Maintaining academic library services during a renovation project." *College & Undergraduate Libraries* 6, no. 1: 65–76.

Latimer, Karen. 2011. "Collections to connections: Changing spaces and new challenges in academic library buildings." *Library Trends* 60, no. 1: 112–133.

Liu, Ziming. 2006. "Print vs. electronic resources: A study of user perceptions, preferences, and use." *Information Processing & Management* 42, no. 2: 583–592.

Lynn, Valerie A., Marie FitzSimmons, and Cynthia K. Robinson. 2011. "Special report: Symposium on transformational change in health sciences libraries: Space, collections, and roles." *Journal of the Medical Library Association* 99, no. 1: 82–87.

Marquez, Joe J., Annie Downey, and Ryan Clement. 2015. "Walking a mile in the user's shoes: Customer journey mapping as a method to understanding the user experience." *Internet Reference Services Quarterly* 20, no. 3–4: 135–150.

Matczak, Jamie. 2018. "Boost! Welcoming, positive, consistent library signage." July 10. https://wvls.org/boost-welcoming-positive-consistent -library-signage/ (Accessed August 21, 2018).

Miller, Eve-Marie. 2016. "Making room for a learning commons space: Lessons in weeding a reference collection through collaboration and planning." *The Serials Librarian* 71, no. 3–4: 197–201.

Miller, Ruth H. 2000. "Electronic resources and academic libraries, 1980–2000: A historical perspective." *Library Trends* 48, no. 4: 645–670.

Montgomery, Susan E., and Jonathan Miller. 2011. "The third place: The library as collaborative and community space in a time of fiscal restraint." *College & Undergraduate Libraries* 18, no. 2–3: 228–238.

Moorefield-Lang, Heather. 2015. "Change in the making: Makerspaces and the ever-changing landscape of libraries." *TechTrends* 59, no. 3: 107–112.

Nicholas, David, Paul Huntington, and Peter Williams. 2002. "The impact of location on the use of information systems: Case study–health information kiosks." *Journal of Documentation* 58, no. 3: 284–301.

Oelschlegel, Sandy, Ann B. Gonzalez, and Elizabeth Frakes. 2014. "Consumer health information centers in medical libraries: A survey of current practices." *Journal of Hospital Librarianship* 14, no. 4: 335–347.

Oldenburg, Ray. 1989. *The great good place: Café, coffee shops, community centers, beauty parlors, general stores, bars, hangouts, and how they get you through the day.* St. Paul, MN: Paragon House Publishers.

Perrin, Andrew, and JingJing Jiang. 2018. "About a quarter of U.S. adults say they are 'almost constantly' online." March 14. http://www.pewresearch .orgfact-tank/2018/03/14/about-a-quarter-of-americans-report-going-on line-almost-constantly/ (Accessed August 15, 2018).

Polger, Mark Aaron. 2011. "Student preferences in library website vocabulary." *Library Philosophy and Practice.* June. 69–84.

Polger, Mark Aaron, and Amy F. Stempler. 2014. "Out with the old, in with
the new: Best practices for replacing library signage." *Public Services
Quarterly* 10, no. 2 (2014): 67–95.

Potter, Ned. 2012. *The library marketing toolkit.* London: Facet Publishing.

Ryerson University Library and Archives. 2017. "Library Brochure." https://
library.ryerson.ca/wp-content/uploads/library-brochure-2017-FA.pdf

Ross, Lyman, and Pongracz Sennyey. 2008. "The library is dead, long live the
library! The practice of academic librarianship and the digital revolution."
The Journal of Academic Librarianship 34, no. 2: 145–152.

Sannwald, William. 1998. "Espresso and ambiance: What public libraries can
learn from bookstores." *Library Administration and Management* 12, no.
4: 200–211.

Sarwari, Khalida. 2015. "Saratoga: Genius bar? Geek squad? No, but library has its own tech toolBar." August 26. https://www.mercurynews
.com/2015/08/26/saratoga-genius-bar-geek-squad-no-but-library-has-its
-own-tech-toolbar/ (Accessed August 15, 2018).

Saunders, Laura. 2015. "Academic libraries' strategic plans: Top trends and
under-recognized areas." *The Journal of Academic Librarianship* 41, no.
3: 285–291.

Schmidt, Aaron, and Amanda Etches. 2014. *Useful, usable, desirable: Applying user experience design to your library.* Chicago: ALA editions.

Schmidt, Aaron. 2015. "The user experience: Positive signs." *Library Journal*
140, no. 14: 25.

Schopfel, Joachim, Julien Roche, and Gilles Hubert. 2015. "Co-working and
innovation: New concepts for academic libraries and learning centres." *New
Library World* 116, no. 1/2: 67–78.

Serfass, Melissa. 2011. "Signs they are a-changin': Is it time to give your
library's signage a makeover?" *AALL Spectrum* 16: 5.

Shill, Harold B., and Shawn Tonner. 2003. "Creating a better place: Physical improvements in academic libraries, 1995–2002." *College & Research
Libraries* 64, no. 6: 431–466.

Slatter, Diane, and Zaana Howard. 2013. "A place to make, hack, and learn:
Makerspaces in Australian public libraries." *The Australian Library Journal* 62, no. 4: 272–284.

Smith, Duncan. 2017. "Public libraries—The genius bar for readers." December 14. https://www.ebsco.com/blog/article/public-libraries-the-genius-bar
-for-readers (Accessed August 15, 2018).

Spivey, Mark A. 2000. "The vocabulary of library home pages: An influence on diverse and remote end-users." *Information Technology and Libraries* 19, no. 3: 151–156.

Stempler, Amy F., and Mark Aaron Polger. 2013. "Do you see the signs? Evaluating language, branding, and design in a library signage audit." *Public Services Quarterly* 9, no. 2: 121–135.

Sullivan, Margaret. 2010. "Merchandising your library resources." *Teacher Librarian* 38, no. 1: 30–31.

Thibodeau, Patricia L. 2010. "When the library is located in prime real estate: A case study on the loss of space from the Duke University Medical Center Library and Archives." *Journal of the Medical Library Association* 98, no. 1: 25–28.

Ursula C. Schwerin Library. 2018. "It's Your Library!" https://library.city tech.cuny.edu/uploads/StudentServices_2.pdf

Van Scoyoc, Anna M., and Caroline Cason. 2006. "The electronic academic library: Undergraduate research behavior in a library without books." *portal: Libraries and the Academy* 6, no. 1: 47–58.

Weare, William H., Paul Moffett, and John P. Cooper. 2016. "Preparing for renovation: Estimating shelf occupancy to inform decision making regarding the redevelopment of library space." *Collection Management* 41, no. 3: 168–181.

Whitchurch, Michael J. 2010. "Planning an information commons." *Journal of Library Administration* 50, no. 1: 39–50.

CHAPTER 8

Using the Web to Market the Library

IN THIS CHAPTER

- The library website as a marketing tool
- Mobile and responsive websites
- User experience design for websites
- Website usability testing methods
- Search engine optimization (SEO)
- Email marketing tools
- Comparison of online advertising methods (website banners and Google Ads)

The Internet provides access to a vast amount of information; it also offers an easy, cost-effective way for people to communicate and interact. The Internet has fundamentally changed the field of marketing, making it easier, faster, and more affordable than ever for marketers to reach more people (Sinha, 2016; Mueller, 2011). However, Internet marketing is not all good. A 2017 consumer survey by the nonprofit association Two Sides surveyed 10,700 consumers across 10 countries and discovered that 45 percent of respondents prefer print-based advertisements over online advertisements; a whopping 71 percent of respondents said that they do not pay attention to online advertisements, and 69 percent find them annoying (Two Sides, 2017). Similarly, although 72 percent of consumers use social media on a regular basis and 47 percent use it multiple times a day, only 3 percent claim that it has an influence on their purchasing decisions (Hagen, 2017); Nielsen's figures in the 2016 Social Media Report are equally discouraging, with only 13 percent of heavy social media users saying that they select online advertisements (Casey, 2017). However, advertising is not the whole story of online marketing; 39 percent of Nielsen respondents reported believing that social media is an important way to learn about new products and services (Casey, 2017).

There is a lesson here for libraries. Although libraries are not necessarily interested in paid advertising, they can and should harness the power of the Internet and social media to communicate their services and resources to their users, and they can and should follow best practices when marketing online.

LIBRARY WEBSITES AS MARKETING TOOLS

A library website serves two functions: first, it is an information resource, providing hours, contact information, and a list of library services and resources and serving as a portal to the library catalog and to commercial research databases. Second, a library website also functions as a marketing vehicle, promoting the library's assets by marketing exhibits, providing downloadable brochures, hosting annual reports, linking to newsletters and press releases, and including photos. According to Welch (2005), the library website is an electronic welcome mat to the community, helping libraries engage with the community, promote fundraising, and publicize events and programs (p. 226)—in other words, supporting the library's advocacy efforts by marketing its offerings (see chapter 10).

The library website might be the first place the users visit, even before visiting the physical location. It must be welcoming, uncluttered, intuitive, organized, and professionally designed. The library's home page is the most important page of the entire library website. Everyone is fighting for a piece of this prime digital real estate. Link placement must therefore be carefully assessed using website usability studies (these will be discussed in detail later in this chapter). The home page should provide access to the most basic information; hours, location, a link to catalog search, a list of services, a list of resources. There should also be a link to an "about the library" page and to a directory of employees that includes contact information.

Recall that chapter 7 explained user experience (UX) design and applied it to the library's physical space. This chapter will explain how UX design should be applied to library websites. One of the key principles of UX design is avoiding clutter and increasing discoverability. Important links should not be buried several levels, or clicks, down; important marketing and public relations links should be on the front page (Welch, 2005). Four categories of marketing and public relations content should be on website front pages: visibility, fundraising, access to information, and contacts (Welch, 2005, p. 227).

Library websites can be used to promote collections, services, events, and programs; for examples of these types of promotions, see Kaba (2011), Kaur (2009), and Abbas, Khalid, and Hashmi (2017). Promotional content on library websites may include virtual exhibits, an electronic newsletter or blog, a website slideshow displayed on the front page, and a website banner. Academic library websites might include special pages for faculty, first-year students, graduate students, and alumni; public libraries might include specific pages for each targeted user group (for example, parents, teenagers, college students, seniors, and new immigrants).

MOBILE AND RESPONSIVE WEBSITES

According to a 2016 survey by Pew Research, 77 percent of U.S. adults and 92 percent of young people between the ages of 18 and 29 use smart phones to access information online (Rainie and Perrin, 2017). This should shape how libraries design their websites, for the websites must be mobile-accessible. There are two ways to do this: web developers can create a "mobile website"—a duplicate website meant for mobile devices—or they can create what is known as a "responsive" website. Mobile websites are abbreviated, simplified versions of the main website that would be viewed on a desktop computer. When the web server recognizes that the client is a mobile device, it serves up the mobile site, which is designed to fit a smaller screen, is more text-heavy (and less image-heavy), and contains only the most important components of the main website. Using this method means that two websites must be created. Content is duplicated, and any updates must be made in two places, making extra work for content managers and website developers.

More recently, responsive website technology has been developed, eliminating the need for a separate mobile website. Responsive design means the developer creates only one website, and that website adjusts to whatever type of device is used to access it. Marcotte (2010) writes that responsive websites "fit" the screens of different devices, including such as mobile phones, tablets, laptops, and desktop computers, responsively adjusting its layout to suit the display specs of each device. Responsive websites are better for both web developers (who need not create, maintain, and update two sites) and for users, because users can access all the same web content on any device. Responsive websites look consistent across different screens (Steimle 2013)—a plus for marketing purposes, as the library website should maintain a consistent visual brand and should communicate the same important information across different devices.

USER EXPERIENCE (UX) DESIGN FOR THE WEB

User experience (UX) design can be defined as the emotional experience of a user when they interact with a particular physical and virtual interface, or as the totality of the user's perceptions as they interact with a product or service (Walton, 2015). The term was coined in Donald Norman's 1988 book *The Psychology of Everyday Things* in the context of the design of everyday consumer products. Norman argued that product design should eliminate confusion and make products easy to use. User experience design is centered around seven tenets: usefulness, desirability, usability, findability, access, value, and credibility (Schmidt and Etches, 2014; Morville, 2004). In this chapter, UX will be applied to websites.

The term "website UX" is often used interchangeably with "website usability," but they have different meanings. Website usability focuses on whether the website has proper navigation and whether the user can access the needed information; usability relates to access, task completion, and ease of use. User experience goes beyond usability, addressing the user's feelings and emotions (Soegaard, 2018). As an example of the difference, when a user clicks on a broken link, a "404 page not found" will be displayed. Usability guidelines would say to fix the broken link; UX design guidelines would also suggest creating a custom error 404 page with the organization's header and footer in order to deliver a more pleasant user experience.

VISUAL DESIGN

One element of UX design is visual accessibility. As per the Americans with Disabilities Act (ADA), websites should be made accessible to visually impaired users by including "alt" tags in the HTML to provide text descriptions for images on the web page. This enables screen readers to do their job (and also aids in search engine indexing). The ADA also recommends using high contrast between the text color and the background (ADA, 2007).

Even non-visually impaired users can benefit from a concern with visual design. For example, users prefer to read text that is chunked together and organized with headings, and that have a consistent font type and color across the website. For reading on the web, fonts should be sans serif styles (such as Arial or Helvetica), although for print media, serif fonts, such as Times New Roman, are more readable (Pearson, 2016).

ORGANIZING TEXT-HEAVY WEB PAGES: THE "F" PATTERN

Users scan web pages from top to bottom, left to right ("F" orientation); this "F" pattern, confirmed by eye tracking research, means the first line of text is the most important, and the organization's branding should therefore be placed at top left (Pernice, 2017). This scanning pattern also means that web pages should have navigation menus positioned either vertically down the left side (the downstroke of the F) or horizontally across the top (the cross stroke of the F). Even in languages that move from right to left, the "F" pattern still prevails (Pernice, 2017). To ensure that users following the "F" pattern do not overlook important content, Pernice (2017) recommends using the following techniques to draw attention to elements not located on the "F":

- Create headings and subheadings
- Use bold text to emphasize content
- Group related content in a box or border
- Put most important content in the first two paragraphs
- Use bulleted or numbered lists to organize content

ORGANIZING IMAGE-HEAVY WEB PAGES: THE "Z" PATTERN

Readers often scan web pages that are not text heavy using the "Z" pattern (Babich, 2017). This type of scan goes horizontally from the left to right, then diagonally to the bottom left, then across the bottom to the right, like the letter "Z." Touchpoints (discussed in chapter 7) also apply to websites. Each point in the "Z" pattern is a touchpoint. On web pages that are more visual, put important information at the four touchpoints of the letter "Z": top left, top right, bottom left, and bottom right.

A BRIEF WORD ABOUT JARGON

In order to be accessible to users, library websites must be free of jargon. According to a lengthy, multi-year study on library jargon, there is a disconnect between the vocabulary that library users understand and the vocabulary that website developers use (Kupersmith, 2012). Other researchers have reached the same conclusions: user vocabulary preferences do not match up with the vocabulary used on library websites (Polger, 2011; Jurkowski, 2007; Polger, 2014; Fauchelle, 2017). To fix this problem, Felder (2012) suggests using a conversational writing style, with short sentences, active verbs, plenty of headings and subheadings, few to no acronyms or idioms, bulleted lists of content, and—most importantly—*plain language*. Especially from the standpoint of marketing, library websites must use the tone and vocabulary that are appropriate for the users being served. Obscure, outdated, and branded library terms like OPAC, ILL, electronic resource, LibGuides, or cute names for library catalogs should not be used. Conducting market research with your library's users (see chapter 3) and asking them about their understanding of library terms, can help library web developers create a vocabulary list that is more user friendly, which in turn will create a more positive user experience.

SEARCH ENGINE OPTIMIZATION (SEO)

Search engine optimization (SEO) is a way to increase online traffic to a website through a search engine's unpaid results. For SEO, web developers proactively work to get their site indexed by search engines to make it more discoverable. Search engines such as Google, Bing, and Yahoo are extremely secretive about their search algorithms, which are sets of rules that determine search result rankings (Davies, 2018). Search engines use a variety of different algorithms involving different website characteristics: the domain name, the content, the back links, the mobile friendliness, the number and quality of outbound links, and technical aspects such as the speed of the website (Barysevich, 2017).

PageRank is one Google's exclusive algorithms (it is named after one of Google's co-founders, Larry Page). It is a metric that is calculated by counting the number of pages that link back to a specific page. The assumption is that a website will have a higher ranking if more websites link back to it (Adams, 2016). Although Google does not disclose the algorithms they use to rank websites (DeMers, 2018), it is known that Google uses over 200 algorithms when ranking websites in search results.

Search engines automatically index (or crawl) web pages on the Internet to harvest metadata and information for the algorithms. According to Morris (2017), the three most important meta tags are the website's keywords, the site description, and the title. The *description* is usually 1 to 2 sentences (135 to 155 characters), written in plain language (aimed at humans) that briefly summarizes the website's purpose and content. Descriptions should be unique and written specifically for each web page (Ratcliff, 2016). *Keywords* are terms that describe the website's content. The *title* (which is not itself a meta tag, but is in between the header tags) describes the website in one sentence.

Here is a list of some sample HTML meta tags that could be placed at the top of each web page to improve the website's SEO:

```
<html>
<head>
<title>City Public Library in City, State,
United States</title>
<meta http-equiv="Content-Type" content="text/
html; charset=utf-8" />
  <meta http-equiv="Content-Type" content="text/
html; charset=ISO-8859-1">
  <meta name=viewport content="width=device-
width, initial-scale=1">
  <meta name="keywords" content="name of city
and state, public library, library, libraries">
<meta name="description" content="This is the
official website for the City Public Library,
in City, State, USA. We have 98 neighborhood
branches throughout the city with 1 research
location. We are open 365 days a week, 7 days
a week.">
</head>
<body>
</body>
</html>
```

WEBSITE ADVERTISEMENTS

There are some commercial methods to advertise your website, including *banner advertisements*, *Google advertisements*, and *social media advertisements*.

BANNER AND POP-UP ADVERTISEMENTS

A banner advertisement is an online advertisement, usually found at the header or footer or in sidebars on web pages. It is operated and produced by an ad server, which requires embedding the ad into the web page hosting the ad. Banner ads entice customers to click on the attractive banner; clicking directs the user to the advertiser's website through a special link that triggers a small payment to the original site where the banner was.

Advertisement-free websites have a cleaner look, are less cluttered, and are easier to load. Advertisements are distracting; they often disrupt the overall flow of the website with competing content. The worst offenders in these areas are large banners, which cover much screen real estate (especially on mobile) and pop-up ads, which are additional browser windows that open up alongside or floating on top of the primary webpage. Some users install software that blocks all pop-up advertisements; this suppresses all advertisements (including banners) and, in some cases, certain components of the web page. Ad blocking software (AdGuard) and browser extensions (AdBlock Plus, uBlock, Ghostery) thus alter the user experience. Someone using an ad blocker will see the website differently from someone who accesses the same website with advertisements. Due to their distracting quality, many libraries do not use banner or pop-up advertising. Instead, most libraries save money by using their existing websites and social media to promote library events.

GOOGLE ADVERTISEMENTS (PREVIOUSLY KNOWN AS GOOGLE ADWORDS)

Google offers different types of advertising options. The simplest is the *text-based search advertisement*. These text-based advertisements appear at the top or the side of the search results page when users search a particular set of terms on Google. Advertisers are only charged when users click on the link to the website—a model known as pay per click (PPC) pricing.

Google also offers *graphic display advertisements* that appear across various platforms and in various forms: on Gmail as text, as a banner, and on Google-owned apps across a network of over two million websites and apps. Graphic display advertisements target specific audiences, hobbies/interests, and demographics. As with all Google advertisements, ad buyers set a budget, and Google sets the reach depending on that budget. Graphic display advertisement campaigns can target users based on particular hobbies and interests, such as pets, music, news, technology, nightlife, and outdoors (Google Advertisements, 2018).

WEB ANALYTICS

Web analytics gives information about how users are finding and accessing the website. Analytic tools give important information that helps website owners assess SEO efforts. Web analytics is an important element of market research, because it enables marketers to understand who their users are: what country they are from, their I.P. addresses, the time of the day they visited, the page they first accessed, and the search terms they used to access the page.

There are many free and commercial web analytics programs. Some programs are self-hosted (installed on the server) and track usage through web log files. Other programs are hosted externally; these require the addition of a small snippet of code on each web page. Inserting the code snippets can be time consuming and tedious, but it offers detailed analysis of each web page containing the code. One of the most popular website analytics programs is Google Analytics. This free tool offers analysis at the page level and reports two types of measures, *dimensions* and *metrics*. The metric measures the user behavior on the web page and the dimension identifies the context. Dimensions include the user's city, state, country, browser, operating system, and device used to visit the website. Metrics for Google Analytics are actual numeric measures, such as the number of sessions, the pages accessed per session, the bounce rate, and the average session duration. Other analytics programs use similar types of metrics: how users found the website, the page they first landed on, the pages they browsed, the search terms used to find the page, and the time spent on the pages.

Below is an alphabetical list of selected website analytics software programs that help track users' website search behavior and usage.

- AWstats (https://awstats.sourceforge.io/)
- Adobe Analytics (https://www.adobe.com/analytics/adobe-ana lytics.html)
- ChartBeat (https://chartbeat.com/)

- Clicky (https://clicky.com/)
- Coremetrics (https://www-01.ibm.com/software/info/coremetrics -software/)
- Crazy Egg (http://www.crazyegg.com/)
- Etracker (https://www.etracker.com/)
- Facebook Page Insights (https://www.facebook.com/yourpage name/insights/)
- Firestats (http://www.firestats.cc/)
- Foxmetrics (https://www.foxmetrics.com/)
- Gauges (https://get.gaug.es/)
- Google Analytics (http://analytics.google.com)
- Heap Analytics (https://heapanalytics.com/)
- HIStats (http://www.histats.com/)
- Hubspot (https://www.hubspot.com/)
- Kiss Metrics (https://www.kissmetrics.com/)
- Open Web Analytics (http://www.openwebanalytics.com/)
- Stat Counter (http://statcounter.com/)
- Twitter Analytics (https://analytics.twitter.com/ for those with Twitter accounts)
- Webalizer (http://www.webalizer.org/)
- Web Trends Analytics (https://www.webtrends.com/)
- W3 Counter (https://www.w3counter.com/)

USABILITY TESTING

Usability testing in all its applications should be part of the market research process. Usability extends to all aspects of the library (Godfrey, 2015), but this chapter focuses on the usability of library websites, examining their layout, design, and organization. Website usability tests give information about how users navigate through your website to find information by assessing how users interact with site design and layout.

Usability tests can take several forms. Some tests are exploratory, holistically evaluating the website's overall effectiveness and usability or measuring how long it takes a user to complete a specific task. Other tests are comparative, comparing two or more interfaces to see which is more usable. This type of comparative usability testing (also known as A/B testing) examines how the user navigates through two versions of a website to perform a specific task. These types often use a control variable, comparing two websites that are identical except for one feature in order to measure the impact of removing that feature (Schmidt and Etches, 2012).

Usability testing can be either moderated or unmoderated. Moderated testing means that evaluators are with the participants, recording their observations as the users test the site, responding to questions, and helping the user navigate the website. Unmoderated testing means that participants are left on their own, with evaluators remotely observing their clicks and navigational pathways. Unmoderated testing may also be asynchronous, because it allows testing administrators to evaluate the results at any time after participants have completed the tasks. Moderated testing, or synchronous testing, is typically more costly and time consuming since each participant is guided by a trained professional (Schade, 2013).

Participants may be randomly or strategically sampled, and they can be recruited either on location or remotely. Administrators can select testers who have a basic understanding of website usability or they can select usability professionals who will give expert opinions. Administrators can also select a sample who will evaluate a prototype website rather than the final product—a less expensive method of testing, because the website need not be fully complete before testing. Administrators may give participants an anonymous questionnaire to complete, either after accessing the website, or they may ask structured interview questions (Becker and Yannotta, 2013; George, 2005; Manzari and Trinidad-Christensen, 2006; Krug, 2014).

EYE TRACKING SOFTWARE

Some tests may use software to track participants' eye movements when visiting a web page, monitoring their pupils and following where on the page they look and for how long. The data is reported in the form of heat maps and saccade pathways. Heat maps use color—green, yellow, and red—to indicate how long the user's eyes lingered on each location on the web page. Saccade pathways show the visual paths followed by the eyes as they move across the web page, and the data is represented by lines and circles. Circles indicate that the user fixed their gaze on a specific spot and lines show how their eyes moved (Wang, Yang, Liu, Cao, and Ma, 2014; Bojko, 2006; Chu, Paul, and Ruel, 2009).

CARD SORTING

Other usability tests may use card sorting, a method that helps administrators understand how users perceive the website's information architecture. Participants are asked to create a category tree by dividing pre-labeled cards into different topical categories. This test helps webmasters understand the navigation, structure, and overall organization of the website (Paladino, Klentzin, and Mills, 2017; Paul, 2008). Card sorting, which can use printed cards or online card sorting tools, can be open, closed, or hybrid tests. In open card sorting, users organize cards into categories they assign themselves; in closed card sorting, users sort cards into pre-defined categories; and hybrid cart sorting combines both open and closed card sorting (Croft, 2014).

EMAIL MARKETING

Opt-in email is an example of what Seth Godin (1999) calls *permission marketing*. With this marketing technique, organizations ask each customer for permission to include their email addresses in the company's database. Once permission is granted, the customer receives commercial messages that promote the company's products and services. In this era of online shopping (according to a 2016 Pew Research study, 80 percent of U.S. adults shop online; Smith and Anderson, 2016), this can be a way for companies to reach large swathes of their customer bases. All commercial transactions require a name and email address, and once a consumer enters their email into the company website, they are giving permission for the company to contact them. They may later be able to remove themselves from these email lists, but the company has their email address.

Email marketing—sending solicited messages to a list of customers who have voluntarily provided their email addresses—is a powerful and relatively inexpensive way to reach customers. Email marketing can be used to build customer loyalty, trust, and brand awareness. It is one of the most powerful ways of directly reaching customers, since subscribers have voluntarily added their emails to the company's list. Emails from companies may be either transactional emails or direct marketing emails. Transactional emails are emails sent for housekeeping reasons: to confirm a purchase or a user's subscription to the email list, or confirm receipt of a customer email or return. Marketing emails, which are often sent via email marketing software, sends curated messages that promote specific products and services. Emailing marketing programs resemble a large mailing list, but unlike listservs, which promote user interaction, email marketing disseminates information one-way; it cannot receive or distribute replies. To ensure that email marketing does not become spam, it needs to be visually appealing, compelling, and well-targeted in order to connect with customers.

PLANNING MARKETING EMAILS FOR LIBRARIES

Compelling, brief messages that connect the library's services and resources with local culture can help draw in more users. According to Lynch (2018), the frequency of marketing emails should be consistently monitored. If subscriber rate decreases, it could mean that there are too many messages being sent out. Libraries should gather data from their particular target audience about email frequency, but a safe median is one to two emails a week. Sending out too many messages will cause information overload for customers and they may unsubscribe (Zhang, Kumar, and Kosguner, 2017). Marketing messages might be planned around the calendar—federal holidays, special cultural festivals such as Thanksgiving, Martin Luther King Jr. Day, Presidents' Day, Lincoln's birthday, Banned Books Week, National Library Week, and Labor Day weekend are all potentially good times to send marketing emails. It is a good idea to compile a list of different topics and tie-ins then create a schedule of when to send marketing emails. For example, on National

Puppy Day, an email message can be sent to promote the Lassie book series for children, an upcoming therapy dogs program, and a library visit from a dog trainer who will teach users how to communicate more effectively with newly adopted dogs.

GETTING PERMISSION

When creating your subscriber list, you should always get permission to collect people's emails, and always give them a way to opt out of emails or unsubscribe to your email list. The Federal Trade Commission's (FTC) CAN-SPAM Act sets the rules for commercial email, bulk email, and commercial messages (which are any email messages whose primary purpose is to advertise or promote a commercial product or service; FTC, 2018). The FTC offers some basic guidelines for email marketing:

1. Provide an authentic header ("From")
2. Convey the nature of the advertisement in the subject line
3. Identify the message as an advertisement in the message itself
4. Include a physical mailing address in the message footer
5. Ensure that there is an unsubscribe option
6. Fulfill unsubscribe requests promptly

PERSONALIZING EMAILS TO THE AUDIENCE

To ensure that email messages do not look spammy, email marketing must be personalized to your audience's needs. It must contain the branding and color scheme of the organization and use original, authentic photographs (not stock photographs).

Messages should avoid large blocks of text, instead breaking text up with photographs. Text should contain headings and subheadings and numbered and bulleted lists. Messages should be responsive in order to be accessible whether a user views the content on a mobile device, tablet, laptop computer, or desktop (Bhuptani, 2018).

INCLUDING A CALL TO ACTION AND TESTING YOUR MESSAGE

As discussed in chapter 5, a call to action (CTA) asks consumers to respond immediately. The task is active and urgent in tone, asking users to call now, email now, or click on the link. A CTA is usually used in the beginning of email marketing messages to grab attention (Mohammadi, Malekian, Nosrati, and Karimi, 2013; Georgieva, 2012).

Always conduct a pre-test to ensure that your message will be properly sent out to the subscriber list. Many programs allow the administrator to conduct these test runs and to preview content before the message is sent. For example, Google's Mail Merge for Gmail allows the administrator to conduct a test run to see if the mail merge was successfully executed. Conducting a pre-test eliminates duplicate messages, making the organization look good (George, 2013).

DEVELOP A POSTING SCHEDULE

Email content should be relevant and timely, and creating a posting schedule that matches the week or month can help ensure that it is. Libraries should follow a consistent posting schedule. Since Throwback Thursday (#TBT) has gained popularity, perhaps sending themed messages on Thursdays, including older photographs of the library from many years ago and facts about library history, could promote the library building. For example, a message might include the fact that on Thursday October 1, 1998, the most popular book checked out was *Harry Potter and the Sorcerer's Stone*.

EMAIL MARKETING METRICS

Marketers may wish to examine the impact of their email marketing efforts. Most email marketing campaign tools offer metrics that give information about what your subscribers do with your messages.

The *open rate* is the percentage of people who actually opened the email message. According to Neely (2014), a good email open rate is between 20 percent and 30 percent. Check your email marketing metrics on a regular basis to determine whether your open rate is improving.

The *click-through rate* (CTR) is the percentage of people who open the message and click on a link inside. A click-through rate of 20 percent to 25 percent is considered adequate, according to Neely (2014). To keep click-through rates high, be sure that your emails are responsive; customers read email messages across many different devices.

The *conversion rate* is the percentage of people who opened the email and performed a task such as completing a form or purchasing a product. In the case of libraries, the conversion rate might be helpful for emails promoting specific events; the conversion rate would be the percentage of recipients who opened the email and completed the registration form with the intention of attending the library program (Harbin, 2018).

Earnings per click is a metric that measures the total earnings of a particular campaign, divided by the total number of emails sent in that specific marketing campaign. For example, if the organization sent 500 messages and earned $10,000, then the earnings per click would be $20. (This metric is not relevant to libraries since they are not selling products or services, but it is an important marketing measure that is worth understanding.)

The *unsubscribe rate*, as the name suggests, is the percentage of customers who unsubscribe from the email list. If your unsubscribe rate is higher than 0.2 percent, you should take a long look at your messages and see what you are doing wrong. Are they too frequent? Spammy? Do they not include useful content targeted to your audience?

The *abuse rate* (or *complaint rate*) is the percentage of subscribers who labeled a particular message as spam. The complaint rate should not go above 1 percent.

The *delivery rate* is the percentage of all emails that successfully reach their intended recipients. The delivery rate should be between 90 percent and 95 percent (Neely, 2014).

A *hard bounce* occurs when a message is sent to an email address that no longer exists. Hard bounces can occur when messages are marked as spam by algorithms; when this happens, the domain that delivers the email marketing messages might be banned. It's important to keep track of hard bounces to sustain the integrity of your mailing list.

A *soft bounce* occurs when an email message cannot be successfully delivered to the recipient because their mailbox is full.

The *forward rate* (or *share rate*) is the percentage of subscribers who click on the "forward to a friend" or "share this" link. The forward rate will likely increase if social media sharing buttons are included in the email message.

The *churn rate* is the total annual percentage loss of subscribers after the unsubscribes, hard bounces, and abuse complaints. The average churn rate is between 20 percent and 25 percent (Neely, 2014).

The *list growth rate* is the total annual percentage increase of subscribers. It is calculated by taking the difference between the losses (unsubscribes and abuse complaints) and new subscribers, divided by the total number of subscribers (Harbin, 2018).

Selected list of Email Marketing Tools

Active Campaign (https://www.activecampaign.com/)
Active Trail (https://www.activetrail.com/)
AWeber (https://www.aweber.com/)
Benchmark Email (https://www.benchmarkemail.com/)
Cakemail (https://www.cakemail.com/)
Campaigner (http://www.campaigner.com)
Campaign monitor (https://www.campaignmonitor.com/)
Constant contact (http://www.constantcontact.com)
ConvertKit (https://convertkit.com/)
Drip (http://www.drip.com/)
Flashissue for Gmail (https://www.flashissue.com/)
Get Response (https://www.getresponse.com/)
iContact (https://www.icontact.com/)
Infusionsoft (https://www.infusionsoft.com/)
Litmus (https://litmus.com/)
MadMimi (http://www.madmimi.com/)
Mailchimp (http://www.mailchimp.com)
MailJet (http://www.mailjet.com/)
Reachmail (https://www.reachmail.net/)
SendinBlue (https://www.sendinblue.com/)
SendGrid (https://www.sendgrid.com/)
Vertical Response (http://www.verticalresponse.com/)

CONCLUSION

Digital tools such as online advertising can be used to promote and raise awareness of the library's services and resources, and this chapter examined one of the most important of these digital tools: the library website, a very cost-effective method with a large reach and a built-in audience. This chapter gave details about how to apply user-centered design to library websites to ensure that this tool is used to maximum advantage. This chapter also discussed using opt-in email marketing, an example of permission marketing, and discussed the elements of successful email marketing campaigns. It also discussed the basics of analytics and SEO—metrics that you can use to assess the success of your online marketing efforts.

REFERENCES

Abbas, Shahzad, Shanawar Khalid, and Fakhar Abbas Hashmi. 2017. "Library websites as source of marketing of library resources: An empirical study of HEC recognized universities of Pakistan." *Qualitative and Quantitative Methods in Libraries* 5, no. 1: 235–249.

Adams, Chelsea. 2016. "What is Google PageRank, how is it earned & does it still matter?" June 3. https://www.bruceclay.com/blog/what-is-pagerank/ (Accessed August 1, 2018).

Americans with Disabilities Act. 2007. "ADA best practices tool kit for state and local governments." May 7. https://www.ada.gov/pcatoolkit/chap5tool kit.htm (Accessed August 21, 2018).

Babich, Nick. 2017. "Z-shaped pattern for reading web content." June 16. https://uxplanet.org/z-shaped-pattern-for-reading-web-content-ce1135f 92f1c (Accessed July 1, 2018).

Barysevich, Aleh. 2017. "4 most important ranking factors, according to SEO industry studies." February 3. https://www.searchenginejournal.com/4-im portant-ranking-factors-according-seo-industry-studies/ (Accessed July 1, 2018).

Becker, Danielle A., and Lauren Yannotta. 2013. "Modeling a library website redesign process: Developing a user-centered website through usability test-ing." *Information Technology and Libraries* 32, no. 1: 6–22.

Bhuptani, Jaymin. 2018. "The current state of email marketing programming: What can and can't be used." March 22. https://www.smashingmagazine

.com/2018/03/email-marketing-programming-best-practices/ (Accessed August 10, 2018).

Bojko, Agnieszka. 2006. "Using eye tracking to compare web page designs: A case study." *Journal of Usability Studies* 1, no. 3: 112–120.

Casey, Sean. 2017. 2016 Nielsen social media report. January 17. http://www .nielsen.com/us/en/insights/reports/2017/2016-nielsen-social-media-report .html (Accessed September 1, 2018).

Chu, Sauman, Nora Paul, and Laura Ruel. 2009. "Using eye tracking technology to examine the effectiveness of design elements on news websites." *Information Design Journal* (IDJ) 17, no. 1: 31–43.

Croft, Pierre. 2014. "Card sorting beginner's guide—Improving your information architecture." October 20. https://www.smashingmagazine .com/2014/10/improving-information-architecture-card-sorting-beginners -guide/ (Accessed July 1, 2018).

Davies, Dave. 2018. " How search engine algorithms work: Everything you need to know." May 10. https://www.searchenginejournal.com/how-search -algorithms-work/252301/ (Accessed July 12, 2018).

DeMers, Jayson. 2018. "How much do we really know about Google's ranking algorithm?" February 7. https://www.forbes.com/sites/jayson demers/2018/02/07/how-much-do-we-really-know-about-googles-ranking -algorithm/#1fcb83f655bb (Accessed July 23, 2018).

Fauchelle, Michael Alexander. 2017. "Libraries of Babel: Exploring library language and its suitability for the community." *Library Review* 66, no. 8/9: 612–627.

Federal Trade Commission. 2018. "CAN-SPAM Act: A compliance guide for business." https://www.ftc.gov/tips-advice/business-center/guidance/ can-spam-act-compliance-guide-business (Accessed September 2, 2018).

Felder, Lynda. 2012. *Writing for the web: Creating compelling web content using words, pictures, and sound.* Berkeley: New Riders.

George, Carole A. 2005. "Usability testing and design of a library website: An iterative approach." *OCLC Systems & Services: International Digital Library Perspectives* 21, no. 3: 167–180.

George, Kevin. 2013. "6 steps to effective email testing." April 24. https:// emailmonks.com/blog/email-marketing/6-steps-to-effective-email-testing/ (Accessed July 26, 2018).

Georgieva, Magdalena. 2012. "An introduction to email marketing: How to execute & measure successful email marketing." http://cache.winntech.net/ docs/ebooks/An-Introduction-to-Email-Marketing.pdf (Accessed August 15, 2018).

Godfrey, Krista. 2015. "Creating a culture of usability." *Weave: Journal of Library User Experience* 1, no. 3. http://dx.doi.org/10.3998/weave.12535642.0001.301 (Accessed August 1, 2018).

Godin, Seth. 1999. *Permission marketing: Turning strangers into friends and friends into customers.* New York: Simon & Schuster.

Google Advertisements. 2018. "Grow your business with Google Ads." https://ads.google.com/home/

Hagen, Eddy. 2017. "Reality check on digital advertising vs print: Trust and influence are much lower with digital." https://www.insights4print .ceo/2017/02/reality-check-on-digital-advertising-vs-print/ (Accessed September 1, 2018).

Harbin, Lane. 2018. https://www.campaignmonitor.com/blog/email-marketing/2018/04/10-metrics-every-email-marketer-needs-to-know/ (Accessed August 2, 2018).

Jurkowski, Odin L. 2007. "School library website terminology." *Library Hi Tech* 25, no. 3: 387–395.

Kaba, Abdoulaye. 2011. "Marketing information resources and services on the web: Current status of academic libraries in the United Arab Emirates." *Information Development* 27, no. 1: 58–65.

Kaur, Kiran. 2009. "Marketing the academic library on the web." *Library Management* 30, no. 6/: 454–468.

Krug, Steve. 2014. *Don't make me think, revisited!: A common sense approach to Web Usability.* Berkeley: New Riders.

Kupersmith, John. 2012. "Library terms that users understand." https://escholarship.org/uc/item/3qq499w7 (Accessed August 23, 2018).

Lynch, Kevin. 2018. "How frequently should you email your list?" April 20. https://www.infusionsoft.com/business-success-blog/marketing/email-marketing/how-often-should-you-email-your-list (Accessed September 30, 2018).

Manzari, Laura, and Jeremiah Trinidad-Christensen. 2006. "User-centered design of a website for library and information science students: Heuristic evaluation and usability testing." *Information Technology and Libraries* 25, no. 3: 163–169.

Marcotte, Ethan. 2010. "Responsive web design." May 25. https://alistapart .com/article/responsive-web-design (Accessed August 20, 2018).

Mohammadi, Mehdi, Kamran Malekian, Masoud Nosrati, and Ronak Karimi. 2013. "Email marketing as a popular type of small business advertisement: A short review." *Australian Journal of Basic and Applied Sciences* 7, no. 4: 786–790.

Morris, Kate. 2017. "SEO Meta Tags." April 13. https://moz.com/blog/seo -meta-tags (Accessed August 1, 2018).

Morville, Peter. 2004. "User experience design." June 21. http://semanticstu dios.com/user_experience_design/ (Accessed August 12, 2018).

Mueller, Daniel R. 2011. "Digital advertising vs. print advertising." September 12. https://smallbusiness.chron.com/digital-advertising-vs-print-advertising -22836.html (Accessed September 1, 2018).

Neely, Pamella. 2014. "11 email marketing metrics ranked in order of impor- tance." October 1. https://www.practicalecommerce.com/11-email-market ing-metrics-ranked-in-order-of-importance (Accessed August 12, 2018).

Norman, Donald A. 1988. *The psychology of everyday things.* New York: Basic Books.

Paladino, Emily B., Jacqueline C. Klentzin, and Chloe P. Mills. 2017. "Card sorting in an online environment: Key to involving online-only student population in usability testing of an academic library website?" *Journal of Library & Information Services in Distance Learning* 11, no. 1–2: 37–49.

Paul, Celeste Lyn. 2008. "A modified delphi approach to a new card sorting methodology." *Journal of Usability Studies* 4, no. 1: 7–30.

Pearson, Chuck. 2016. "Typography on the web." September 21. https:// medium.com/rareview/typography-on-the-web-4cd494d6b165 (Accessed August 1, 2018).

Pernice, Kara. 2017. "F-shaped pattern of reading on the web: Misunderstood, but still relevant (even on mobile)." November 12. https://www.nngroup .com/articles/f-shaped-pattern-reading-web-content/ (Accessed August 2, 2018).

Polger, Mark Aaron. 2011. "Student preferences in library website vocabu- lary." *Library Philosophy and Practice.* https://digitalcommons.unl.edu/ libphilprac/618/ (Accessed August 23, 2018).

Polger, Mark Aaron. 2014. "Controlling our vocabulary: Language consis- tency in a library context." *The Indexer* 32, no. 1: 32–37.

Rainie, Lee, and Andrew Perrin. 2017. "10 facts about smartphones as the iPhone turns 10." June 28. http://www.pewresearch.org/fact-tank/2017/06/28/10 -facts-about-smartphones/ (Accessed August 20, 2018).

Ratcliff, Christopher. 2016. "How to write meta descriptions for SEO (with good and bad examples)." May 26. https://searchenginewatch .com/2016/05/26/how-to-write-meta-descriptions-for-seo-with-good-and -bad-examples/ (Accessed August 12, 2018).

Schade, Amy. 2013. "Remote usability tests: Moderated and unmoderated." October 12. https://www.nngroup.com/articles/remote-usability-tests/ (Ac- cessed August 1, 2018).

Schmidt, Aaron, and Amanda Etches. 2012. *User Experience (UX) Design for Libraries*. Library and Information Technology Association (LITA).

Schmidt, Aaron, and Amanda Etches. 2014. *Useful, usable, desirable: Applying user experience design to your library*. ALA editions.

Sinha, Mridu. 2016. "Online marketing vs. print advertising: Which is best media to achieve max. ROI?" July 1. https://www.linkedin.com/pulse/online -marketing-vs-print-advertising-which-best-max-mridu-sinha-/

Smith, Aaron, and Monica Anderson. 2016. "Online shopping and e-commerce." December 19. http://www.pewinternet.org/2016/12/19/online-shopping-and -e-commerce/ (Accessed July 1, 2018).

Soegaard, Mads. 2018. "Usability: A part of the user experience." August 24. https://www.interaction-design.org/literature/article/usability-a-part-of-the -user-experience (Accessed August 25, 2018).

Steimle, Josh. 2013. "Why your business needs a responsive website before 2014." November 8. *Forbes*. https://www.forbes.com/sites/josh steimle/2013/11/08/why-your-business-needs-a-responsive-website-be fore-2014/

Two Sides. 2017. "Print and paper in a digital world: An international survey of consumer preferences, attitudes and trust." https://twosides.info/wp -content/uploadvertisements/2018/05/Two_Sides_Print_and_Paper_In_A_ Digital_World_UK-edition-web.pdf (Accessed July 1, 2018).

Walton, Graham. 2015. "What user experience (UX) means for academic libraries." *New Review of Academic Librarianship* 21, no.1: 1–3.

Wang, Qiuzhen, Sa Yang, Manlu Liu, Zike Cao, and Qingguo Ma. 2014. "An eye-tracking study of website complexity from cognitive load perspective." *Decision support systems* 62: 1–10.

Welch, Jeanie M. 2005. "The electronic welcome mat: The academic library website as a marketing and public relations tool." *The Journal of Academic Librarianship* 31, no. 3: 225–228.

Zhang, Xi, V. Kumar, and Koray Cosguner. 2017. "Dynamically managing a profitable email marketing program." *Journal of Marketing Research* 54, no. 6: 851–866.

CHAPTER 9

Social Media Marketing

IN THIS CHAPTER

- Introduction to social media
- Explanations of the major social networking sites and how to use them
- Posting strategically
- Automating social media posting
- Social media policy guidelines and sample policies
- Social media advertisements
- Social media analytics

INTRODUCTION TO SOCIAL MEDIA

Social media sites, also known as social networking sites, allow companies, organizations (like libraries), celebrities, and public figures to communicate directly with their target audience. Social media is an extension of the web; it's part of Web 2.0, a newer generation of websites that provide two-way communication. Web 2.0 started in the early 2000s with the advent of weblogs (also known as blogs). Blogs were user-generated websites that were topical in nature and were updated periodically, like a newspaper or magazine. Anyone could create a blog and document their life or activities—a kind of online journal. Some blogs became so popular that they began generating income, and some bloggers became celebrities. For example, Perez Hilton's famous celebrity gossip blog started in 2004 (Widdicombe, 2010), and he became a household name. Julie Powell's blog, which documented her project of preparing every meal from Julia Child's cookbook, became a *New York Times* bestseller and a major Hollywood film, *Julie and Julia*, enabling Julie Powell to quit her day job and become a full-time author (Biography.com, 2014).

Some celebrities and other public figures have bypassed publicists and public relations departments, instead connecting directly with their audiences through social media. Before Web 2.0, websites were a one-way mode of communication; organizations provided information for user consumption, and the user remained a passive receiver. With social media, the user participates in content creation and is able to engage organizations directly in conversation. Social media also allows the user to produce content of their own. Users can now write articles and publish them using free blog software such as Wordpress or Blogger. They can microblog in 280 characters on Twitter, they can post photos and share their experiences via Facebook and Instagram, produce professional quality video and post it on YouTube, or they can record professional audio programs and deliver them as podcasts. Libraries can use all of these social media tools for marketing.

FACEBOOK

Facebook is a social networking website that was originally developed as a online student directory—a "face book"—at Harvard University, by then-undergraduate students Mark Zuckerberg, Eduardo Saverin, Dustin Moskovitz, Andrew McCollum, and Chris Hughes (Brügger, 2015). It was originally restricted to students with Harvard.edu email addresses, but it soon opened to any student with a .edu address, and finally to the public. It is now a publicly traded company with more than two billion daily active users (Osman, 2018). Facebook is an empty platform (meaning that it supplies no content—all its content is user generated) that enables people to communicate with each other, interact, engage, share information, and develop online communities.

Facebook enables organizations like libraries to directly engage with their users, communicating, promoting events, providing information, and creating community. Facebook is free for individuals and organizations, and libraries can create individual profiles (not recommended, as these are meant to be personal pages for individual users), organizational pages, or groups. The difference between *pages* and *groups* is subtle. A *group* is a page that is managed by an individual profile (or many individual profiles); the profiles of all group members and managers (called moderators) are visible to all group members (and sometimes, in the case of public groups, to anyone). *Pages*, which are a relatively new development from Facebook, are designed to be slightly less interactive; individuals can "like" the page, which is run by individual whose personal Facebook account is not attached to the page. In other words, the page owners' identities are masked. A group can be traced back to an individual profile, but a page cannot. Libraries can register as either a page or a group; both have similar options for communicating with their users.

Facebook's user-generated content is populated through text-based status messages, links to external websites, photos, and video content. Its mission is "to give people the power to build community and bring the world closer together, to stay connected with friends and family, to discover what's going on in the world, and to share and express what matters to them" (Facebook Investor Relations, 2018). Recently, Facebook introduced Facebook Stories, user-generated photos or videos that update the user's status, then disappear after 24 hours. For users to keep content posted as a Facebook Story, they must save it on their camera or send it to a Facebook friend. This new feature responds to Snapchat and other social media tools, offering filters and special lenses that users can apply to photos or videos of themselves (Newton, 2017).

According to a 2018 Pew Research Study, about 68 percent of U.S. adults use Facebook (Smith and Anderson, 2018; Gramlich, 2018). Most users visit Facebook once a day (74 percent), so libraries should probably post once a day (Smith and Anderson, 2018; Gramlich, 2018). Most Facebook users are between 30 and 49 years old (Smith and Anderson, 2018).

Facebook Posting Guidelines

Ideally, users should post to Facebook five to ten times per week (Hughes 2016). Most users are online on Thursday and Friday afternoons between

1 pm and 3 pm, so this is a good time for libraries to post to ensure that their messages are seen. Content can be manually posted or posts can be scheduled using social media management software (discussed later in this chapter). Libraries' Facebook posts should be written in an informal, conversational tone, be user centered, promote specific services and resources to their local community, should include an original photograph, hyperlinks to external content, hashtags, and should be guided by a social media policy.

Facebook Advertising

In Facebook advertising, individuals and organizations set a predefined budget amount; Facebook then works within that budget to disseminate the ads to a specific audience. Facebook ads can be charged by the click or by the impression (cost per click or cost per impression). Another advertising option involves *boosting* existing posts (paying for these posts to have a larger audience reach). *Boosted posts* are the most basic, flexible ad available on Facebook, although it does not resemble a typical advertisement.

To create more formal Facebook advertisements, advertisers select a format (single image, slideshow, video) and the ad text. Users can select a predefined audience based on geography, gender, language, and age range. Facebook ads may be designed to meet various types of campaign objectives: to increase brand awareness or reach, to boost traffic to a web page, to increase user engagement, to get people to install an app, to promote company-produced videos, to collect potential customer leads, to convert passive users into active customers, to advertise specific items from a catalog, or to promote specific store locations based on users' geolocations.

Libraries that have Facebook pages (not groups) can create free posts with text, image, and video. These posts can easily be transformed into advertisements that will be automatically shown to a specific target audience, defined by the customer. This type of advertising may be useful for libraries that want to promote one database or raise attendance at an important fundraising event that benefits the library. These types of one-shot Facebook ads are affordable; customers select their budget and Facebook offers options (type of advertisement, extent of reach, and time period) that fit into that budget (Facebook Business, 2018a).

Some libraries have successfully used Facebook ads to target particular markets. For example, Chan (2011) ran a two-month Facebook advertising campaign promoting library services to a targeted audience (of students who had Facebook accounts) who were not registered library users (Chan, 2011). Similarly, Young, Tate, Rossmann, and Hansen (2014) used Facebook advertising to increase their library's audience and to raise awareness of their services and resources. They found that boosted posts were more effective than advertisements.

TWITTER

Twitter is a free microblogging tool that enables users to post short posts (280 characters, up from the original 140 characters), which are known as tweets. It is used by 24 percent of U.S. adults (Smith and Anderson, 2018) and has 328 million monthly active users (Osman, 2018). The group who uses it most frequently is 18- to 29-year-olds, 40 percent of whom are on Twitter (Pew Research Center, 2018).

Libraries have been using Twitter for many years to promote events, services, and resources and engage directly with their users. This free tool lets libraries communicate time-sensitive information and post links that are relevant to library users. To make themselves discoverable, libraries should select a handle (username) that is aligned with their library's name. Twitter imposes a 15-character limit for usernames/handles, so some libraries may use acronyms in their handles. Usernames should match the library's brand.

Twitter's dashboard provides some analytics information: the number of tweets, Following, Followers, Likes, Lists, and Moments. The three important features are

- Following: the Twitter users that you follow
- Followers: Twitter users who follow you
- Lists: topical sub-lists, created by the user from the larger Following list (usually topic-specific: you might create an "academic libraries" list, or a "library bloggers" list)

Tweeting/ Liking/Retweeting

A tweet is a short message posted by a user to Twitter. A retweet (RT) is a repost of an original tweet to another user's timeline—similar to sharing on Facebook. Retweets usually mean that another user endorses, likes, agrees with, or feels impassioned about a particular tweet. Twitter limits users to no more than 2,400 tweets per day, including retweets (Twitter, 2018). A like (clicking the empty heart beneath a tweet) indicates that another user likes (or agrees with) a tweet. This is a separate action from retweeting. Organizations should tweet three times a day (Hughes, 2016; Parsons, 2016), and they should only retweet content that has not been retweeted more than six times (McCoy, 2016).

Organizations should aim for a ratio of three retweets per tweet (Hertvik, 2014). This means that libraries should post one original tweet per day and retweet the tweets of similar organizations throughout the day. Academic libraries, for example, may tweet about a particular library service, resource, or event and retweet news about local events in the community and anything related to education, the local college campus, and the local community—anything relevant to their targeted audience.

According to Estes, Schade, and Nielsen (2009), an ideal tweet should

- focus on one subject
- contain a concise message
- provide an optional short hyperlink to external content
- contain an attractive image
- contain a hashtag that describes the content and makes the tweet discoverable

Here is a specific example that follows these criteria:

Celebrate #bannedbooks @nameoflibrary #nameoflibrary by visiting our display on the 1st floor and slideshow on our website http://bit .ly/nameoflibrary

You can judge the quality of your tweets by examining the ratio of replies to retweets. If the number of replies to a tweet is higher than the number of retweets, then the quality of the original Tweet is bad (Isaac, 2018). High-quality tweets compel users to retweet. Tweets containing images receive 35 percent more retweets and tweets with video links 28 percent more retweets than plain text tweets (Rogers, 2014). According to Dan Zarrella (2009), retweeted tweets often contained hyperlinks to external content and while most tweeting occurs during business hours and in the evening, most retweeting takes place between 3 pm and midnight (p. 20). Thursday is the day with the most tweet activity and Friday has the highest volume of retweets (p. 21).

Mentions / Replies / Direct Messages

A mention (@) is when a Twitter user posts about another user, or replies to that user. The "@" symbol, which notifies the tagged user, is used for both "replying" to or "mentioning" another user. Replying differs from a direct message (DM). Replies appear on the timeline of users who follow both the tweeter and the tagged person; a direct message is a private exchange between two Twitter users that does not appear on either user's Twitter feed.

Hashtags

A hashtag is a keyword that describes the content of a user's tweet. Like tags, hashtags assign descriptive words to specific posts in order to make them discoverable. Hashtags always start with a number sign (#) with no space between the # and the word. Not all tweets need hashtags, but including them allows other users interested in particular topics to find your tweets. Twitter allows searches for usernames, hashtags, and keywords.

Choosing Hashtags

There are many resources that can help you identify cultural festivals and national holidays that can be hashtagged in libraries' relevant promotional tweets. Chase's Calendar of Events is one of the most authoritative directories, containing 12,500 entries from 196 countries with something for every day of the year: historical events, civic observances, and famous birthdays, and special days, weeks, and months, including public holidays for each nation. This reference tool has published an updated edition each year since 1957, and purchasers of the print edition also receive access to a companion website (Chase and Chase, 2018).

When you are logged into Twitter, you will see trending hashtags listed at the bottom left corner of the home page. The trending hashtags are somewhat personalized; Twitter shows you trends based on user location and who you follow. Third-party websites such as Trends24 (https://trends24.in) identify trending hashtags based only on geographic location; for example, New York City's URL is https://trends24.in/united-states/new-york/. The page's list of local trending hashtags is updated hourly. Below is a selected list of popular library-related hashtags that may be used for marketing purposes. Remember, a successful tweet should be succinct and should include short, active text with an image, video, or external link and a hashtag.

- ALA's Library Card Sign Up Month (September): #librarycard signup
- National Library Week: #nlw, #nationallibraryweek
- Banned Books Week: #bannedbooks #bannedbooksweek
- Love My Library: #lovemylibrary #librarylove
- I Love Libraries: #ilovelibraries
- Daily Read Days: #mondayreads, #tuesdayreads #wednesdayreads #thursdayreads #fridayreads #saturdayreads #sundayreads
- Library Life: #librarylife
- Libraries Transform: #librariestransform
- Libraries Strong: #librariesstrong
- Monday Morning: #MondayMorning
- Throwback Thursday: #TBT
- Monday Motivation: #MondayMotivation
- Shelfie (selfie in a library): #shelfie

Twitter Advertisements

Twitter Promote Mode ($99/month) is an automatic service that promotes the tweets you would normally post anyway. Promoted tweets are targeted to audiences in *either* select geographic markets (such as the United States, Japan, or the United Kingdom) or users with particular interests and hobbies, but not both. Interest-targeted promotions allow advertisers to select up to five "interests/hobbies," and location-targeted promotions allow advertisers to select up to five metropolitan areas (Twitter Advertisements, 2018).

Twitter advertising campaigns are formal advertising campaigns that are priced based on the options you choose. Twitter advertisements should not contain hashtags (#) or mentions (@) because the goal is to keep users from clicking out of the advertisement. Campaigns allow advertisers to select a target audience based on geography, followers of particular Twitter accounts, or interests (Twitter Advertisements, 2018). There are eight different types of campaigns to choose from:

1. **Awareness**: This type of campaign aims to get as many users to view your tweet as possible. Advertisers pay for the number of impressions, because more impressions means more exposure, more followers, more retweets, and more profile clicks and website visits (Twitter Advertisements, 2018).

2. **Website Clicks or Conversions**: These campaigns, which work on both desktop and mobile platforms, are designed as call-to-action campaigns. Tweets are targeted to specific audiences who will click on the provided link and visit the website. Advertisers pay for the number of website link clicks (Twitter Advertisements, 2018).

3. **Followers**: These campaigns, which are designed for both desktop and mobile platforms, aim to attract more followers (not organically). Advertisers only pay for new followers (Twitter Advertisements, 2018).

4. **Tweet Engagement**: These campaigns, which are designed for both desktop and mobile platforms, are tweets that are promoted to spark engagement (retweets, replies, likes, and new followers). Advertisers pay for initial engagements from the campaign tweets, not for organic engagements (Twitter Advertisements, 2018).

5. **App Installs**: This type of campaign is geared toward mobile devices, for the advertisers want users to download their app. These tweets are promoted to a target audience who are likely to download the app. Advertisers pay only for the number of app clicks or installs (Twitter Advertisements, 2018).

6. **App re-engagement**: Designed for mobile users, these campaigns are aimed at getting existing Twitter followers to engage with your app. The campaign is targeted to a specific audience of users who are likely to engage with the app. Advertisers only pay for the number of app clicks (Twitter Advertisements, 2018).

7. **Video View**: Designed for both desktop and mobile devices, this type of campaign is aimed at increasing the number of video views by auto-playing promoted videos when users scroll through their Twitter feed. Twitter defines a "video view" as a video that is watched in 50 percent view for more than 2 seconds and a 3s/100 percent view as when a video is watched in 100 percent view for more than 3 seconds. Advertisers only pay for the number of views on promoted videos (Twitter Advertisements, 2018).

8. **In-Stream Video**: This type of campaign, designed for both desktop and mobile devices, also aims to increase the number of video views, but these video ads are played in the video player rather than being presented as a banner link. These advertisements can be played before the actual video (pre-roll), during the video (mid-roll), or after the video (post-roll). Advertisers pay for the number of in-stream video views (Twitter Advertisements, 2018).

INSTAGRAM

Instagram is a photo and video sharing tool, owned by Facebook, with 700 million monthly active users (Osman, 2018). Unlike other social media, users can only post to Instagram from mobile devices, although Instagram photos can be viewed across many devices, including desktop computers. Marketing photos posted to Instagram should be captioned with descriptive text and hashtags that are relevant to the content. Instagram is highly visual, so it is important to use high-quality photos (Hughes, 2016). Once a day, users should post a high-quality image, taking advantage of the photo filter options pre-installed in the app, or an Instagram Story, which is a short video, lasting between 15 seconds and 60 seconds. Instagram Videos (as distinct from Stories) can last as long as 60 seconds, but Hsiao (2018) recommends that marketing videos be no longer than 30 seconds.

Libraries can get creative with the visuals they use to promote their libraries' services, resources, physical spaces, events, and programs. For example, a library might promote an upcoming program by uploading an image or a short video clip relating to the event, or promote a specific book title, aligning it with the release date of a film (i.e., *Fifty Shades of Grey* film paired with the book series), using a shot of the book cover. Instagram allows viewers to repost content (similar to Facebook sharing or retweeting) to ensure that the library gets credit for photos that others repost, tag, or otherwise identify your photos. Some libraries even personalize their postings to connect with users, humanizing staff by posting staff photos, which promotes library employees and helps increase morale and staff engagement (Cribbs, 2017).

Popular Library Hashtags on Instagram

Instagram, like Twitter, uses creative hashtags and descriptive text to make posts discoverable. Instagram hashtags can be similar to hashtags Twitter (see list on p. 244), there are some Instagram-specific hashtags for libraries:

#librariesofinstagram
#bookstagram
#shelfie
#libraries
#lovelibraries
#librarylove
#instabook
#librarylife
#bookface

VIDEO MARKETING: YOUTUBE AND VIMEO

YouTube is a video-sharing website with more than 1 billion active users monthly (Osman, 2018). According to a 2018 Pew Research study, 73 percent of U.S. adults use YouTube. Approximately 94 percent of YouTube users are between the ages of 18 and 24; 81 percent of all users who use YouTube also use Facebook (Smith and Anderson, 2018). Although much YouTube content infringes copyrights, some videos are original and authentic, for this social media tool was designed to give any amateur film maker or video blogger the opportunity to share their artistic creations with the world.

Another popular video sharing service is called Vimeo. This tool has become quite popular in the last few years, and it is more refined, sophisticated, and professional than YouTube in many ways. The main differences between YouTube and Vimeo are below.

YouTube is a free platform for individuals and businesses and is the second most visited website on the Internet (next to Google, which is first). It attracts an audience from 88 countries and is accessed in 76 languages (YouTube Press, 2018). Since YouTube is owned by Google, it is more discoverable than Vimeo. Both offer privacy settings and basic analytics (Simon, 2018). Although YouTube's free service contains many ads, there is an affordable ad-free service available.

Vimeo contains more curated and specialized video content, catering to documentary film makers and videographers. Its commercial version ($170/year) restricts users to no more than 20GB of video uploads per week or 1TB per year. Their community guidelines encourage positive commenting, and they do not tolerate negative and inflammatory comments. However, its audience is relatively small—only about 120 million monthly users. Vimeo offers more privacy options than YouTube, but their advanced analytics cost money, while YouTube's are free (Simon, 2018).

For libraries, YouTube seems to be the most practical choice for uploading marketing videos. It is more discoverable, has more reach, and offers free analytics. The rest of this chapter will assume that you are designing your campaign around YouTube videos and will use that terminology.

Although most YouTube videos are uploaded for entertainment or instruction, libraries can also create videos for marketing purposes. Many studies have examined how libraries produce instructional videos (Charnigo, 2009; Maness, 2006; Tewell, 2010; Bowles-Terry, Hensley, and Hinchliffe, 2010; Little, 2011; Martin and Martin, 2015; Cho, 2013; Henrich and Prorak, 2010), but only a few published studies document how libraries create marketing videos.

Libraries might produce short videos that provide a virtual tour of the library building, that promote a specific archival or special collection that is unique to the community, or that promote their virtual chat reference service. For library videos that offer virtual tours, presenters, who can be either library workers or students, can promote the library "as a space for interaction, intellectual exploration, socialization, and a place where students can access print and online collections and take advantage of librarians' expertise and knowledge" (Little 2011, p. 71).

Examples of Library Video Marketing

Several libraries have successfully created video marketing campaigns. For example, Meyers Martin (2012) discusses how her academic library produced one-minute marketing videos that were informative and entertaining. In the planning phase, they selected a service or resource to market, wrote a script of between 170 and 200 words, and created an animated storyboard using Adobe After Effects. In the production phase, they used a high definition (HD) video camera, tripod, and boom microphone to get high-quality visuals and sound, and used cue cards for actors to ensure that all necessary lines were spoken within the one-minute time frame. The library's student employees edited the videos using Sony's Vegas Pro 9 editing suite. The author estimates that each video required 25 to 35 hours per person on the planning and production teams. The library branded its one-minute videos as "Message in a Minute," and all the videos share an opening scene inspired by the television program *60 Minutes* (p. 595). The library produced six "Message in a Minute" videos between September 2010 and April 2012. Between 2010 to 2012, these "Message in a Minute" videos had 2,744 total views on YouTube. Afterward, the library surveyed 31 faculty members who viewed the videos, asking 10 questions that were a mix of closed- and open-ended questions (Meyers Martin 2012, p. 597). The open-ended questions were the following:

1. What did you like (or dislike) about the video?
2. How can it be improved?
3. What suggestions do you have for other video topics?

4. Please provide any comments concerning the video, or any other library resources and services

Similarly, Perry (2011) discussed the process of Arizona State University Libraries' creation of their "Library Minute" videos, a series of 30 episodes of one-minute library promotional videos. She writes that video producers' planning process should include the following steps:

*   decide on the specific purpose for each video
*   ensure each video will be discoverable (plan hashtags, SEO keywords, etc., in advance)
*   evaluate the needs of the selected audience and create meaningful and useful content that will meet those needs
*   make a detailed plan to ensure that videos will be between 60 and 90 seconds long
*   secure professional video equipment (camera, lighting, sound, and editing software) for good production quality

To promote underutilized library services to patrons, Dalal and Lackie (2014) recommend using library marketing videos. Following a needs assessment, Dalal and Lackie (2014) found that their users were unaware of many of their library's resources and services, and according to data from student focus groups, even students who visited the library almost daily were unaware of many services (p. 227). To raise students' awareness, they decided to change their long step-by-step video tutorials into short promotional videos and to target distance learners, branding the videos The Rider Libraries Minute (TRLM). They used storyboarding to develop the shots, shot the video using a Kodak Zi8 Pocket Video camera with a microphone headset for voiceovers, and used Camtasia Studio for editing the video and for screen captures. Camtasia offers a production wizard with a "share to YouTube" option, which automatically uploads an MP4 video file to YouTube, which enables the user to set the video to different privacy settings: public, unlisted, or private. The authors ensured that the media they included was in the public domain or was usable under a Creative Commons License (Dalal and Lackie 2014, p. 232); YouTube also conducts an automatic copyright verification that scans uploaded audio and video for copyrighted material. The authors promoted the videos on their LibGuides, library website, as one of the orientation videos for the Office of Distance Education, and via social media. They also gave special presentations and promoted the videos specifically to faculty.

Sandy, Krishnamurthy, and Rau (2009) describe creating a self-guided video library tour on a budget of $2,000. They used a Canon XL2 video camera for all filming and recorded more than eight hours of footage on a digital video cassette (DVC). They used Final Cut Pro to edit the footage. The final virtual tour video was 2,100 words and just under 10 minutes. It was not posted to YouTube, but saved onto a video player; the library used Sony Video MP3 players, which were lent to patrons at the library's circulation desk, to play the tour video on a two-inch video screen. The video was also shown on a jumbo screen in the library instruction room at designated times and dates.

The Lloyd Sealy Library at John Jay College of Criminal Justice, part of the City University of New York, produced a creative virtual tour video for their library in August 2009. Produced in black and white *film noir* style, the video showed one person playing a Sherlock Holmes character and interacting with the reference librarian, who answered questions while promoting the library's services and resources. The video portrayed the library user as a detective because John Jay College is a criminal justice school (Lloyd Sealy Library, 2009).[1]

Best Practices in Video Marketing for Libraries

In a content analysis of 373 library-related videos on YouTube, Colburn and Haines (2012) found that 51 involved professional development, 252 contained library themes but were created by non-library workers, 9 were personal videos by librarians, 6 were anonymous library videos, and 55 were promotional videos. The "promotional videos" category was divided into the following groups:

- General promotion
- Library orientation/virtual tour
- Patron generated
- Promotion of services/resources
- Event promotion (before or after event)
- News
- Instructional

The instructional videos were included in the sample of promotional videos because instructional videos can be used for both teaching and marketing purposes (Colburn and Haines, 2012). Through an analysis of view counts (2008 through 2010), referral links (a useful way to track how users access specific videos), and comments, the authors found that 96 percent of promotional videos had comments enabled and that 79 percent of them had comments on them; 50 percent of those comments were positive, 6 percent were negative, and 44 percent were neutral (Colburn and Haines 2012, p. 17). The authors found that referrals came primarily not from the originating libraries, but from other websites within the library profession (Colburn and Haines, 2012 p. 18). Links should be shortened using a link shortening program such as Bitly, which offers both free and subscription service shortlinks. The subscription services create custom shortlinks that provide statistics on the number of times users click on that link to download or view the content. For more information about shortening and tracking links, visit http://www.bitly.com. The authors argue that for maximum impact from marketing videos, the library website should provide clear links to specific videos, and the videos should be used in classes, LibGuides, faculty orientations, and library welcome blogs (Colburn and Haines, 2012, p. 23).

In their book *Video Marketing for Libraries*, Dalal, O'Hanlon, and Yacobucci (2017) discuss best practices in creating library marketing videos. They argue that content is the most important factor: content must be compelling, valuable, and relevant to keep viewers engaged (p. 20). High-quality videos make a better impression than poorly produced videos, so they recommend using appropriate video cameras, lighting, and sound equipment. Understanding your intended audience and identifying the specific purpose of your marketing video is crucial. There is no point in creating a marketing video for a service or resource that is not useful for your users. As chapter 3 demonstrates, market research can help you identify the gaps between what you offer and what your users need.

The authors recommend that videos be succinct, for well-planned short videos can convey as much information as longer videos (the top 50 YouTube videos average only two minutes and fifty-four seconds; p. 21). To ensure succinctness and information density, your planning team (which should include members from various groups to ensure a diversity of talent and expertise) should create a graphical organizer, or storyboard, of the video, including descriptions of each shot (p. 50). The authors also recommend planning to assess the videos' impact: helpful metrics include video view counts, how users access your video, type of devices used, referral URLs, and any type of user engagement can help you understand the success or failure of your marketing videos. To ensure maximum impact, the final video should be discoverable via Internet searches and should be linked from the library's website and social media accounts. In order to make videos accessible to all users, they should include captioning, transcripts, or audio transcriptions (p. 25). The authors divide library marketing videos into four types:

- **Virtual tours** promoting the library's physical space, collections, and services
- **Demonstrations** that show the high points of a service or resource (these videos should be no longer than one minute)
- **Interviews or testimonials** from users, for personal stories are the most compelling
- **Parodies** videos of libraries or librarians who are making fun (of themselves or someone else) (see Librarians Do Gaga, from 2010: https://www.youtube.com/watch?v=a_uzUh1VT98)

YouTube Video Advertisements

YouTube advertisements accompany YouTube videos, usually before the video begins. Anyone can register for a YouTube account and make money from ads on their videos, providing they follow the guidelines. Uploaded videos are reviewed; once the uploader confirms that they have the appropriate rights (both audio and visual) to legally use the content, it will appear on the YouTube account, which becomes a "channel" as soon as it has content. To make money, the uploader must select each video and turn on monetization. Monetized videos are subject to copyright laws and other rules; the uploader must legally own the content, must be able to use it commercially, must use only royalty-free or original music, and must have explicit permission to use any intellectual property not their own. Nudity and violence are not appropriate for either YouTube advertisements or YouTube videos.

YouTube offers six types of advertisements:

Display advertisements. These ads are designed for desktop viewing and are located to the right of the feature video, above the video suggestions list.

Overlay advertisements. These ads, designed for desktop viewing, are semi-transparent advertisements located on the lower portion of the video.

Skippable video advertisements. These ads, which work on all devices, can be skipped after 5 to 10 seconds and can be embedded at the beginning, middle, or at the end of the video.

Non-skippable video advertisements. Designed for desktop and mobile devices, these 15 to 20 second advertisements can be embedded before, during, or after the video and are the most annoying for users, because the user is required to view them.

Bumper advertisements. These ads, designed for desktop and mobile devices, are 6-second ads that are non-skippable and are displayed only before the video is shown.

Sponsored cards. These ads, which work on desktop and mobile devices, are clickable slides, or "cards," that display during the video. Ads can include up to 5 cards that can have text, images, or clickable links, and each card interrupts the video for a moment (YouTube Help, 2018).

PINTEREST

Pinterest is a social media site, based on the idea of a bulletin board or corkboard, that allows users to organize and group photos (called "pins") into subject-specific collections ("pinboards"). This ability to organize images, links, and so forth into themed pinboards sets Pinterest apart from Instagram, the other major image sharing site (Thornton, 2012). Launched in March 2010, the site had 175 million monthly active users in 2017 (Kaplan, 2017). A 2018 Pew Research study examined the usage breakdown of four social media tools; Pinterest, Snapchat, YouTube, and What'sApp. They found that 29 percent of all U.S. adults use Pinterest. User demographics are as follows: of the 29 percent who use Pinterest, 16 percent are men and 41 percent are women; 34 percent between the ages of 18 and 29, 34 percent between 30 and 49, 26 percent between 50 and 64, and 16 percent over 65 years of age (Pew Research Group, 2018). Users (known as "pinners") upload images, copy and paste from web pages, and re-pin images from other boards to their own (like reposting or retweeting). Like Facebook, Twitter, and Instagram, Pinterest also allows users to follow the pinboards of other users with similar interests.

Pinterest is a highly visual tool that libraries can use to promote services and resources. Before using Pinterest, however, libraries should consider copyright issues and whether they can legally pin a copyrighted image (Dudenhoffer, 2012; Thornton, 2012; Hansen, Nowlan, and Winter, 2012). Recently, Pinterest has made this somewhat easier, adding a "nopin" script that allows content creators to protect their copyrighted images by blocking users from pinning them. One library that successfully navigated Pinterest for marketing is the University of Regina Library in Regina, Saskatchewan, Canada. To promote the library and engage their users, the authors created a "What are you reading?" board and asked followers to post the covers of books they were reading. They made sure to pin only original images that they created, images available under a Creative Commons license, images in the public domain, and images protected under "fair dealing"—what is called "fair use" in the United States (Hansen, Nowlan, and Winter, 2012). The authors provide best practices for pinning images:

- Give credit to the original source
- Describe the pin
- Upload high-quality images
- Respect privacy
- Update often

Thornton (2012) analyzed the Pinterest accounts of 57 libraries to discover how libraries use Pinterest. She found that libraries provide images of campus authors and visiting writers; book covers; library events, library renovations, and library space; library staff; and photographs from archives and special collections (p. 170).

POSTING STRATEGICALLY

Fostering Engagement

When posting on social media, it's important to foster engagement and interactivity with your users. Use an informal, casual, and even playful posting tone (Jacobson, 2011; King and Poulin, 2011; Houk and Thornhill, 2013; King, 2015; Kroski, 2009; Khan and Bhatti, 2012). Too much formality may discourage your audience from interacting with you, and posts should invite interaction and engage users in a conversation (Huang, Chu, Liu, and Zheng, 2017; Guo, 2018; Brubaker and Wilson, 2018; Benetoli, Chen, and Aslani, 2018; Anderson, 2017; Sørensen, 2016).

Dealing with Conflict

Interactive social media accounts will have to deal with upset users who wish to complain. The best thing to do is acknowledge their feelings and propose solutions to their problems. Social media administrators should be empathetic, but they should respond on behalf of the organization, not as an individual. If the social media administrator does not have enough information to respond to a request, the customer should be referred to someone else who is accessible via email or telephone. Never engage in hostile communications with users on social media; it is unprofessional and tarnishes the organization's reputation.

Social Media Automation Tools

There are many tools, both free and subscription-based, that help automate the management of multiple social media accounts. They web-based tools offer scheduling options that enable users to automatically post to multiple social media accounts at the same time. Posts can be scheduled days, weeks, and months in advance. However, your social media accounts should *not* be completely automated; marketers need to check in with their target audience and engage in real conversations. Automation tools help alleviate the drudgery of manually maintaining multiple social media accounts, but always keep your finger on the pulse of your organization's social media accounts (Olenski, 2018; Cisnero, 2014). Here is a list of selected automation tools:

1. AgoraPulse (https://www.agorapulse.com/)
2. Buffer (http://www.buffer.com)
3. CoSchedule (https://coschedule.com/)
4. CrowdFire (https://www.crowdfireapp.com/)
5. Hootsuite (http://www.hootsuite.com)
6. MavSocial (http://mavsocial.com/)
7. SpredFast (http://www.spredfast.com)
8. SproutSocial (http://www.sproutsocial.com)
9. Social Drift (https://socialdrift.com/)
10. TweetDeck (for Twitter) (https://tweetdeck.twitter.com/)

Social Media Guidelines and Policies

Social media guidelines are brief recommendations for employees who post content on organizational social media accounts. Authors nearly unanimously recommend that organizations create social media guidelines (or more detailed social media policies) that provide explicit direction about how and what employees can post to organizational social media accounts (Beese, 2015; Vites, 2017; Bergstrom, 2017; Kroski, 2009; Steiner, 2012). Social media policies are more detailed, providing information about the organization's social media "voice," what employees can (and can't) post, how frequently employees should post, confidentiality and transparency, how to deal with potential conflict, and crisis management. Social media policies outline the organization's goals and mission in using social media. Many social media policies and guidelines include a code of conduct for employees who manage and post to organizational social media accounts, addressing how to handle inflammatory comments and providing guidelines on how to be respectful, ethical, honest, and protect privacy when posting on social media (Beese, 2015). The goals of a social media policy are protecting the organization's reputation, encouraging employee advocacy, promoting the products and services being offered, raising awareness, and engaging with the targeted audience (Solar, 2018).

SOCIAL MEDIA METRICS; REACH, IMPRESSIONS, ENGAGEMENT

Libraries and other organizations often post tirelessly on social media, taking a rather scattershot "post and hope" approach to cutting through the noise and having their posts be seen. Instead, savvy marketers consult social media metrics such as *reach, impressions*, and *engagement* to understand the impact of their posts, so that they can target the days and times when posts are most likely to be seen. Social media metrics allow libraries to understand their audience demographics: when they go online, from what device, and what they react to. Social media managers can use this information to decide how often to post and what types of content to post (based on which posts generate the most engagement). Metrics allow marketers to make decisions on their marketing activities.

Generally speaking, social media *impressions* is the total number of times your content has been displayed, and *reach* is the total number of users who actually see your content. On Facebook, *impressions* (the number of times the posting has been displayed in users' timelines) can be organic (when posts appear in the timelines of friends or followers), paid (when impressions is increased with paid advertisements), or viral (when many users who are not friends or followers share your post into their own networks; York, 2018). On Twitter, *impressions* are the number of times your tweet has appeared in Twitter feeds (Twitter does not provide data on reach). On both platforms, *engagement* is the number of interactions users have with the content—comments/replies, likes, and shares/retweets (Morrison, 2015). Engagement is a metric for how well an organization is connecting with its customers on social media. High engagement does not guarantee an immediate increase in customers or sales, but it can help raise brand awareness, and maintain positive, long-term relations, supporting a relationship marketing approach to retaining customers (Achen, 2017). Each major platform has its own set of analytics tools to measure social media engagement: Facebook Insights, Twitter Analytics, Instagram Analytics, and YouTube Analytics.

Facebook Insights (http://www.facebook.com/yourpagename/insights)

Facebook Insights tracks user interactions on Facebook pages. It helps social media administrators understand the best time to post, the best day of the week to post, and the type of content that appeals most to your users. Facebook Insights offers a breakdown of the most recent posts (the previous week or the previous 28 days) by the number of users each post reached, the number of users who engaged with each post, and the virality percentage of each post (Facebook Business, 2018b):

1. Page likes: broken down by geographic location, age group, and gender
2. Virality: the number of people who created a story about your post
3. Post engagements: number of likes, shares, and comments
4. Reach: the number of unique visitors who access the page, broken down by organic, paid, and viral means
5. Page followers: these numbers represent more engagement than a simple like or share; following a page means the page appears on the user's personal feed
6. Check-Ins: number of users who have physically checked in to a location

Twitter Analytics (http://analytics.twitter.com)

Twitter Analytics, which was originally created for business accounts, was made available for all accounts in 2014 (Burnham, 2014). It analyzes the performance and quality of a user's tweets and provides details on how users interact with those tweets. Updated daily, it provides a 28-day snapshot of the total tweets, impressions, profile visits, mentions (@), follower activity, top tweets, and top follower, along with an analysis of all tweet activity.

Twitter defines its metrics as follows:

1. **Impressions**: total number of times a Tweets is displayed by anyone
2. **Engagement**: total number of times a user interacts with a tweet in some way, including clicking anywhere on the tweet (tweet expansion, links, hashtags, avatar, and username) as well as retweets, likes, replies, and follows
3. **Engagement rate**: Number of engagements divided by total impressions

Twitter Analytics also analyzes the demographics of all Twitter users, of your followers, and of your organic audience. It breaks down each of these groups according to their gender, hobbies, country, region, household income, language, mobile carrier, and device used to access Twitter. Twitter divides audiences into different personas, which include

- Parents
- Generation X
- Professionals
- Millennials
- Baby Boomers
- Adults 18–54
- Small businesses
- Seniors
- Business decision makers
- College graduates
- > 100K income

In addition to offering fairly granular analysis of individual accounts' performance, Twitter analytics also analyzes the traffic (tweets, impressions, and engagement) associated with tweets about various events, including entertainment, holidays, conferences, politics, sports, movies, and recurring trends.

Instagram Insights (only available on the app and to Business Profiles)

Instagram Insights, Instagram's native analytics tool, is only available to business profiles as of 2018. However, individual accounts can seamlessly convert to business profiles as long as they can link to a Facebook page (not an individual profile). Insights provides metrics at the level of the individual post and at the account level. For individual posts, Instagram provides metrics for impressions (how many people saw the post), Instagram reach percentage (impressions divided by number of followers), and engagements (the number of times a post is liked, commented on, shared, or saved). At the account level, Instagram offers three metrics that should be monitored: engagement rate (percentage of followers that interact with posts), follower growth rate (percentage of new followers added during a specific time period), and audience metrics (number of followers; demographics of followers, including location, age, gender; and time of day followers are most active; Baird, 2018).

In addition to Instagram's native analytics tools, many external tools provide Instagram metrics. Hootsuite, for example, which is known for automating social media posts, provides more detailed analytics than Instagram Insights (Baird, 2018). Other third-party Instagram analytic tools include:

1. Facebook Advertisements Manager (https://business.facebook.com/)
2. Hootsuite Analytics (https://hootsuite.com/products/social-media-analytics)
3. InconoSquare (https://pro.iconosquare.com/)
4. Keyhole (https://keyhole.co/)
5. Picture.Io (https://picture.io/)
6. Plann (https://www.plannthat.com/)
7. Sprout Social (http://www.sproutsocial.com)
8. Socialbakers (https://www.socialbakers.com/)
9. SquareLovin (https://squarelovin.com/)
10. Buffer for Instagram (https://buffer.com/instagram)

YouTube Analytics (http://www.YouTube.com/analytics)

YouTube's native Analytics program provides a graphical interface that displays metrics that give you detailed information about who is watching your videos (demographics), where they are watching, on what devices, how they are finding the videos, and how much of each video they watched, called "watch time reports." Ideally, users should finish watching each video—if they don't, that's a signal that your videos are too long, not valuable or relevant enough, or not engaging enough. Libraries need to frequently evaluate their analytics to determine whether their marketing videos are still current, effective, engaging, discoverable, and relevant. Analytics provide valuable information for marketers because they reveal how a user found the YouTube video, the device they watched it on, the time of day, and their geographic region. As mentioned above, the videos with higher rates of viewership give important information about how to shape future marketing videos. For example, if your shorter videos have higher viewership, that lets you know to make future videos shorter. Analytics reveal valuable data that helps marketers make decisions about future marketing.

YouTube also gives information about the impressions click-through rate (how frequently users watch a video after viewing a YouTube thumbnail), the total number of impressions for each video (YouTube defines this as the number of times YouTube video thumbnails were clicked on the YouTube website; clicks on YouTube videos from external sources do not count in impressions), and the unique impressions for each video (the approximate number of unique viewers; this figure does not include people who watch the video more than once).

YouTube also offers Interaction Reports (another name for engagement), which measure subscribers, likes, dislikes, favorites, videos added to playlists, comments, and sharing. YouTube offers weekly, monthly, quarterly, and annual metrics, or users can select a custom date range to evaluate a specific time period—perhaps the period of a specific campaign (Google, 2018).

SAMPLE SOCIAL MEDIA GUIDELINES AND POLICIES

DAVID & LORRAINE CHENG LIBRARY SOCIAL MEDIA GUIDELINES, WILLIAM PATTERSON UNIVERSITY LIBRARIES

Purpose: David & Lorraine Cheng Library recognizes Social Media as a vital tool in communicating and engaging with the University community and general public. In striving to attain the Library's strategic goals, we seek to utilize social media to foster collaboration, and increase awareness of Library resources and services.

Liability and Comments: The Library assumes no liability for comments made by any third party on any pages or posts linked to Cheng Library Social Media Accounts. The Cheng Library actively monitors comments and posts related to its Social Media accounts and reserves the right to remove from its social media pages any comments or content posted by third parties that are contrary to the Mission, Vision, and Goals of the Library or University.

Responses: Questions sent to our social media accounts can typically expect a response or referral within 24–48 hours.

Purpose: These guidelines are for faculty and staff serving on the David & Lorraine Cheng Library Social Media Team and any other Library personnel that may engage in Social Media activities pertaining to any Social Media account of the Cheng Library. Defined: Social Media is defined herein as any third party hosted online technology that facilitates social interaction. Social Media Sites include, but are not limited to, Facebook, Twitter, and Instagram. These guidelines will also govern any additional social media tools used by the Social Media Team, upon approval of the Library Council, Dean, and the University Marketing and Public Relations Department. Use: Social Media activities conducted on behalf of the Cheng Library will adhere to the following Guidelines:

- All activities will conform to William Paterson University Social Media Policies, Best Practices Guidelines, and code of conduct.
- All activities will align with the Mission, Vision, and Goals of the Cheng Library and the University.
- All information disseminated via any Social Media outlets will conform to the Cheng Library's policies regarding patron privacy.
- Access to Cheng Library Social Media sites will be managed by the Social Media Team coordinated by the Reference & Outreach Librarian.
- The development of a "Best Practices Guide," based upon the aforementioned guidelines, will be implemented to elaborate upon and guide specific activities.

Structure of Social Media Team: The Social Media Team will be led by the Reference & Outreach Librarian and will be composed of selected Faculty and Staff of the Cheng Library. The team will be representative of department/units whose activities focus upon patron service and interaction.

Liability/Accountability: The Social Media Team is responsible for maintaining account credentials, and insuring access is allocated to designated individuals as necessary. Team Members and any individual designated by the Cheng Library will ensure that all social media posts and/or activities engaged in on behalf of the Cheng Library align with these guidelines.

SOCIAL MEDIA POSTING GUIDELINES, STONY BROOK UNIVERSITY LIBRARIES

The University Libraries are committed to providing an active learning environment that supports the needs of the Stony Brook University community. Social media from the University Libraries is intended to enhance communication and outreach efforts and engage the greater academic community.

Social media can be defined as any web-based application, site, software, or account used to disseminate information through online social interaction, created using highly accessible publishing techniques. Examples include, but are not limited to: blogs, Instagram, Twitter, Facebook, YouTube, and Pinterest.

The same laws, professional expectations, and guidelines for interacting with students, parents, alumni, donors, media, and other university constituents apply online as in person.

Posts on social media sites should be professional in tone and in good taste. Before posting, please take a moment to review the Stony Brook University's Brand website at https://www.stonybrook.edu/brand/. Refrain from posting items that are not related to the University Libraries' mission statement. All posts should reinforce our academic mission and advance our strategic goals.

Before you do anything with or for the University Libraries social media, you must remember and embody what the Stony Brook FAR BEYOND brand represents: ambitious ideas, imaginative solutions, and exceptional leadership. In every post you create, promote, and distribute to the world, regardless of channel, keep this essence in mind and use it as a filter for both your content and its message. All posts must adhere to the University's conduct code and our guiding principles of community.

Do not use copyrighted photos and/or images. If an image is posted, and is not owned by SBU or the University Libraries, the image will link directly back to the original site. If the image is not from a website, then permission will be requested from the copyright holder before the image is posted.

SOCIAL MEDIA MANAGERS

Responsibilities for Social Media Managers

Social Media Managers will post the social media campaigns for the day, any event promotions as well as any ad hoc posts requested for the day.

Anyone in the Library can submit a social media request through the Social Media Request Form. Social Media Managers will monitor and respond to these requests on their designated day. If there is a question regarding whether a request should be posted, please email the Social Media Chair.

Social Media Managers will also check the Library website for any news/blogs posted as well as other banners posted by the Web Services Librarian.

Login information for all social media account can be found in our shared Social Media folder on Google Drive. Instagram requires the use of an iPad or mobile device.

Guidelines for Liking/Retweeting Posts

1. Support Stony Brook University student success in the Library and throughout campus
2. Support University departments and their initiatives/events
3. Support Stony Brook Librarians in their Library initiatives and accomplishments
4. Support library associations—ALA, ACRL, etc.
5. Support local public libraries and other academic libraries

Guidelines for Event Postings/Promotion

1. All events should be posted with banner created by Web Services Librarian.
2. All events should be promoted

   a. 2 weeks prior to event
   b. 1 week prior to event
   c. Day of event (before event takes place!)

Please include link to sign up for event as well as tagging any presenters, librarians, collaborators and departments.

Handles/Tags

Please include possible hashtags and tagging groups/people.

- The purpose of tags and hashtags is to draw attention and to promote the Library. They help to make it easier for people to find the Library on Social Media!
- *Tags (handles):* @stonybrooku (university); @kristinlearn27 (person); @spd_stonybrook (department)

- **Hashtags:** #fridayreads; #mondaymotivation; #libraryweek #summer (you can create your own!)

Photos

Make sure photos are in the public domain, copyright free or owned/taken by University Libraries. You can browse photos on

- ○ staffweb
- ○ Pexels
- ○ Wikimedia

- Instagram—Needs a photo and should have less text. More student focused

UNIVERSITY OF TORONTO LIBRARIES

SOCIAL MEDIA POLICY

Overview of social media at UTL

We are dedicated to providing engaging and relevant services and resources to our users. As access, production, and consumption continues to be digitally mediated, we endeavor to meet our users where they are—online. Instead of being the sole authors of the University of Toronto Libraries story, we are inviting and encouraging all of those who walk in and out of our physical and virtual spaces to participate in the telling of our story through their own content: words, photos, and videos on various established and emergent social media platforms.

Purpose of using social media at UTL

The purpose of this guide is to provide University of Toronto Libraries staff with best practices and guidelines related to the integration, maintenance, and removal of social media channels for institutional use. This guide also outlines recommended procedures for creating, managing, marketing, and assessing social media content.

Goals of using social media at UTL

- To inform, engage, communicate, and create a dialogue with our users and community about libraries, events, services, facilities, resources, and staff
- To improve user experience, by having an outlet for users to provide direct and immediate feedback, and the ability for UTL to directly and immediately address this feedback
- To extend the physical location of the library and build community into digital realms and meet our internal and external stakeholders (i.e., librarians, visiting scholars, students, alumni)

Please refer to the Strategic Marketing and Communications Plan 2012–2015 for a more in-depth overview, located on the Communications and Marketing Support: University of Toronto Libraries LibGuide.

This guide was created by the following librarians involved in the Student Outreach Group:

Rachel Beattie, Heather Buchansky, Nelly Cancilla, Jesse Carliner, Holly Inglis, Judith Logan, Vincci Lui, Stephanie Quail, Kathleen Scheaffer, Margaret Wall, and Tracy Zahradnik.

Creating a social media plan

Before you start to create accounts or generate content, it can be useful to create a social media plan with the sections listed below that will drive the strategy behind your social media accounts. A social media plan should ideally illustrate:

- Your library's target market
- SMART objectives for your social media account for a specific time period

Library's target market

Your library can define your target market in a variety of ways. Some of the factors to consider when creating a profile of your library's target market are:

Type of library user(s)	Part-time students; full-time students; international students; tenured faculty; adjunct faculty; staff; alumni
Attendance	Part-time students; full-time students; part-time instructors; full-time instructors
Level of study	Undergraduate, graduate, postgraduate, continuing education
Programs the library supports	Health sciences, business, arts & humanities
Information-seeking behaviors	First-year undergraduate students, professional graduate students, research graduate students, faculty
Demographics	Age, gender, ethnicity, living arrangement (commuter vs. residence); see if you can get more detailed demographic information from your registrar's office
Psychographics	Interests; hobbies; behaviors; values (librarians may have an educated idea about the psychographics of their users already; however, proper assessment and monitoring of your social media accounts will help you)

SMART objectives

Specific	Be precise about what you want to achieve
Measurable	Make sure the objective is quantified and can be easily measured (refer to Assessment section in this document)
Achievable	Make sure you have the resources and personnel at your library to achieve the stated objective(s)
Relevant	Make sure the objective is aligned to your library's overall outreach and engagement goals
Time-sensitive	State when the objective must be achieved by

Example of SMART objectives:

- Gain 50 Twitter followers that are part of the library's target community over the next six months by tweeting relevant content for students and faculty twice a day, Monday–Friday
- Increase traffic to the library's research guides by 10 percent for the fall 2014 semester by promoting guides through Facebook, Twitter, and library blog posts

Account profile and display

A consistent visual identity helps convey who we are to local and global audiences. It also builds credibility. Please consider the following customized areas below when creating or editing a profile area on a UTL social media account.

Creating a profile or username

In order for our users and social media followers to easily identify that a social media channel is part of U of T, as well as UTL, it can be beneficial to include "*U of T*" within the profile name and/or username, especially on Twitter when the handle may not always resonate with people.

Here are instructions on how to change your Twitter profile name and username (aka Twitter handle).

Banner photos

Photos of library buildings, study spaces, or people within these spaces are good options for social media banners/backgrounds. Please make every effort of representing students that reflect the U of T community. And, if people are easily identifiable within the photos, make sure they have signed the UTL photo/video release form, allowing the photo they are in to be used publicly for promotional purposes. Also ensure that the image dimensions are optimal by referring to this social media image size guide.

For central libraries

Please consider using a pre-established UTL banner for your social media account, when a banner is required (below), to help create consistency and credibility.

All other libraries within the system are free to use the UTL banner as well.

Example of a banner photo:

Profile photo

Library buildings and spaces can be used in the profile photo. The library name (i.e., Gerstein) or acronym (i.e., BIC) will also help followers easily identify your account within their feed.

Example of a profile photo:

OISE Library Twitter profile photo

Bio field

The bio field or "About" area is a space to highlight the unique features of your library, and perhaps the people behind the social media account.

Include relevant links to your library website to establish credibility, and list hashtags for followers to use (ex. #uoftlibraries). And, note that it is the "official channel" of the library.

Examples of a bio field:

U of T Libraries Twitter bio	*Gerstein Library Twitter bio*
U of T Libraries @uoftlibraries The official Twitter channel of the University of Toronto Libraries. Librarians Judith, Heather, Lisa, and Margaret respond to tweets Monday-Friday, 9am-5pm EST ⚲ Toronto, Ontario, Canada ⊘ library.utoronto.ca ⊘ Joined October 2009	**Gerstein Library UTL** @GersteinLibrary Gerstein Science Information Centre-The largest Science and Medicine Library at U of T. Librarians Elena, Allison, and Heather are tweeting! ⚲ Toronto, Ontario, Canada ⊘ gerstein.library.utoronto.ca ⊘ Joined April 2009

Thomas Fisher Rare Book Library Instagram bio

The "About" area on Facebook allows for a longer description, as well as listing hours and location. Please refer to the Media Commons and Thomas Fisher Rare Book Library Facebook pages for examples and ideas.

Creating and generating content

Persona and tone

Opt for a friendly, yet professional persona across all of your social media platforms. Contractions are fine. Personal pronouns—especially "we"—give a sense of warmth and personality to your writing.

Scheduling

Be aware of what's going on in your community on a day-to-day and semester basis, and create timely posts to match the concerns of your community.

For example, students will be more interested in posts about quiet study spaces during exams. Scheduling software programs, such as Hootsuite, can be used to schedule your communications for several platforms in advance. (Note: Instagram posts can now be prescheduled in Hootsuite, though it isn't as seamless as it is for other platforms, such as Twitter.)

It may also be useful for your library to create a social media editorial calendar. An editorial calendar will help you organize when you should promote specific events and what platforms you will use for promotional purposes.

Retweets/reposts/shares

Other accounts at the university and library are a good source for informational retweets/shares. Following leaders in the field that your patrons are in is a good source as well. Beware social media hoaxes: If you're retweeting big news (a death, a major event), confirm the story using trustworthy news sources. It's okay to brag a bit, so feel free to share or retweet compliments or other interesting posts or photos from followers directed at your account.

We recommend Repost app for reposting Instagram posts, as it embeds image credit onto the image itself, communicates directly with Instagram, and allows you to paste the original caption into your own post.

Replying

When to reply

Reply to posts that have been directly addressed to your social media account (i.e., your Twitter handle has been used in the tweet).

If there is a positive tweet or comment that your library may want to use in its promotions, ask for permission to use their comments as testimonials. It is best to ask at that moment, as it may be difficult to locate the comment later on.

Who to reply to

Make sure that the user is a real person, not a spambot or someone with an ulterior motive. Always look at the user's profile and recent posts before replying.

How to reply to angry users

Social media provides a needed space for people to vent their frustrations and be heard. You will encounter angry messages or posts directed at your library and/or its practices. This is an opportunity to build a relationship, even if that seems daunting at first. Some key tips:

- Acknowledge user and "kill 'em with kindness"
- Give the needed information immediately or promise to find out what is happening and keep them updated

Helpful links:

How to respond to angry customers on Twitter (presentation by Verist Labs, via Slideshare, see http://www.slideshare.net/veristlabs/how-to-respond-to-an-angry-customers-on-twitter-4747442)

How to respond to public complaints on Twitter (article by Kyle Lacy, *Twitter Marketing for Dummies*, 2nd ed., see http://www.dummies.com/how-to/content/how-to-respond-to-public-complaints-on-twitter.html)

5 ways brands respond to social media comments (article by Seek Social Media, see http://www.seeksocialmedia.com/respond-negative-social-media-comments/)

Use of hashtags

Hashtags make your content more discoverable. Use hashtags that are appropriate for the content of your post. It's always a good idea to use #UofT instead of just writing "U of T," so other users searching for posts about #UofT can easily find your content.

Example of hashtag usage:

U of T Archives tweet

UTL institutional hashtag

The hashtag #UofTLibraries can be used to allow other UTL libraries to search and find your content for retweets and reposts on Twitter and Instagram

Sharing content among UTL social media channels

If you have an event, post, or issue that needs "amplification," contact the other social media managers or student outreach group members on the UTL listserv: UTL-STUDENTOUTREACH-L@listserv.utoronto.ca

Generating content

Posting regularly is an important part of maintaining a fresh and relevant social media presence. Here are some suggestions for generating new content on a regular basis:

- Employ student staff to come up with and draft post ideas. You can even have them take pictures or videos to include in the post* (if people are easily identifiable within the photos/video make sure they have signed the UTL photo/video release form [see http://guides.library .utoronto.ca/c.php?g=251124&p=1673140], allowing the photo to be used publicly for promotional purposes)
- Listen to what your community is talking about on the social media platform you're using and write about those concerns. For example, if you see a lot of complaints about the elevators in your building, post about their maintenance issues
- Set up Google alerts for topics related to your field or use an RSS reader such as Feedly to follow online newspapers, websites, and blogs that your target audience may be interested in
- Create standing post types. For example, the @uoftlibraries Twitter feed posts FAQs on the weekends
- Content types you might want to publicize on social media: faculty publications, new books, events at the library or in the faculty department you work with, and articles of interest to your users
- Add photos to your Twitter posts and links, as it usually generates more interest and retweets*

*Please refer to University of Toronto's Digital Media Bank 'Understand Rights and Releases' (see https://mediabank.utoronto.ca/pages/help.ph p?section=Understanding+Rights+and+Releases) for more information related to obtaining signed consent for photos.

Make sure to use a link shortener, such as uoft.me, to make your posts more appealing to read. If you decide to include links that lead followers back to your library's website, you can use Google Analytics to see how many users are entering your site through a social media link.

Linking accounts and duplication of content

If you have multiple platforms with different audiences, it is a good idea to link these platforms so you can reach as broad an audience as possible with one post/tweet/etc. There is some debate about this practice, though, as your followers could see the same post on different platforms and see your content as redundant and annoying.

Maintenance

If you find that your social media account is being neglected, you might want to think about closing it entirely. It's better not to have an account than to have an outdated one. Please refer to the assessment section of this document to learn more about assessment techniques you can use to determine if you need to deactivate a social media account.

Accessibility

Third-party software programs, including social media platform like Facebook, Twitter, and Instagram, are not part of the Accessibility for Ontarians with Disabilities Act (AODA). However, there are certain things we can do with social media posts to make them more accessible to our followers, including:

- use camel casing with hashtags, such as #LibrariesOfInstagram
- use contextual hashtags
- provide a brief description of what is in a photo (especially for Instagram, as there is more space)

Promotions and marketing

Listed below are ideas on how to promote social media channels

Print marketing

(add icon, handle or links to following print materials):

- Flyers

- Workshop handouts
- Table top tent signs for desks, tables, and workstations

- Business cards (can be done through special requests)
- Bookmarks
- Due date slips
- Buttons

- Stickers
- Posters (for primary promotion and standardization for inclusion for other printed library informational

Digital marketing

(add hyperlinked icon when possible):

- LCD screens
- Workshop slides
- Staff newsletter (e.g., *In the Loop*)
- Email signatures
- Social media cross-promotion (post Instagram photos on Twitter)

- Screensavers or splash pages on library computer workstations
- Web banners

- Widgets in LibGuide

Building followers and community

- Promotion through followings (Twitter, Instagram, Pinterest)
- Subscribing (YouTube) and liking or joining groups (Facebook)
- "Like" or "Favorite" other user's content, and offline word of mouth communication
- Focus on members of your targeted audience
- Share your page and accounts with existing followers and friends and ask them to like or share with their friends
- Offer incentives
- Have contests

Target audience

- Current and prospective University of Toronto faculty, staff, and students Alumni
- International researchers and visiting scholars. Other community members
- Relevant organizations like associations, media outlets, cultural institutional units (i.e., departments, offices, student groups)

When to promote

At specific times during the term or year, such as:

- Acceptance packages for students
- Orientation materials
- Graduation notifications (i.e., how to stay involved with the libraries)
- TRY or other conferences and staff development events

On a regular basis:

- Exhibitions and displays
- Events
- Instructional sessions
- Library tours

Frequency and timing of posts

There are certain times of the day where posts and tweets receive more attention, so it would be best to schedule around these times. It varies from social media platform. Here is an interesting infographic (see https://www.ned-potter.com/blog/social-media-the-best-times-to-post) on when the best times to post items to: Facebook, Twitter, Instagram, LinkedIn, Pinterest, and Google+.

Other considerations

- Budget: integrate with existing outreach campaigns or separate?
- Collaboration and consultation: ensure through communication that your marketing campaign does not conflict with other libraries or groups on campus. Email the UTL social media listserv.
- Coordination: a social media marketing shared calendar could be created to be consulted when planning social media marketing initiatives, or remember to email the student outreach group listserv.
- Refer to communications policies for marketing at U of T, UTL, and your individual library (ex. Communications @ UTL guide, see http://guides.library.utoronto.ca/communications)

Assessment

Assessing the success of your social media strategy is crucial, as maintaining various social media accounts can be time consuming. By collecting data on your social media properties and turning the data into usable metrics, libraries within the UTL system can make evidence-based decisions on areas, such as:

- Types of content to include
- Frequency of posts
- When to discontinue a social media account
- Success of specific outreach campaigns

The following sections will discuss how to assess social media properties in a library context, while also providing librarians with a list of assessment tools and some sample Google Forms for collecting assessment data.

Quantitative and qualitative data to collect

Assess the value and effectiveness of your library's social media activity by using both quantitative and qualitative metrics:

Quantitative data to collect	Qualitative data to collect
Number of followers, likes	Consistency of library's tone and personality in posts
Amount of content posted	Quality of mentions (use of library's hashtag by followers or non- followers)
Types of content posted (links, images, posts)	Sentiment (Klout score - see Assessment tool spreadsheet, see https://docs.google.com/spreadsheets/d/1NSHjgrwff lOsZ4JQXS7bkIy4_wWRE1Y_5U6Dxn_qlSU/edit ?usp=sharing
Shares of content (reply tweets, Facebook shares, repins)	Library's interaction with target users (number of retweets, comments directed at students, faculty, etc.)
Referrals (users clicking through to library's website via a link on a social media account)	
Amount of staff time used to monitor accounts and create content	

Gathering data

Track internal social media activity data

- Use a Google Form to track staff time and activity on social media
- Sample forms have been created; feel free to copy and customize according to your library's needs
- Track data for all social media interactions on a daily basis to determine how much staff time is being spent on maintaining social media accounts (recommended)

- Every term, export the statistics into a spreadsheet and use appropriate tools and infographics to summarize the statistics and compare with previous terms

Track external social media activity data

- There are a variety of tools for tracking external social media activity depending on the platform

  ○ We have created a spreadsheet outlining some of the tools available for evaluating social media reach, effectiveness, popularity, and user engagement

- Depending on the types of data you would like to collect (retweets, new followers, likes, shares, etc.), you may want to collect data on a weekly basis or have weekly reports sent to you using tools such as Hootsuite or SumALL
- Additionally, with tools such as Facebook Insights you can download data for a 180-day period and analyze larger periods of time
- Every term, analyze your collected data and use appropriate tools and infographics to summarize the statistics and compare with previous terms

Assessing collected data

- Choose appropriate platform assessment tools to gather data on your social media accounts and the amount of staff time being used to maintain the accounts.
- Evaluate the internal and external social media data according to the criteria you have developed that is appropriate for your library.
- Tie your assessment to the social media objective(s) you have created for your library's social media strategy.
- Benchmarking: evaluate statistics every term to note any trends or whether or not you are achieving the social media objectives you have established.
- Evaluate the continued worth of each platform based on resources used (i.e., staff time) and engagement with library's target users to decide whether to change your approach to the platform or to deactivate/cancel the account from your social media portfolio.

Using the data

It is best to evaluate relative value and effectiveness of social media activity every term (every four months) and annually before yearly planning meetings. Here are some things to consider when collecting and using data:

- Set your criteria based on the unique needs of your library (who are your users, what is the size of your faculty/college/department, what level of staffing do you have?
- Compare yourself against libraries of similar size and how your social media influence compares (numbers of followers, likes, retweets, Klout score)
- Develop criteria for deletion, so that you can determine if your library can cut back on its social media activities in certain platforms
- Set your goals for improvement and put a plan in place for achieving the goals
- Set up policies and procedures for transferring responsibility for account(s) to another staff member if the current staff member is unable to maintain the platform due to other responsibilities

Remember, criteria for evaluation may be different for each platform.

APPENDIX

Social media contacts at UTL

Please contact the following individuals for questions or assistance with your library's social media channel(s):

Heather Buchansky, Student Engagement Librarian heather.buchansky@utoronto.ca | 416-946-7788

Contact for: subscribing to UTL student outreach group listserv

Jesse Carliner, Communications & Reference Librarian jesse.carliner@utoronto.ca | 416-946-3803

Contact for: creating any new social media accounts

Current UTL social media sites

This UTL social media directory page outlines social media platform at libraries across U of T. See https://www.utoronto.ca/social-media-directory/libraries

CONCLUSION

This chapter examined how libraries can promote library events, services, and resources via social media. Posting on platforms such as Facebook, Twitter, Instagram, Pinterest, and YouTube provides a way for libraries to directly connect with the communities it already serves in a cost-effective way. The chapter also gave an overview of social media platforms and the advertisement options they offer. It recommended that, if possible, libraries should consider experimenting with social media advertisements such as Facebook ads, Twitter promote mode, or Twitter campaigns. Social media advertisements provide an added boost in spreading the library's message, is more affordable than print promotions or advertising, and can be automated with tools such as HootSuite, which save staff time by scheduling social media posts across different platforms. Some automation tools are free and some have affordable subscription plans, but they all support the library's social media marketing efforts. Set up a library marketing committee to develop a social media posting schedule (in an Excel spreadsheet or on Hootsuite) to streamline the process even more.

This chapter also recommended (again) that libraries conduct market research to be sure that your users are on social media. The premise of social media marketing is that engaged users "share" your posts, increasing engagement by creating a ripple effect. This chapter also recommended various specific strategies for each platform. For Instagram, it recommended taking professional photos, being mindful of lighting, and using appropriate hashtags for discoverability. For YouTube, it recommended producing short, professional videos that provide bursts of information that is both current and relevant to your users' needs. It recommended prominently linking all social media platforms on the library's home page and promoting them in print and online publications. Posts on different platforms can cross-promote one another: Embedding YouTube video on libraries' Facebook pages helps users learn about your YouTube presence, and having your Facebook page linked in all library YouTube videos promotes the Facebook page. Create consistent handles, such as "nameoflibrary," across all social media accounts in order to make social media accounts more discoverable. Finally, this chapter examined social media analytics tools and recommended that library marketers use them to better understand how their users interact with the library's social media accounts. This information will enable you to make their social media marketing as relevant and impactful as possible and keep it from getting lost in the online noise.

NOTE

1. To watch these videos, see https://www.YouTube.com/watch?v=tX8gm GNson8

REFERENCES

Achen, Rebecca M. 2017. "Measuring social media marketing: Moving towards a relationship marketing approach." *Managing Sport and Leisure* 22, no. 1: 33–53.

Anderson, Cordelia. 2017. "Moving from a promotion strategy to an engagement strategy." *Reference & User Services Quarterly* 57, no. 2: 89–92.

Baird, Fergus. 2018. "The 7 best Instagram Analytics tools (and metrics you need to track)." July 16. https://blog.hootsuite.com/instagram-analytics -tools-business/ (Accessed August 1, 2018).

Beese, Jennifer. 2015. "Your guide to creating a social media policy." September 24. https://sproutsocial.com/insights/social-media-policy/ (Accessed August 25, 2018).

Benetoli, A., T. F. Chen, and P. Aslani. 2018. "How patients' use of social media impacts their interactions with healthcare professionals." *Patient Education & Counseling* 101, no. 3: 439–444.

Bergstrom, Breonna. 2017. "How to build a thorough social media policy to prevent emergencies." June 15. https://coschedule.com/blog/social-media -policy/ (Accessed August 1, 2018).

Biography.com. 2014. "Julie Powell." July 7. https://www.biography.com/ people/julie-powell-20903379 (Accessed August 1, 2018).

Bowles-Terry, Melissa, Merinda Kaye Hensley, and Lisa Janicke Hinchliffe. 2010. "Best practices for online video tutorials in academic libraries: A study of student preferences and understanding." *Communications in Information Literacy* 4, no. 1: 17–28.

Brubaker, Pamela Jo, and Christopher Wilson. 2018. "Let's give them something to talk about: Global brands' use of visual content to drive engagement and build relationships." *Public Relations Review* 44, no. 3: 342–352.

Brügger, Niels. 2015. "A brief history of Facebook as a media text: The development of an empty structure." *First Monday* 20, no. 5. http://www .firstmonday.dk/ojs/index.php/fm/article/view/5423/4466

Burnham, Kristin. 2014. "Twitter Analytics Now Available To Everyone." August 28. https://www.informationweek.com/software/social/twitter-analytics -now-available-to-everyone/d/d-id/1306797 (Accessed August 1, 2018).

Chan, Christopher. 2011. "Using online advertising to increase the impact of a library Facebook page." *Library Management* 32, no. 4/5: 361–370.

Charnigo, Laurie. 2009. "Lights! Camera! Action! Producing library instruction video tutorials using Camtasia studio." *Journal of Library & Information Services in Distance Learning* 3, no. 1: 23–30.

Chase, William D., and Harrison V. Chase. 2018. *Chase's calendar of events.* Lanham, MD: Rowman & Littlefield Publishers.

Cho, Allan. 2013. "YouTube and academic libraries: Building a digital collection." *Journal of electronic resources librarianship* 25, no. 1: 39–50.

Cisnero, Kristina. 2014. "The DOs and DON'Ts of social media automation." September 18. https://blog.hootsuite.com/social-media-automation/ (Accessed August 5, 2018).

Colburn, Selene, and Laura Haines. 2012. "Measuring libraries' use of YouTube as a promotional tool: An exploratory study and proposed best practices." *Journal of Web Librarianship* 6, no. 1: 5–31.

Cribbs, Bonnie. 2017. "12 must follow library Instagram accounts." June 20. http://www.rivistas.com/12-must-follow-library-instagram-accounts/ (Accessed August 1, 2018).

Dalal, Heather A., and Robert J. Lackie. 2014. "What if you build it and they still won't come? Addressing student awareness of resources and services with promotional videos." *Journal of Library & Information Services in Distance Learning* 8, no. 3–4: 225–241.

Dalal, Heather A., Robin O'Hanlon, and Karen L. Yacobucci. 2017. *Video marketing for libraries: A practical guide for librarians.* Vol. 33. Lanham, MD: Rowman & Littlefield.

Dudenhoffer, Cynthia. 2012. "Pin it!: Pinterest as a library marketing and information literacy tool." *College & Research Libraries News* 73, no. 6: 328–332.

Estes, Janelle, Amy Schade, and Jakob Nielsen. (2009). *Social media user experience.* Fremont, CA: Nielsen Norman Group. https://media.nngroup .com/media/reports/free/Social_Media_User_Experience.pdf

Facebook Business. 2018a. "Facebook advertisements." https://www.face book.com/business/products/advertisements (Accessed August 23, 2018).

Facebook Business. 2018b. "Facebook Insights." https://www.facebook.com/business/a/page/page-insights (Accessed August 23, 2018).

Facebook Investor Relations. 2017. "FAQs." https://investor.fb.com/re sources/default.aspx (Accessed August 23, 2018).

Google. 2018. "YouTube Analytics." https://support.google.com/YouTube/answer/1714323 (Accessed August 12, 2018).

Gramlich, John. 2018. "5 facts about Americans and Facebook." April 10. http://www.pewresearch.org/fact-tank/2018/04/10/5-facts-about-americans -and-facebook/ (Accessed August 1, 2018).

Guo, Miao. 2018. "How television viewers use social media to engage with programming: The social engagement scale development and validation." *Journal of Broadcasting & Electronic Media* 62, no. 2: 195–214.

Hansen, Kirsten, Gillian Nowlan, and Christina Winter. 2012. "Pinterest as a tool: Applications in academic libraries and higher education." *Partnership: The Canadian Journal of Library and Information Practice and Research* 7, no. 2. https://doi.org/10.21083/partnership.v7i2.2011

Henrich, Kristin J., and Diane Prorak. 2010. "A school mascot walks into the library: Tapping school spirit for library instruction videos." *Reference Services Review* 38, no. 4: 663–675.

Hertvik, Joe. 2014. "The Twitter retweet to tweet ratio for business is >=3:1." September 21. http://joehertvik.com/twitter-retweet-to-tweet-ratio/ (Accessed August 24, 2018).

Houk, Kathryn M., and Kate Thornhill. 2013. "Using Facebook page insights data to determine posting best practices in an academic health sciences library." *Journal of Web Librarianship* 7, no. 4: 372–388.

Hsiao, Jason. 2018. "The what, why and how of Instagram video for small businesses." April 30. *Forbes Magazine.* https://www.forbes.com/sites/forbescommunicationscouncil/2018/04/30/the-what-why-and-how-of-insta gram-video-for-small-businesses/#17ff0b9ae15d (Accessed August 1, 2018).

Huang, Hong, Samuel Kai Wah Chu, Lesley Yuyang Liu, and Philip Yi Zheng. 2017. "Understanding user-librarian interaction types in academic library microblogging: A comparison study in Twitter and Weibo." *Journal of Academic Librarianship* 43, no. 4: 329–336.

Hughes, Brian. 2016. "How to optimize your social media posting frequency." March 16. https://socialmediaweek.org/blog/2016/03/optimize-social-media -time/ (Accessed August 2, 2018).

Isaac, Mike. 2018. "The ratio establishes itself on Twitter." February 9. *New York Times*. https://www.nytimes.com/interactive/2018/02/09/technology/the-ratio-trends-on-twitter.html (Accessed March 12, 2018).

Jacobson, Terra B. 2011. "Facebook as a library tool: Perceived vs. actual use." *College & Research Libraries* 72, no. 1: 79–90.

Kaplan, Jon. 2017. "175 million people discovering new possibilities on Pinterest." https://business.pinterest.com/en/blog/175-million-people-discovering-new-possibilities-on-pinterest (Accessed August 1, 2018).

Khan, Shakeel Ahmad, and Rubina Bhatti. 2012. "Application of social media in marketing of library and information services: A case study from Pakistan." *Webology* 9, no. 1: 1–8.

King, David Lee, and Eric T. Poulin. 2011. "Facebook for libraries: It's easy to use social media's most popular tool to connect with your community." *American Libraries* 42, no. 5/6: 42–45.

King, David Lee. 2015. *Managing your library's social media channels*. ALA TechSource.

Kroski, Ellyssa. 2009. "Should your library have a social media policy?" *School Library Journal* 55, no. 10: 44–46.

Kupersmith, John. 2012. "Library terms that users understand." https://escholarship.org/uc/item/3qq499w7 (Accessed August 23, 2018).

Little, Geoffrey. 2011. "The revolution will be streamed online: Academic libraries and video." *The Journal of Academic Librarianship* 37, no. 1 (2011): 70–72.

Lloyd Sealy Library. 2009. "John Jay College Lloyd Sealy Library Tour." August 18. https://www.YouTube.com/watch?v=tX8gmGNson8 (Accessed August 1, 2018).

Maness, Jack M. 2006. "An evaluation of library instruction delivered to engineering students using streaming video." *Issues in Science and Technology Librarianship* 47: 156–163.

Martin, Nichole A., and Ross Martin. 2015. "Would you watch it? Creating effective and engaging video tutorials." *Journal of Library & Information Services in Distance Learning* 9, no. 1–2: 40–56.

McCoy, Julia. 2016. "How many times should you retweet & repurpose your content?" April 5. http://www.sitepronews.com/2016/04/05/how-many-times-should-you-retweet-repurpose-your-content/ (Accessed August 15, 2018).

Meyers Martin, Coleen. 2012. "One-minute video: Marketing your library to faculty." *Reference Services Review* 40, no. 4: 589–600.

Morrison, Kimberlee. 2015. "Cutting through the social media jargon: What are reach, impressions and engagement?" September 15. https://www.ad

week.com/digital/cutting-through-the-social-media-jargon-what-are-reach
-impressions-and-engagement/ (Accessed July 15, 2018).

Newton, Casey. 2017. "Facebook launches stories to complete its all-out assault on Snapchat." March 28. https://www.theverge.com/2017/3/28/15081398/ facebook-stories-snapchat-camera-direct (Accessed August 25, 2018).

Olenski, Steve. 2018. "Top 25 social media tools for marketers." February 24. *Forbes Magazine.* https://www.forbes.com/sites/steveolenski/2018/02/24/ top-25-social-media-tools-for-marketers/ (Accessed August 15, 2018).

Osman, Maddy. 2018. "28 powerful Facebook stats your brand can't ignore in 2018." February 15. https://sproutsocial.com/insights/facebook-stats-for -marketers/ (Accessed August 1, 2018).

Parsons, James. 2016. "How many times per day should you post to Twitter?" April 28. https://follows.com/blog/2016/04/times-day-post-twitter (Accessed August 10, 2018).

Perry, Anali Maughan. 2011. "Lights, camera, action!: How to produce a library minute." *College & Research Libraries News* 72, no. 5: 278–283.

Pew Research Center. 2018. "Social media fact sheet." February 5. http:// www.pewinternet.org/fact-sheet/social-media/ (Accessed August 12, 2018).

Pew Research Group. 2018. "Who uses Pinterest, Snapchat, YouTube and WhatsApp." http://www.pewinternet.org/chart/who-uses-pinterest-snap chat-YouTube-and-whatsapp/ (Accessed August 12, 2018).

Rogers, Simon. 2014. "What fuels a Tweet's engagement?" March 10. https:// blog.twitter.com/official/en_us/a/2014/what-fuels-a-tweets-engagement .html (Accessed August 12, 2018).

Sandy, John H., Mangala Krishnamurthy, and Wayne Rau. 2009. "An innovative approach for creating a self-guided video tour in an academic library." *The Southeastern Librarian* 57, no. 3: 29–39.

Simon, Justin. 2018. "YouTube vs. Vimeo: What's the difference?" May 18. https://www.techsmith.com/blog/youtube-vs-vimeo-whats-the-difference/ (Accessed August 12, 2018).

Smith, Aaron, and Monica Anderson. 2018. "Social media use in 2018." March 1. http://www.pewinternet.org/2018/03/01/social-media-use-in-2018/ (Accessed August 1, 2018).

Solar, Aria. 2018. "5 key components to an agile social media policy for employees." January 9. https://getbambu.com/blog/social-media-policy-for -employees/ (Accessed August 4, 2018).

Sørensen, Mads P. 2016. "Political conversations on Facebook—the participation of politicians and citizens." *Media, Culture & Society* 38, no. 5: 664–685.

Steiner, Sarah K. 2012. *Strategic planning for social media in libraries.* Tech Set Vol. 15. American Library Association.

Tewell, Eamon. 2010. "Video tutorials in academic art libraries: A content analysis and review." *Art Documentation: Journal of the Art Libraries Society of North America* 29, no. 2: 53–61.

Thornton, Elaine. 2012. "Is your academic library pinning? Academic libraries and Pinterest." *Journal of Web Librarianship* 6, no. 3: 164–175.

Twitter. 2018. "About Twitter limits." https://help.twitter.com/en/rules-and -policies/twitterlimits (Accessed August 23, 2018).

Twitter Advertisements. 2018. "Promote mode." https://advertisements.twit ter.com/subscriptions/mobile/intro (Accessed September 5, 2018).

Vites, Emma. 2017. "How to create a social media policy that empowers employee advocacy." February 16. https://business.linkedin.com/marketing -solutions/blog/linkedin-elevate/2017/how-to-create-a-social-media-policy -that-empowers-employee-advoc (Accessed August 10, 2018).

Widdicombe, Ben. 2010. "The business of blogging." December 2. *Financial Times.* https://www.ft.com/content/b76a135e-fd5b-11df-b83c-00144feab 49a (Accessed August 1, 2018).

York, Alex. 2018. "Reach vs. impressions: What's the difference in terms?" February 15. https://sproutsocial.com/insights/reach-vs-impressions/ (Accessed July 15, 2018).

Young, Scott W. H., Angela Tate, Doralyn Rossmann, and Mary Anne Hansen. 2014. "The social media toll road: The promise and peril of Facebook advertising." *College & Research Libraries News* 75, no. 8: 427–434.

YouTube Help. 2018. "YouTube advertising formats." https://support.google .com/YouTube/answer/2467968 (Accessed September 12, 2018).

YouTube Press. 2018. "YouTube for Press." https://www.youtube.com/yt/ about/press/ (Accessed September 1, 2018).

Zarrella, Dan. 2009. *The science of retweets.* http://danzarrella.com/science -of-retweets.pdf (Accessed August 20, 2018).

CHAPTER 10

Advocacy

An Integral Component of Marketing Your Library

In a world where private, for-profit companies like Google, Amazon, and YouTube loom ever higher over the information landscape, funding and support for libraries cannot be neglected. According to a Pew Research survey, 77 percent of people go online to find information (Perrin and Jiang, 2018), and commercial services such as Amazon, Netflix, and YouTube offer content that libraries cannot compete with. However, this does not mean that "you can find everything online" (Hagerty, 2017) or that "we don't need libraries anymore" (Graboyes, 2016; Denning, 2015). Libraries offer services that companies like Google cannot match, and libraries and librarians must proactively promote their worth and value to society.

Promoting libraries is a form of advocacy, and advocacy is a tool of library survival. The Trump administration's recent threat to eliminate federal funding for the Institute of Museum and Library Services (IMLS) would have been catastrophic for most libraries and museums. The threat was not carried out because of advocacy efforts. Spurred by public advocacy from the American Library Association, people stepped up, flooding their senators and representatives with calls and letters, influencing lawmakers to reinstate IMLS funding. In March of 2018, President Trump signed a $240 million funding package for the IMLS, which would fund the organization through the end of September of 2018 (Bullard, 2018).

Library advocacy is intimately related to marketing, fundraising, and public relations, for it involves influencing others to support libraries. According to Edgett (2002), advocacy is "the act of publicly representing an individual, organization, or idea with the object of persuading targeted audiences to look favorably on—or accept the point of view of—the individual, the organization, or the idea" (p. 1). Advocacy aims to garner the support of decision makers by convincing them of the organization's positive value. Like fundraising, advocacy attempts to persuade donors to give money to the library. Like public relations, it attempts to increase the library's profile in the community. And like marketing, advocacy aims to "sell" people on actively supporting libraries (Siess, 2003).

But one need not be professionally trained as a marketer, fundraiser, or public relations expert to engage in advocacy. *Anyone* can be an advocate. Indeed, library marketing can only be successful when each staff member becomes an advocate; a "cheerleader" for the organization who helps spread the message to others in the community. To be effective library advocates, staff should collectively plan how to respond with positive rhetoric when faced with criticism, budget cuts, and doubt. Library advocacy strategies may include having library staff create and rehearse a consistent elevator speech; writing a vivid, powerful mission statement that sums up the value of your library; creating a clear vision statement about where your library would like to be in the next five to ten years; and creating effective responses to questions about why libraries are relevant in the digital age. Advocacy may manifest through library events (discussed in chapter 5), media appearances, newspaper articles, presentations, in-person interactions, library websites, billboards, posters, brochures—really, all traditional marketing activities are examples of library advocacy:

- Friends of the Library groups and library foundations
- Staff training (frontline advocacy, elevator speeches, telling library stories)
- Word-of-mouth marketing
- Formal advocacy campaigns
- Media interactions
- Meeting with legislators

Library advocacy, then, is a form of marketing—marketing your library to gain support from your stakeholders, possible donors, politicians, and community.

FRIENDS OF THE LIBRARY AND LIBRARY FOUNDATIONS

A Friends of the Library organization will increase the number of advocates for your library. A Friends group is a nonprofit, volunteer-driven membership organization that raises money to fund library events and programs not covered by the library's operating budget (Lowman and Bixby, 2011). Friends groups are recommended by the ALA's *United for Libraries* division, which sponsors an annual week of celebration to promote Friends groups. The ALA website provides toolkits to start Friends groups at both public and academic libraries, and offers resources, book club reading lists, organizational tools, an electronic discussion group, and a listing of Friends groups across each state (ALA, 2014).

Friends groups are thus grassroots advocacy groups that run small events that raise money for the library. Some libraries may also have library foundations, which are nonprofit organizations that manage public and private donations to strategically plan for the library's future.

TRAINING STAFF AS ADVOCATES

Library employees must be trained as advocates, just as they should be trained to speak to the media. As advocates, staff must speak effectively on behalf of their libraries and convince others to pass the message along. Frontline advocacy—advocacy training for staff who work directly with the public—focuses on teaching staff to assert the library's value at public service points. It empowers library employees who normally might not engage in advocacy activities. Dr. Camila Alire, ALA President for 2009–2010, initiated the frontline advocacy toolkit for libraries, with materials aimed at frontline librarians in public, academic, school, and special libraries (Wong and Todaro, 2010). Every user interaction and every circulation or reference transaction is an opportunity for frontline staff to make a positive impact on users.

Frontline library employee advocates must be familiar with the problems facing libraries today, including budget cuts, staffing problems, increasing resource costs, and reduced hours of operation (Alire, 2009). Frontline advocacy content must be integrated into interactions with library users, and frontline advocates should develop scripts, phrases, and comments, connected to services and resources, that fit into these typical customer interactions. These scripts must be optimistic, not gloomy, and information must be up to date. Advocates should listen to customer concerns and feedback and pass them along to administration, and advocacy interactions with library users should be observed and assessed by colleagues.

One advocacy tool that all frontline library employees can master is how to deliver an effective two-minute elevator speech (Hicks, 2016). According to Muccio (2016), one trick to having an effective elevator speech in your pocket is frequent practice, and frontline library employees should rehearse their talking points whenever they can (Muccio, 2016). According to Muccio (2016), there are five steps to developing a perfect elevator pitch: practice your pitch in front of a mirror; lead with a one-sentence summary; ask your audience a question about their awareness level about the issue you are pitching; listen carefully to their response; and mention one unique feature that will stick in their minds (Muccio, 2016).

Another tool that should be developed in staff advocacy training is the ability to tell library stories: either statistical stories about library usage or personal stories about how the library has helped users. Fichter and Wisniewski (2014) explain the power of statistically based library stories that also include images. According to Fichter and Wisniewski (2014), infographics are the most engaging way to present statistics. Instead, they recommend presenting data in a compelling narrative fashion, using text and graphics to deliver a clear message to a specific audience in an accessible way (using text alternatives and distinguishing data without relying on color) with completely de-identified user data (Fichter and Wisniewski, 2014).

According to the ALA advocacy training packet, the most effective stories are not about what the library does, but about the people who use the library and the impact the library has had on their lives (ALA, 2008). Library stories aim to dispel library stereotypes and to assert the library's value. Testimonials, interviews, and conversations are great examples of compelling library stories. The ALA library advocacy training packet gives the following tips: keep the stories simple, do not include people's real names, and have a good punch line, know your audience, personalize the story so that it is authentic, and practice delivering the story in an informal, conversational style (ALA, 2008).

According to Singh (2006), however, the most powerful stories about library usage are personal stories by patrons, which can be shared by staff in various ways: compliment boards, booklets at checkout desks, displays on library walls, and testimonials on library websites. Singh started an essay contest for the British Columbia Library Association, co-sponsored by the Canadian Broadcasting Corporation. The contest, *Beyond Words*, asked for people to submit essays that expressed how their public library helped them. Over 350 people submitted personal stories. The winning stories (which can be read on the website www .beyondwords.ca) were published in a booklet that was sent to each library in British Columbia (Singh, 2006).

WORD-OF-MOUTH MARKETING (WOMM)

Word-of-mouth marketing, or consumer advocacy, is unpaid promotion from a satisfied customer who recommends a product or service to others via literal word-of-mouth (conversations), testimonials, or written reviews. High levels of inter-consumer interactions are known as "buzz" (Carl, 2006). Deliberate word-of-mouth marketing strategies aim to recruit product ambassadors who will spread a positive message to other consumers (Alire, 2007). Word-of-mouth marketing is one of the most positive forms of marketing available; according to the 2011 Nielsen Global Trust in Advertising Survey, 92 percent of consumers trust products or services recommended by family or friends (Nielsen, 2012). Word-of-mouth marketing is affordable and reaches a wide audience. It is also extremely powerful, because it's immediate, it's honest, and it's customer driven (Barber and Wallace 2009).

According to Kumar, Petersen, and Leone (2007), there are four types of customers, in order of their level of engagement: *Affluents*, *Advocates*, *Champions*, and *Misers*. *Affluents* are frequent customers who are poor marketers; *Advocates* are infrequent customers who are strong marketers; *Champions* are frequent customers who are strong marketers; and *Misers* are infrequent customers who don't market. These categories could be adapted to use in library marketing; some library users are strong advocates but never step inside the library, while others may use the library daily but complain about its services. As chapter 3 explained, detailed user feedback from surveys may enable us to accurately segment our users. For example, if we find in a survey that engineering students use the library as a study hall rather than using it to access the databases, we can identify them as a particular user segment and can tailor our marketing strategies to reach that segment. Kumar, Petersen, and Leone (2007) illustrate how a targeted marketing campaign can transform affluents into champions, advocates into affluents, and misers into advocates, increasing customers' use of library services and their willingness to advocate for the library to others.

According to Keller (2007), who helped design an assessment instrument called "TalkTrack," word-of-mouth is an extremely powerful advocacy tool because it is customer centered. TalkTrack is an ongoing survey of American consumers ages 13–69 that reports word-of-mouth conversations (which include face-to-face, phone, and online interactions) about products and services: each day, 100 respondents record their word-of-mouth interactions about particular brands. Responses are coded based on gender, age, race/ethnicity, and education, and findings are reported on a weekly basis. Keller found that over the course of a week, an American consumer participates in 121 word-of-mouth conversations, most of them about food and dining, media and entertainment, sports, hobbies, beverages, and retail. Keller was surprised to find that 63 percent of word-of-mouth was positive, which refuted the myth that people only speak up about complaints.

Many important inter-customer interactions take place on social media. In 2006, Keller found that 10 percent of word-of-mouth interactions were happening online; the number is likely far higher now. According to Whitler (2014), online word-of-mouth marketing should focus on the Three Es; *engage*, *equip*, and *empower*. Companies need to *engage* by listening to their customers on social media; it doesn't work to post one-way communications on Facebook or Twitter without interacting with customers who respond. They also need to *equip* their customers with tools so they can be heard, such as a special Twitter handle (such as @CompanyNameSupport) or a customer support website (Whitler, 2014). Finally, companies need to *empower* their customers by giving them opportunities to participate in the company's growth. For example, in 2012, Lay's potato chips organized a "Do Us a Flavor" campaign on Facebook that asked consumers to create a new flavor of potato chip, with a $1 million prize for the winner (Lafferty, 2012). The engage, equip, and empower model offers guidelines to enable libraries to connect authentically, efficiently, and inexpensively with customers online, and to convert them from simple customers into word-of-mouth advocates for your library. (chapter 9 discusses social media marketing in more detail.)

ADVOCACY CAMPAIGNS

Frontline employee advocates engage with users in small ways, from greeting them as they enter the library building to spending extra time helping them, and in these interactions, they have the opportunity to enlist customers as advocates to spread what Seth Godin calls an "idea virus"—the message that customers pass to other customers. As Godin points out, this kind of consumer-driven marketing is far more effective than traditional company-sponsored marketing (Godin, 2001). Libraries can adapt the power of consumer-driven marketing by training frontline staff, who work directly with library users, to spread the library advocacy idea virus and encouraging customers to engage in word-of-mouth marketing.

A successful advocacy campaign must present a strong image of the library (Dimattia, 2011). Campaigns should create a consistent theme (i.e., Libraries Transform) and communicate that theme from the start and in all materials. Successful advocacy campaign share the following factors: a vision, a list of prioritized messages, a target audience, a set of talking points, and training for advocates who will deliver the messages (Dimattia, 2011). Chapter 5 describes several existing library campaigns (the Campaign for America's Libraries, the Libraries Transform campaign, Save IMLS, National Library Card Sign Up Month, and National Library Week) that your library can use in its advocacy efforts, or that can serve as models for your own advocacy campaigns. Advocacy campaigns (which, unlike awareness campaigns, have a specific call to action) often target specific groups (stakeholders, politicians, legislators, policy makers, and decision makers), often in order to acquire funding. They may also recruit the general public to advocate to funders and decision makers.

SPEAKING WITH THE MEDIA

Libraries benefit from media coverage, especially when facing challenging circumstances like budget cuts or other crises. It is much better to address problems directly rather than ignoring the media (which can propel rumors and speculation; Duke and Masland, 2002). In fact, libraries should proactively contact the media to give statements in times of crisis (Soehner, Godfrey, and Bigler, 2017). These statements ideally should be written by a professional—a library publicist (who normally writes press releases and acts as the point person for media inquiries) or, in larger libraries, by someone from the communications department (which writes news articles and press releases). The statement may be delivered by the library director, who usually speaks on behalf of the library or, in larger university libraries, by the communications director (who usually works with the university's external relations or communications department to craft official statements).

The American Library Association's Advocacy Handbook (2008) offers the following recommendations for speaking to the media:

- Rehearse beforehand
- Use notes for the main interview talking points
- Represent the library, not yourself
- Smile and remain positive
- Deliver a consistent message
- Know the audience of the publication where your interview will appear
- Be ready to answer difficult questions with statistics or specific examples
- Stick to the facts and avoid responding to leading questions
- Messages should be brief, but avoid one-word responses
- Admit when you don't have the information
- Deliver key messages at least three times
- Acknowledge bad news, but frame as positively as possible

SPEAKING TO LEGISLATORS

Library staff sometimes have opportunities to speak directly to legislators. For example, the ALA National Library Legislative Day (NLLD) provides an opportunity for library employees to engage in meaningful conversations with their members of Congress to discuss the importance of library funding. NLLD is a two-day advocacy event, held annually in the spring, that brings together librarians, library trustees, donors, and legislators in Washington, D.C. Library personnel spend the first day learning and practicing strategies for efficient advocacy; on the second day, they meet with their members of Congress to lobby for library support (ALA, 2018).

Another resource that helps library employees in their advocacy efforts is EveryLibrary, a nonprofit social welfare organization that works on local library ballot initiatives—the first and only national organization to do so. With contributions from all types of donors (individual, corporate, union, and political), they offer resources, training, and tools to help libraries advocate for more funding and resources.

According to Sandow (2011), library trustees and library directors are the most appropriate library personnel to meet with legislators. However, anyone familiar with the issues facing the library can be an advocate if they have the opportunity to connect with lawmakers. The most successful discussions with lawmakers follow some simple principles. First, it is crucial to avoid jargon, because lawmakers are probably unfamiliar with library lingo. Second, focus on a single issue to keep the interaction short and impactful (ALA, 2008).

Sandow (2011) offers recommendations to increase the likelihood that a library advocate will capture the ear of a lawmaker:

- Work as a team to ensure that a library representative attends every city council meeting
- Provide factual information to educate public officials about an issue facing libraries today
- Get to know your local council members, state legislators, and Congress people; attend their fundraising events and invite them to library events
- Ensure that the library is visible at every community event
- Be friendly

The chapter has pulled together the elements of library marketing described in this book under the umbrella of library advocacy. While library advocacy involves promotion and marketing of libraries, it is also something more: Advocacy uses the strategies of marketing and promotion to change minds, to influence others to support libraries. Library advocacy is a form of lobbying, one aimed at convincing people in positions of power (funders, legislators, policy makers, and administrators) to increase library funding. Anyone can become a library advocate, and advocacy is the underlying passion that drives library marketing efforts.

REFERENCES

Alire, Camila A. 2007. "Word-of-mouth marketing: Abandoning the academic library ivory tower." *New Library World* 108, no. 11/12: 545–551.

Alire, Camila. 2009. 23 (advocacy) things (tips) for frontline employees. December 13. http://www.ala.org/advocacy/advleg/advocacyuniversity/front line_advocacy/frontline_public/twentythree (Accessed July 1, 2018).

American Library Association. 2008. *Library advocate's handbook.* http://www.ala.org/aboutala/sites/ala.org.aboutala/files/content/ola/2008lah.pdf (Accessed July 1, 2018).

American Library Association. 2014. "United for libraries resources for friends groups." September 14. http://www.ala.org/united/friends (Accessed July 1, 2018).

American Library Association. 2018. "National library legislative day." March 27. http://www.ala.org/advocacy/advleg/nlld (Accessed July 1, 2018).

Barber, Peggy, and Linda Wallace. 2009. "The power of word-of-mouth marketing." *American Libraries* 40, no. 11: 36–39.

Berg, Kati Tusinski. 2009. "Finding connections between lobbying, public relations and advocacy." *Public Relations Journal* 3, no. 3: 1–19.

Bullard, Giuliana. 2018. IMLS receives funding increase for remainder of FY 2018. March 23. https://www.imls.gov/news-events/news-releases/imls-receives-funding-increase-remainder-fy-2018 (Accessed July 1, 2018).

Carl, Walter J. 2006. "What's all the buzz about? Everyday communication and the relational basis of word-of-mouth and buzz marketing practices." *Management Communication Quarterly* 19, no. 4: 601–634.

DiMattia, Susan. 2011. "Advocacy and image: Partners in creating a value proposition." *Information Outlook* 15, no. 2: 14–16.

Denning, Steve. 2015. "Do we need libraries?" April 28. https://www.forbes
.com/sites/stevedenning/2015/04/28/do-we-need-libraries/ (Accessed July
1, 2018).

Duke, Shearlean, and Lynne Masland. 2002. "Crisis communication by the
book." *Public Relations Quarterly* 47, no. 3: 30–35.

Edgett, Ruth. 2002. "Toward an ethical framework for advocacy in public
relations." *Journal of Public Relations Research* 14, no. 1: 1–26.

Fichter, Darlene, and Jeffrey Wisniewski. 2014. "Telling your library's story
one number at a time." *Online Searcher* 38, no. 4: 74–76.

Godin, Seth. 2001. *Unleashing the ideavirus: Stop marketing AT people! Turn
your ideas into epidemics by helping your customers do the marketing thing
for you.* New York: Hachette Books.

Graboyes, Robert. 2016. "Column: Do we need librarians now that we have
the internet?" Oct 24. https://www.pbs.org/newshour/economy/column
-need-librarians-internet (Accessed July 1, 2018).

Hagerty, James R. 2017. "Google, shmoogle: Reference librarians are busier
than ever." *The Wall Street Journal Eastern Edition*, November 16.

Hicks, Deborah. 2016. "Advocating for librarianship: The discourses of advocacy and service in the professional identities of librarians." *Library Trends*
64, no. 3: 615–640.

Keller, Ed. 2007. "Unleashing the power of word of mouth: Creating brand
advocacy to drive growth." *Journal of Advertising Research* 47, no. 4:
448–452.

Kumar, V., J. Andrew Petersen, and Robert P. Leone. 2007. "How valuable is
word of mouth?" *Harvard Business Review* 85, no. 10: 139–146.

Lafferty, Justin. 2012. "Lay's joins growing trend of brands crowdsourcing
through Facebook." *Adweek*, July 20. https://www.adweek.com/digital/
lays-crowdsourcing-chips/ (Accessed July 1, 2018).

Lowman, Sara S., and Mary D. Bixby. 2011. "Working with friends groups:
Enhancing participation through cultivation and planning." *Journal of Library Administration* 51, no. 2: 209–220.

Muccio, Josh. 2016. "Pitch perfect: 5 steps to a perfect elevator pitch." *Forbes.*
June 16. https://www.forbes.com/sites/under30network/2016/06/16/pitch
-perfect-5-steps-to-a-perfect-elevator-pitch/#7e8c4f61471f

Nielsen Company. 2012. "Consumer trust in online, social, and mobile advertising grows." April 10. http://www.nielsen.com/us/en/insights/news/2012/
consumer-trust-in-online-social-and-mobile-advertising-grows.html (Accessed July 1, 2018).

Perrin, Andrew, and JingJing Jiang. 2018. "About a quarter of U.S. adults say
they are 'almost constantly' online." March 14. http://www.pewresearch

.org/fact-tank/2018/03/14/about-a-quarter-of-americans-report-going-on-line-almost-constantly/ (Accessed July 1, 2018).

Sandow, Dennis. 2011. "Advice for political relationships and activities." *New Jersey Library Association Newsletter.* Spring. http://njla.org/sites/default/files/spring2011.pdf (Accessed July 1, 2018).

Siess, Judith A. 2003. *The visible librarian: Asserting your value with marketing and advocacy.* American Library Association.

Singh, Sandra. 2006. "Telling the library's story." *Library Journal* 131, no. 5: S42.

Soehner, Catherine, Ian Godfrey, and G. Scott Bigler. 2017. "Crisis communication in libraries: Opportunity for new roles in public relations." *The Journal of Academic Librarianship* 43, no. 3: 268–273.

Whitler, Kimberly A. 2014. "Why word of mouth marketing is the most important social media." *Forbes*, July 17. https://www.forbes.com/sites/kimberlywhitler/2014/07/17/why-word-of-mouth-marketing-is-the-most-important-social-media/#2fc36b1954a8 (Accessed July 1, 2018).

Wong, Patty, and Julie Todaro. 2010. "Frontline advocacy is everybody's job." *American Libraries* 41, no. 6/7: 82–84.

Index

Aaker model, 174

Abas, Shahzad, 215

academic libraries: database usage statistics, 82; entrances to, 202–3, 204; media outlets and, 93; roles and responsibilities of librarians in, 187; target audiences, 48, *49*; user segments, 90–91. *See also specific libraries; specific universities*

ACS (American Community Survey), 76

activity planning feedback, 126

ad blocking software, 221

advertising campaigns: about, 26–27, 93, 146–49; on Facebook, 240–41; rebranding, 149–50; on Twitter, 244–46

advocacy campaigns: about, 31–32, 144–46, 175–76, 291–92, 297–98; ALA and, 294–95; legislators, speaking with, 299; media, speaking with, 298; word-of-mouth marketing, 295–97

affiliations. *See* partnerships

affluents, 295–96

airlines and branding, 176

ALA. *See* American Library Association (ALA) campaigns

Alire, Camila, 293

Amazon gift cards, 177

American Community Survey (ACS), 76

American Factfinder, 77–78

American Library Association (ALA) campaigns: advocacy, 294–95; Banned Books Week, 143–44; Campaign for America's Libraries, 145–46; Celebrity READ campaign, 151–52, *152–55*; Friends groups and, 293; Libraries Transform, 141; National Library Legislative Day, 299; National Library Week, 146; READ posters, 144; Save the Institute of Museum and Library Services, 144–45

American National Election Studies (ANES), 79

Americans with Disabilities Act (ADA) compliance, 205, 217

analytics, 141, 179, 258–62

ANES (American National Election Studies), 79

About the Author

Mark Aaron Polger is the First Year Outreach Librarian at the College of Staten Island, City University of New York (CUNY). He has written and presented internationally on topics such as library marketing strategies, faculty outreach, information literacy campaigns, library jargon, and library signage. Polger is very involved in integrating marketing activities into the library profession. Since 2014, he has coordinated the annual PR Xchange Event at ALA Annual and co-chairs the PR Xchange Awards Competition, a library marketing contest sponsored by ALA's LLAMA division. Since 2015, he has been a member of the planning team of the Library Marketing and Communications Conference (LMCC). In 2017, he founded the first open-access, peer reviewed journal *Marketing Libraries Journal*. Originally from Montreal (Canada), he holds a BA and MA in Sociology, a B.Ed. in Adult Education, an MLIS, and is currently completing his third year of PhD course work at SUNY University at Buffalo, where he is studying the Learning Sciences. He has been working as a professional librarian for the last twenty years. Polger moved to New York City in 2008.

Made in the USA
Monee, IL
29 June 2022

98775764R00194